AF339062

BRECHT SOURCEBOOK

Bertolt Brecht's career intersects a wide range of political and cultural practices and history including German folk culture, vaudeville, jazz, the rise of Hollywood and mass culture, two World Wars, Nazi Germany, the emergence of international travel, and the beginnings of global culture. As one of the most prolific and influential writers, directors, and theorists of the twentieth century, Brecht is mandatory reading for anyone interested in cultural and political life.

This anthology brings together an indispensable collection of articles, plays and interviews portraying the development and the complexity of Brecht's ideas. Included are two plays not easily available in English: *The Beggar* or *The Dead Dog* and *Baden Lehrstück*.

The collection covers:

- the development of Brecht's aesthetic theories
- Brecht's aesthetic theories in practice
- Brecht's collaborations with Kurt Weill, Paul Dessau and others
- the adoption and adaptation of Brecht's ideas in England, Japan, Russia, the United States, and Latin America.

This book is an ideal companion to Brecht's plays, and provides an invaluable reconsideration of his work.

Contributors include: Lee Baxandall, Eric Bentley, Hans-Joachim Bunge, Paul Dessau, Martin Esslin, Henry Glade, Barclay Goldsmith, Mordecai Gorelik, Karen Laughlin, W. Stuart McDowell, Erica Munk, Jean-Paul Sartre, Ernst Schumacher, Diana Taylor, Tadashi Uchino, Kurt Weill, Carl Weber.

Carol Martin is Associate Professor of Drama at New York University, the co-editor of *Studies in Dance History*, the book review editor of *The Drama Review* and the author of *Dance Marathons: Performing American Culture of the 1920s and 1930s*.
Henry Bial is Instructor of Drama at New York University. He is currently completing his dissertation on Jewish-American popular performance.

Worlds of Performance
General Editor: Richard Schechner

WORLDS OF PERFORMANCE

What is a "performance"? Where does it take place? Who are the participants? Not so long ago these were settled questions, but today such orthodox answers are unsatisfactory, misleading, and limiting. "Performance" as a theoretical category and as a practice has expanded explosively. It now comprises a panoply of genres ranging from play, to popular entertainments, to theatre, dance, and music, to secular and religious rituals, to "performance in everyday life", to intercultural experiments, and more.

For nearly forty years, *The Drama Review* (*TDR*), the journal of performance studies, has been at the cutting edge of exploring these questions. The Worlds of Performance Series is designed to mine the extraordinary riches and diversity of TDR's decades of excellence, bringing back into print important essays, interviews, artists' notes, and photographs. New materials and introductions bring the volumes up to date. Each World of Performance book is a complete anthology, arranged around a specific theme or topic. Each World of Performance book is an indispensable resource for the scholar, a textbook for the student, and an exciting eye-opener for the general reader.

Richard Schechner
Editor, *TDR*
Series Editor

Other titles in the series:

Acting (Re)Considered edited by Phillip B. Zarrilli
Happenings and other Acts edited by Mariellen R. Sandford
A Sourcebook of Feminist Theatre and Performance: On and Beyond the stage edited by Carol Martin
The Grotowski Sourcebook edited by Richard Schechner and Lisa Wolford
A Sourcebook of African–American Performance: Plays, People, Movements edited by Annemarie Bean

BRECHT SOURCEBOOK

Edited by Carol Martin and Henry Bial

London and New York

First published 2000 by Routledge
11 New Fetter Lane, London EC4P 4EE

Simultaneously published in the USA and Canada
by Routledge
29 West 35th Street, New York, NY 10001

Routledge is an imprint of the Taylor and Francis Group

Typeset in Times by Solidus (Bristol) Limited
Printed and bound in Great Britain by TJ Press International Ltd, Padstow, Cornwall

British Library Cataloguing in Publication Data
A catalogue record for this book is available from the British Library

Library of Congress Cataloguing in Publication Data
Bertolt Brecht : a critical anthology / Carol Martin and Henry Bial.
p. cm. -- (Worlds of performance)
Includes bibliographical references and index.
1. Brecht, Bertolt, 1898–1956--Criticism and interpretation.
I. Martin, Carol, 1952– . II. Bial, Henry, 1970– .
III. Series.
PT2603.R397Z56325 1999
832¢.912--dc21 99-41388
CIP

ISBN 0-415-20042-3 (hbk)
ISBN 0-415-20043-1 (pbk)

To
Sophia and Sam

and to

Ernest and Martha Bial

CONTENTS

ACKNOWLEDGEMENTS

When we began this project, we knew that the pages of *TDR* over the past 40 years would provide an incredible range of information on Brecht and how he was introduced in the U.S. In the late 1950s and early 1960s, *TDR* (then the *Tulane Drama Review*) was instrumental in making work by and about Brecht available to an English-speaking audience. Under the editorship of the late Robert W. Corrigan, the journal frequently published such work, including a special issue (T13) devoted exclusively to Brecht in 1961. Erika Munk, Managing Editor of *TDR* in 1967 and 1968, helped compile two additional special issues on Brecht (T37 and T38), which subsequently became the anthology *Brecht* (Bantam, New York, 1972). Many of the articles in this volume originally appeared in one of these three special issues, and we gratefully acknowledge the work of the editors of *TDR*.

We regret that the *Brecht Sourcebook* cannot include all the work by and about Brecht which has appeared in the pages of *TDR*. Given the rich source of material, we had to make many hard choices. We thank Talia Rodgers and her staff at Routledge and Suzanne Winnacker, among others too numerous to name, for their helpful suggestions on this book. We also thank those authors who contributed new work, or granted permission to reprint material published elsewhere to help us bring this collection up to date.

We gratefully acknowledge the many authors, editors, and publishers who assisted us as we navigated the murky waters of copyright information. Jerold Couture, attorney for the Brecht Estate, was especially helpful in enabling us to secure reprint permissions for the five Brecht-authored pieces in this collection.

Our colleagues in the Departments of Drama and Performance Studies at New York University have provided invaluable support. Two people deserve special thanks for their practical assistance: Cindy Brizzell (now at Yale) and Aitor Baraibar. The editorial staff of *TDR*, including Mariellen Sandford, Marta Ulvaeus, Julia Whitworth, Sara Brady, and Jennifer Chan, were also very helpful. A special thanks to Katherine Hui-ling Chou, whose comments on "Brecht, Feminism, and Chinese Theatre" were most insightful and generous.

Finally, without the support of Richard Schechner and Christine Dotterweich Bial, this project could not have come to fruition.

"Are Stanislavsky and Brecht Commensurable?" by Eric Bentley originally appeared in the *Tulane Drama Review* 9, no. 1: 69–76 (T25, 1964); this piece also appeared in *Thinking About the Playwright* (1987) by Eric Bentley pp. 130–4, and is reprinted here by permission of Northwestern University Press and the author.

"Brecht's Concept of *Gestus* and the American Performance Tradition," by Carl

Weber originally appeared in *Gestus* 2, no. 3: 179–85 (Fall 1986), and is reprinted by permission of the author.

"Prologue to *The Caucasian Chalk Circle*," by Bertolt Brecht, tr. Eric Bentley first appeared in English in the *Tulane Drama Review* 4, no. 2: 45–9 (T6, 1959); this piece also appeared in *Parables for the Theatre: Two Plays by Bertolt Brecht*, translated by Eric Bentley (University of Minnesota Press, Minneapolis, 1948, 1965), pp. 99–104, and is reprinted here by permission of University of Minnesota Press and Eric Bentley.

"Brecht and Chicano Theater," by Barclay Goldsmith originally appeared in *Modern Chicano Writers*, edited by Joseph Sommers and Tomas Ybarra-Frausto (Prentice-Hall, Englewood Cliffs, NJ, 1979), pp. 167–75, and is reprinted by permission of the author.

"Brechtian Theory and the American Feminist Theatre," by Karen Laughlin originally appeared in *Re-Interpreting Brecht*, edited by Pia Kleber and Colin Visser (Cambridge University Press, Cambridge, 1990), pp. 147–60, and is reprinted by permission of Cambridge University Press.

The following articles, cited in the order in which they appear in this book, were previously published in *TDR* and are reprinted by permission of *TDR*/MIT Press and/or the authors.

"On Chinese Acting," by Bertolt Brecht, tr. Eric Bentley 6, no. 1: 130–6 (T13, 1961). Additional permission granted by Eric Bentley and Arcade Publishing.

"Theatre for Learning," by Bertolt Brecht, tr. Edith Anderson 6, no. 1: 18–25 (T13, 1961). Additional permission granted by Arcade Publishing.

"An Epic Theatre Catechism," by Mordecai Gorelik 4, no. 1: 90–5 (T5, 1959).

"Beyond Bourgeois Theatre," by Jean-Paul Sartre, tr. Rima Dell Reck 5, no. 3: 3–11 (T11, 1961).

"*Gestus* in Music," by Kurt Weill, tr. Eric Albrecht 6, no. 1: 28–32 (T13, 1961).

"Composing for BB: Some Comments," by Paul Dessau, tr. Hella Freud Bernays 12, no. 2: 152–5 (T38, 1968).

"Actors on Brecht: The Munich Years," by W. Stuart McDowell 20, no. 3: 101–16 (T71, 1976).

"Bertolt Brecht's *J.B.*," by Lee Baxandall 4, no. 4: 113–17 (T8, 1960).

"*Baden Lehrstück*," by Bertolt Brecht, tr. Lee Baxandall 4, no. 4: 118–33 (T8, 1960). Additional permission granted by Lee Baxandall and Arcade Publishing.

The Beggar or *The Dead Dog*, by Bertolt Brecht, tr. Michael Hamburger 12, no. 2: 120–3 (T38, 1968). Additional permission granted by Arcade Publishing.

"The Dialectics of *Galileo*," by Ernst Schumacher, tr. Joachim Neugroschel 12, no. 2: 124–33 (T38, 1968).

"The Dispute Over the Valley: An Essay on Bertolt Brecht's Play *The Caucasian Chalk Circle*," by Hans-Joachim Bunge, tr. Bayard Q. Morgan 4, no. 2: 50–66 (T6, 1959).

"Brecht and the English Theatre," by Martin Esslin 11, no. 2: 63–70 (T34, 1966).

"The Death of Mother Courage," by Henry Glade 12, no. 1: 137–42 (T37, 1967).

"The Actor's Involvement: Notes on Brecht – An Interview with Joseph Chaikin," by Erika Munk 12, no. 2: 147–51 (T38, 1968).

CONTRIBUTORS

LEE BAXANDALL has translated several of Brecht's works, including *Baden Lehrstück* (reprinted in this volume) and *The Mother* (Grove, 1965). He is a former editor of *Studies on the Left*, as well as the author of *Marxism and Aesthetics* (1968).

ERIC BENTLEY is the editor of the Grove Press edition of Brecht's works and author of *Bentley on Brecht* (Applause Books, New York, 1998), a collection of his writings on Brecht over a 55-year period. Born in England in 1916, he was inducted into the (American) Theatre Hall of Fame in 1998. His best-known play is *Are You Now or Have You Ever Been* (Harper and Row, 1972); his best-known book is *The Playwright as Thinker* (Reynal and Hitchcock, 1946). He is currently (1999) working on a show *To Those Who Come After: The Voice of Bertolt Brecht* with music by Weill, Eisler, Wolpe, and Milhaud.

HENRY BIAL (co-editor) teaches in the Department of Drama at New York University, where he is completing his Ph.D. in Performance Studies. He is currently researching the communication of Jewish culture through American theatre, film, and television.

BERTOLT BRECHT (1898–1956) was born in Augsburg, Germany. His early plays, including *Baal* (1923) and *Drums in the Night* (1923), were written and produced in Munich, where he had gone to study medicine. In 1924, he moved to Berlin, where he began to develop his idea of epic theatre through such works as *The Threepenny Opera* (1928) and *The Rise and Fall of the City of Mahagonny* (1927, rev. 1930), as well as several Lehrstücke, or "teaching plays." During the Nazi regime he went into exile, spending 1933–41 in Denmark and 1941–7 in the United States, where he worked briefly in Hollywood. After being called to testify before the House Un-American Activities Committee in 1947, Brecht left the United States for Switzerland, before returning to Berlin late in 1948 to stage *Mother Courage and Her Children* (first performed in Zurich, 1941), which opened in January 1949. Later that year, Brecht formed the Berliner Ensemble, which he directed until his death from a heart attack in 1956.

HANS-JOACHIM BUNGE was, at the time "The Dispute over the Valley" was published in T6 (1959), the director of the Brecht archives at the Berliner Ensemble.

JOSEPH CHAIKIN, actor and director, was born in Brooklyn in 1935 and educated at Drake University. For nearly a decade, he directed one of the most influential experimental theatre groups in the United States, the New York City-based Open Theatre, which he founded in 1963 after working as an actor with the Living Theatre. Among other distinctions, Chaikin is a six-time Obie Award recipient, including the very first Lifetime Achievement Obie Award in 1977; he has also been awarded two Guggenheim Fellowships, the National Endowment for the Arts' first Annual Distinguished Service to American Theatre Award, The Edwin Booth Award, and honorary Ph.D.'s from Drake University and Kent State University. His book, *The Presence of the Actor*, was re-released by TCG Publications in 1991. Chaikin was the first American director to be included in the Cambridge University Press "Directors in Perspective" series on the world's most influential theatre directors.

PAUL DESSAU (1894–1979) composed the music for Brecht's *Mother Courage*. Dessau was born in Hamburg, Germany. After World War I he became a composer at the "Kammerspiele" in Hamburg. From 1919 with Otto Klemperer he was a conductor in Cologne. In 1968 when this article was originally published he had been living in East Germany for 20 years and working as a composer. He identified himself as a Communist.

MARTIN ESSLIN is the author of numerous books on theatre, including *Brecht: The Man and His Work* (1960), *The Genius of the German Theatre* (1968), and *Mediations: Essays on Brecht, Beckett and the Media* (1981). He is a former head of drama for the BBC and Professor Emeritus of Drama at Stanford University.

HENRY GLADE was, at the time his article appeared in T37 (1967), chairman of the Department of Modern Languages at Manchester College, Indiana, and the recipient of a Ford Foundation travel grant to study the reception of recent German literature in the Soviet Union.

BARCLAY GOLDSMITH teaches at Pima Community College in Tuscon, Arizona. He is a member and director of the Borderlands Theatre.

MORDECAI GORELIK (1899–1990) was born in Russia and enjoyed a long career as prominent stage designer in the United States. In addition to designing shows for the Provincetown Players, the Group Theatre, and numerous Broadway shows, he was the author of *New Theatres for Old* (1940), and an early advocate of Brecht's epic theatre in America.

KAREN LAUGHLIN is Associate Professor of English at Florida State University, where she teaches courses in drama, women's studies, and film. She is co-editor of *Theatre and Feminist Aesthetics* (Fairleigh Dickinson Press, 1995) and has also published numerous articles and book chapters on the works of Beckett, Glaspell, Fornes, Henley, and other modern playwrights. Her current project is a book-length study of pain, power, and imagination in Beckett's plays.

W. STUART McDOWELL is Chair of Theatre, Dance and Motion Pictures at Wright State University; director and co-writer of *1913: The Great Dayton Flood*, (American College Theatre Festival, Kennedy Center) with recorded narration by Martin Sheen, Ossie Davis, and Ruby Dee. Founder and Artistic Director of Riverside Shakespeare Company of NYC, McDowell has directed and translated numerous Brecht plays.

CAROL MARTIN is Associate Professor of Drama at Tisch School of the Arts/NYU. She is the author of *Dance Marathons: Performing American Culture of the 1920s and 1930s* (University of Mississippi Press, 1994), which won a De La Torre Bueno Citation for best book on dance of the year, and the editor of *A Sourcebook of Feminist Theatre and Performance: On and Beyond the Stage* (Routledge, 1996). She is currently the book review editor of *TDR* (MIT Press) and the co-editor of *Studies in Dance History*, the book series of the Society of Dance History Scholars.

ERIKA MUNK is the editor of *Theater*, a thrice-yearly publication of the Yale School of Drama, where she is Associate Professor of Dramaturgy and Dramatic Criticism. Her most recent writing on theater has appeared in *The Nation*, the *Village Voice*, and the *Brecht Yearbook*. Her political journalism from Bosnia, Croatia, and China appeared in the *Village Voice*, where she earlier served as theatre editor and critic, 1978–90. In the 1960s and 1970s, she edited the journals *TDR*, *Performance*, and *Scripts* and published anthologies on Brecht and Stanislavsky.

JEAN-PAUL SARTRE (1905–80) was a French philosopher, playwright, novelist, and critic, who refused the 1964 Nobel Prize for Literature. His many published works include *Nausea* (novel, 1938), *Being and Nothingness* (1943), *No Exit* (play, 1947), and *Critique of Dialectical Reason* (1960).

ERNST SCHUMACHER, an East German critic, is the author of numerous critical works, among them *Die Dramatischen Verusche Bertolt Brechts 1918–1933* (1955) and *Bertolt Brecht's "Leben des Galilei" un Andere Stücke* (1965).

DIANA TAYLOR is Professor and Chair of Performance Studies at Tisch School of the Arts/NYU. She is the author of *Theatre of Crisis: Drama and Politics in Latin America* (University Press of Kentucky, 1991), which won the Best Book Award given by the New England Council on Latin American Studies and Honorable Mention in the Joe E. Callaway Prize for the Best Book on Drama, and of *Disappearing Acts: Spectacles of Gender and Nationalism in Argentina's "Dirty War"* (Duke University Press, 1997). She has also edited three volumes of critical essays on Latin American, Latino, and Spanish playwrights.

TADASHI UCHINO is Associate Professor of Theatre Studies at the Department of Interdisciplinary Cultural Studies, Graduate School of Arts and Sciences, University of Tokyo, Japan. Now a contributing editor to *TDR*, he studied at the Department of Performance Studies, NYU, 1986–7 and 1997-98 both times as a Fulbright Fellow. He has written extensively on theatre culture both in Japan and in the U.S. His most recent publications include *The Revenge of Melodrama: Theatre of the Private in the 1980s* (in Japanese, 1996) and *The Return of the Political: A Short History of American Avant-garde Performance Since the 1960s* (in Japanese, 1999).

CARL WEBER has been Professor of Directing and Dramaturgy at Stanford University since 1984. He was an assistant director with Bertolt Brecht, 1952–6, and a director with the Berliner Ensemble, 1956–61. He has directed for leading American repertory theatres and Off and Off-off Broadway, and was Master Teacher of Directing at NYU's Tisch School, 1966–84. He translated and edited four volumes of writings by Heiner Müller, and the volume *Drama Contemporary: Germany* (Johns Hopkins University Press). His essays have appeared in all of the leading theatre journals.

KURT WEILL (1900–50) was born in Dessau, Germany. A composer, he collaborated with Bertolt Brecht on *The Rise and Fall of the City of Mahagonny* and *The Threepenny Opera*. With his wife, Lotte Lenya (1900–81), Weill emigrated to the United States in 1935 to escape Nazi persecution. In the U.S., his theatrical works included *Knickerbocker Holiday* (with Maxwell Anderson) and *Street Scene* (with Elmer Rice and Langston Hughes).

INTRODUCTION

Carol Martin and Henry Bial

Bertolt Brecht (1898–1956), born to a middle-class family in the German town of Augsburg, is a seminal figure in the development of political theatre theories and practices around the world. Brecht was a total theatre man: director, playwright, manager, theorist, critic, and poet. He challenged Aristotelian assumptions, developing practices and theories of how acting could consciously make spectators critical observers and active participants in the creation of meaning on stage and in the audience. Through the actor's use of "alienation," and *Gestus*, the playwright's use of "epic" structure, and the spectator's consequent active filling-in of the links between parts, Brecht reoriented twentieth-century understanding of performance away from the authority of the playwright to the circulation of meaning among playwright, actor, and spectator.

Brecht's work was formed in the political and artistic context of Germany in the early part of the twentieth century. Germany was capitalist and industrial but with very active radicals – both on the right and the left. After World War I and the signing of the Treaty of Versailles in 1919 which forced the burden of war reparations on Germany, limited its armed forces, awarded land to France, and placed German colonies under the control of the League of Nations, fascism emerged as a pernicious reaction and eventually controlled German daily and political life, including all forms of artistic expression. As the right gained power, leftist artists and certain kinds of popular culture grew more defiant in their practices.

Political playwrights like Brecht had to find an aesthetic and a means of production appropriate to the advantages and limitations of live theatre. Film had successfully usurped the portrayal of the "real" without the distractions of odors, dust, noise, chaos, and insupportably high production costs in relation to the number of potential viewers. Theatrical realism was outdone by this new medium. In Brecht's view, much of German theatre was bourgeois and obsolete, no longer capable of treating the complexities of modern, tumultuous Germany. There were new political and social realities that needed to be addressed.

Influenced by his reading of Marx in the 1920s, Brecht took the view that history is fluid, negotiable, and controllable. Instead of the Aristotelian model of tragic destiny, Brecht considered life as a dialectic between rudimentary existence and the complexity of living: "First comes eating, then morality"[1] ("Erst kommt das Fressen und dann kommt die Moral") is Brecht's famous maxim, explored in different ways in many of his plays.

To disrupt the sentimental identification of spectators with characters, Brecht challenged actors to address spectators about the characters and the contents of the play. Together spectators and actors would then reflect upon the characters' situations as these were informed by historical and material, rather than psychological or spiritual, conditions. The epic structure of Brecht's plays, influenced both by Erwin Piscator (1893–1966) and Sergei Eisenstein's (1898–1948) film montage theory, rejected linear narrative in favor of seemingly disassociated scenes, of which spectators had to make sense in much the same way as they make sense of cuts, dissolves, and flashbacks in film.

For Brecht, theatre was an occasion for rational thought, not emotional catharsis. But this does not mean that Brecht's theatre was bloodless or without passion; his was not an intellectual theatre without feeling. Brecht's early productions were met with both riotous approval and disavowal: audiences booed, cheered, yelled at one another, and discussed the plays well beyond the performance. Brecht loved it. He was after participation and engagement – in and about a new world order. He wanted his theatre to be politically engaged, economically viable, and aesthetically "entertaining."

Brecht was by no means alone in his search for a new theatre. He was among many who moved to Berlin where there was a heady mix of both international artists and intellectuals and high and low culture. Brecht arrived in Berlin in 1924 when the city was a crossroads between East and West, a boiling pot of significant social, political, and artistic experimentation.

Max Reinhardt (1873–1943), for example, despite his illusionistic theatre being deemed dated by the 1920s, was still searching for new forms of theatrical expression. He was enamored with the black vaudeville he had seen on a trip to the U.S. in 1924. *Shuffle Along* (1921) with performer Josephine Baker (1906–75), music by Eubie Blake (1883–1983) and lyrics by Noble Sissle (1889–1975), was a revelation to him: it was physical, rhythmic pantomime with a unique kind of emotional expression. When Baker showed up to perform in Berlin, Reinhardt offered to train her.[2]

Piscator's productions at Berlin's Volksbuhne suited Brecht's interests. Piscator defined epic theatre as the text of the play disclosing its sociopolitical circumstances. His productions featured technical innovations such as the use of film and dramaturgical agit-prop devices such as placards to disrupt conventional narratives. Brecht took from Piscator the term "epic" and used it to describe the theatre form he was developing. This was not just a matter of playwriting and dramaturgy, but also of acting and staging.

Popular culture was equally important to Brecht: as a boy in Augsburg he attended local fairs where performers used placards and narrated theatrical stories. Later, as an adult in Berlin, he became familiar with the sardonic cabarets critical of fascist culture; the films of Charlie Chaplin were well known; black American musicians such as Duke Ellington frequented the city; the comedian Karl Valentin became a close friend with whom Brecht sometimes performed. Thus vaudeville, cabaret, sports, and circus were all fodder for his theories and practice; his evaluation of them was according to the needs of his theatre.

Though Brecht envisioned a theatre for the contemporary scientific age his work proceeded from, albeit indirectly, the experimentation of the nineteenth century. During this period two major dramatic movements were born: naturalism, in which new evolutionary and medical theories informed the struggle of characters to survive, established by Emile Zola and others; and (as distinct from naturalism), realism, which sought to represent the world as it is rather than as it should be. Realistic theatre used real objects on stage, and ushered in the aesthetic of the invisible fourth wall.

Naturalism and realism were mimetic and representational dramatic movements. There were also the symbolists who viewed art as a vehicle for mystical considerations and hence rejected both naturalism and realism. And there was expressionism, which initially sought to differentiate itself from impressionism by the overt portrayal of emotional experience. Both symbolism and expressionism portrayed interior states. Thus the genetic and historical considerations of naturalism and realism were either abandoned entirely or inflected with mystical or emotional rationale. Brecht's early plays were expressionist combined with social content. The states of his characters were aptly portrayed as consequences of their material conditions, and the style of his actors was presentational rather than representational.

Brecht's theatrical experiments in Germany would soon be cut short. As the Nazis gained power, Brecht and the circle of left-wing artists (many of them Jewish) with whom he was associated were forced to flee. Brecht left in February 1933 on the day after the Reichstag fire to settle in Denmark, his main residence until 1939.[3] Brecht eventually moved to California in 1941, living in the U.S. until October 31, 1947, the day after his appearance as one of nineteen Hollywood witnesses subpoenaed by the House Un-American Activities Committee (HUAC).

In 1935 Brecht took a sojourn from Denmark to Leningrad and Moscow. It was in Moscow that Brecht saw the *jingju* (Chinese opera) performer Mei Lanfang (1894–1961) who fully embodied Brecht's theory of acting, in which the actor consciously presents the behavior of the character on the stage. This examination by the actor of the character prevented the complete transformation of an actor into the role, creating instead a portrayal that included both emotional empathy and analytical distance. Mei embodied the acting theory Brecht had been developing: "Verfremdung," translated into English as "alienation" and French as "distanciation."

Brecht spent a significant part of his adult life in exile, living abroad as a stranger. He must have experienced a personal sense of alienation and distance; a sense of gesture detached from language, of the familiar being strange. He was not alone in this. Brecht was part of a large movement of intellectuals and artists across many national borders in many directions. Piscator, who also fled Nazi Germany, set up his Dramatic Workshop in New York in 1938. Among his students was Tennessee Williams. Piscator returned to West Germany in 1951, becoming head of the Freie Volksbuhne in 1962, using epic theatre techniques of the 1920s to develop the German documentary theatre of the 1960s.

While German artists and intellectuals fled Nazi Germany for the U.S., many American intellectuals and artists had already aligned themselves with political movements abroad. Esther Sherman (1897–1982) transformed herself by darkening her skin, wearing saris, performing Indian dance and changing her name to Ragini Devi. She authored *Dances of India* (1928), one of the first books on Indian dance, and then moved to India where she supported the Independence movement against the British. Isadora Duncan (1877–1927) left the U.S in 1899 to live in Paris, Berlin, and eventually Moscow, where she helped celebrate the Russian Revolution and the overthrow of the tsar with a performance at the Metropolitan Opera House.[4] Josephine Baker (1906–75) was among American expatriots in Paris, and became an important member of the French Resistance during World War II.

The 1920s and 1930s were times when both the creation of indigenous art unique to specific histories *and* modernization were important to many, but they were also times in which, through international travel, artists gravitated to different aesthetic systems and political identifications. As Brecht's work became known beyond Germany, his ideas were adapted to accommodate very different political and social realities.

Brecht's approach to theatre can be characterized, in part, by a radical reinvention of existing performance forms. Borrowing freely from traditions both popular and elite, local and distant, he reshaped classic genres, texts, and techniques to suit his immediate political and aesthetic goals. Just as Brecht drew upon other cultures to help formulate his theories and practices, his work was adapted by theatre practitioners to suit their distinctive contexts. This two-way process of assimilation and adaptation resituates the subject of the movement of ideas and practice away from problems of interpretation to, in the case of Brecht, the problems of the circulation of political aesthetics in a global setting.

THE ESSAYS

The essays in this collection reflect the emergence of Brecht's work beyond the borders of Germany and the German language. The circumstances in which Brecht's ideas were imported and in which translations of his work were made is one of the stories of this anthology. Another story is the malleability of ideas in general and Brecht's in particular as his work was adapted in Latin America, Japan, China, the United States, the United Kingdom, and the Soviet Union.

The six articles in the first part of this book, "Brecht's Aesthetic Theories," situate the relationship between Brecht's travels – to Moscow, New York, Los Angeles – and the transnational movement of his ideas. At a formal dinner party in 1935, Brecht saw Mei, the celebrated *jingju* (Chinese opera) performer, give a spontaneous demonstration of his acting. What Brecht saw Mei do confirmed his notion that disturbing the distance between actor and character was an effective technique for resituating spectators' sympathies. Instead of "real life," Brecht saw in Mei's acting a manipulable system of signs and referents: a "transportable bit of technique". This was especially significant in relation to Brecht's emergent theories of "alienation" and of *Gestus*, actions that are both themselves and emblematic of larger social practices. In "On Chinese Acting,"[5] written after Brecht saw Mei display his remarkable skills, Brecht describes his first encounter with Chinese opera. This article contains Brecht's earliest published use of the now-familiar term "*Verfremdungseffekt*", or alienation-effect, also often translated as V-effect.[6]

By means of his "alienation effect" Brecht sought a radical separation of actors from characters enabling each to operate independently. Actors should not "live" characters but "demonstrate" them to spectators. The demystification of acting technique was a key part of Brecht's goal. For Brecht, acting should be both scientific and popular – demonstrative and clear, as he believed scientific hypotheses were. Actors should be in control and fully conscious of their technique, as Brecht presumed scientists were. Spectators could then respond with an expertise analogous to sports fans:

> When people in sporting establishments buy their tickets they know exactly what is going to take place; and that is exactly what does take place once they are in their seats: viz. highly trained persons developing their peculiar powers in the way most suited to them, with the greatest sense of responsibility yet in such a way as to make one feel that they are doing it primarily for their own fun. Against that the traditional theatre is nowadays quite lacking in character.[7]

In "Theatre for Learning," unpublished in Brecht's lifetime, Brecht asserted that because technique is international, the theatre of New York,

Moscow, and Berlin possessed certain similarities. This argument has perhaps come of age with discussions of globalization that have more recently recast our perceptions of local cultures. In Brecht's time, however, the idea that technique could exist apart from nation and apart from any specific form, was unprecedented. While borrowing and adapting theatrical techniques was a basis for modern innovation of many artists in many places, Brecht's conceptual framing of practice as transcending specific geographic locations points to his orientation toward international perspectives and a variety of cultural experiences. What was modern, for Brecht, was hypothetically without borders. Yet Brecht belies the implications of his idea when he declares that only in Berlin, and only for a short time, did "the modern theatre" find its most powerful expression: the epic theatre. The contradiction of wanting to claim international stature based on artistic practices with universal appeal and at the same time to construct an art form that demonstrates national identity also marks the career of many of Brecht's contemporaries in both the East and the West. Brecht seemingly thought globally, but his work was also very much the product of Berlin at that time.

As Brecht's plays and theoretical writings were translated and published in English, a new group of practitioners and scholars attempted to identify the salient characteristics of epic theatre that distinguished it from other experimental forms. Mordecai Gorelik, a Russian-born American director, and stage and film designer, carefully explains Brecht's ideas about epic theatre to Americans. Gorelik, the primary designer for the Group Theatre, was one of the first advocates for epic theatre in the United States. His "Epic Theatre Catechism" addresses "the many misconceptions [about epic theatre] now current among theatre people".

Eric Bentley's "Are Stanislavsky and Brecht Commensurable?" outlines Brecht's ideas in relation to Stanislavsky's System. Bentley argues that, despite seeming opposition, epic theatre and the Stanislavsky System do not necessarily present the actor with an either-or choice. Bentley reminds us that both approaches to acting must be understood in political as well as aesthetic terms. Most notably, Bentley describes the curious position occupied by Stanislavsky in the Soviet artistic pantheon of the 1950s. He sets this against Brecht's uneasy relationship with the East German Communist Party as a way of explaining some of the perceived differences between the two aesthetic approaches.

Cold War politics played a part in the initially mixed and muddled American response to Brecht's theories in the 1950s. But the roots of this response go back even earlier, to Brecht's visit to New York in 1935–6 and his subsequent years spent in Los Angeles during World War II. Carl Weber recounts Brecht's disenchantment with both Broadway and Hollywood's commercialization of American popular performance forms. Brecht had initially respected these forms as fine examples of his concept of *Gestus*, but he later became disillusioned with them.

Finally in this section, the French philosopher, playwright, and novelist Jean-Paul Sartre (1905–80), in a lecture originally delivered at the Sorbonne in the Spring of 1960, applauds epic theatre as anti-bourgeois while questioning whether or not alienation is possible, or even desirable, if Brecht were to depict a society with which he felt empathy. Sartre's first play *Bariona* (1940) was written for and performed by prisoners in a German stalag (POW camp), where Sartre was also imprisoned for his work with the French Resistance. Sartre felt, as did Brecht, that theatre was most successful at directly and immediately communicating the need for social action to a mass audience.[8] Political similarities between Sartre and Brecht can be seen in Sartre's plays (including *The Flies* (1943), *No Exit* (1944), and *The Devil and the Good Lord* (1951)), particularly in Sartre's insistence on historicization and focus on dramatic gesture. But while Sartre's dramas are subversive in content, they are traditional in form. The lecture "Beyond Bourgeois Theatre" was given late in Sartre's career as a playwright, and represents an attempt to reconcile politically his own dramatic style with Brecht's more radical aesthetic.

The second part of this book, "Brecht's Theories in Practice," examines how Brecht's theoretical ideals were realized in his creative practice. Articles by composers Kurt Weill and Paul Dessau, both of whom worked with Brecht, depict the integral role that music played in his theatre, as well as the search beyond the borders of Germany for musical inspiration. In "*Gestus* in Music" Weill argues that music should magnify and focus the *Gestus* of a dramatic action. Weill's illustrative example, "Alabama Song" from *The Rise and Fall of the City of Mahagonny* (1930), shows the strong influence of American jazz on his compositions. Though this transcultural borrowing goes unremarked in the 1929 essay, it represents an early example of how American popular performance traditions provided source material for the Brecht–Weill collaborative team. Dessau, who wrote music for *Mother Courage and Her Children* (1941), *The Caucasian Chalk Circle* (1948), and other Brecht plays, describes how Brecht would suggest source material from a wide range of musical traditions. This was especially true for *The Caucasian Chalk Circle* in which much of the music was based on Azerbaijanian folk dances. Dessau's orchestration calls for several folk instruments, including guitar, mandolin, and accordion.

In "Actors on Brecht: The Munich Years," W. Stuart McDowell presents a series of interviews he conducted in 1975 with three actors from Brecht's Munich productions (1922–4): *Drums in the Night* (1922), *Mysteries of a Barber Shop* (film, 1923), *In the Jungle of Cities* (1923), and *Edward II* (1924). Erwin Faber, Hans Schweikart, and Blandine Ebinger describe their experiences as the first actors to attempt to mold their performances to Brecht's vision.

In his *Lehrstücke*, or "plays for learning," Brecht was most directly politically Marxist. In these short often terse texts, Brecht tried to put his aesthetic and political theories into theatrical practice. Lee Baxandall characterizes *Baden Lehrstück*, performed at the 1929 Baden-Baden music festival, as a play which reveals Brecht's personal political conflicts. Baxandall's introduction to *Baden Lehrstück* is paired with his own translation of the text.

The Beggar or *The Dead Dog* is one of Brecht's earliest known dramatic writings. In it, a beggar outside the gates of a palace confounds the Emperor by refusing to acknowledge his authority. Through the Beggar's eloquent refusal to acknowledge the difference in status between the two men, we see a model for epic theatre. The Beggar dares to describe the Emperor and his realm in objective terms. The Emperor, representing the bourgeois audience, finds himself on the defensive without really knowing why.

Central to Brecht's idea of epic theatre is Marx's concept of the dialectic as an analytical tool. Brecht's focus on cycles of historical development and change, informed in part by an "ideological superstructure" which is the theatre, led him to re-evaluate and re-interpret past narratives as a method for gaining greater understanding of existing social conditions, and how to change them. Though this approach to history characterizes nearly all of Brecht's theatrical work, Ernst Schumacher argues that *Life of Galileo* (1943), one of Brecht's most linear and plot-driven plays, actually comes closest to achieving this ideal of a dialectical theatre. The way the plot of *Galileo* foregrounds the decisions the characters make stresses the mechanisms of social change. The dialectical construction of character forces spectators to consider their actions in relation to historical situations.

This section concludes with the controversial Prologue to Brecht's *The Caucasian Chalk Circle*, which had its world premiere in 1948 at Carleton College in Northfield, Minnesota. In 1948, when Bentley published *Parables of the Theatre* (Minnesota), the first American text devoted exclusively to Brecht, the Prologue was omitted at Brecht's request, in deference to his scheduled appearance before the House Un-American Activities Committee. The Prologue remained unpublished in English until Bentley's translation appeared in the *Tulane Drama Review* in 1959, accompanied by Hans-Joachim Bunge's essay "The Dispute Over the Valley: An Essay on Bertolt Brecht's Play *The Caucasian Chalk Circle*." Bunge surveys critical responses to the Prologue and argues that it is an integral part of the play, comparing the 1954 Berlin production – which included the Prologue – with the 1955 Frankfurt-am-Main production – which omitted it. This volume reprints Bunge's essay in tandem with Brecht's Prologue, though at the request of Bentley, a more recent version of his translation has been used.

Finally, part three, "Brecht Interpreted Abroad," locates Brecht's work in different historical contexts and geopolitical locations.

Frequently, this involves the adaptation of Brecht's ideas to meet local economic, aesthetic, and political needs. In his 1966 essay "Brecht and the English Theatre" Martin Esslin describes how the theatrical left interpreted and misinterpreted Brecht's work during the decade immediately following his death. Very few English critics, playwrights, or directors had access to Brecht's theoretical writings, as they were not widely available in translation until the 1964 publication of Willett's *Brecht on Theatre*. Yet Brecht's plays were embraced during the 1950s and 1960s, in part because the artistic vitality of the Berliner Ensemble provided an example of an artistically viable state-supported theatre.

Misreading is also the occasion for continuing interpretation and historical examination. Henry Glade suggests as much in his 1967 article on the production of Brecht's plays in Moscow, where the political constraints of the Soviet regime led to many loosely translated and freely adapted productions. Following Brecht in his demand that the classics be adapted to the times, Glade finds that a syncretic blend of new theatre and old traditions produces creative and successful productions.

Barclay Goldsmith takes this a step further, as he identifies the Brechtian "spirit" of much Chicano theatre in the 1960s and 1970s. Goldsmith sees both epic theatre and Chicano theatre as political performances drawing on popular entertainment forms which depart from the conventions of naturalism. But, as Goldsmith notes in his essay, the political circumstances of Chicanos in the United States are vastly different from those of the working class in Weimar Germany, and this necessitates the need for significant differences in texts and performance conventions. Taken together the first three articles in this section portray how contemporaneous authors viewed significant developments in the adoption and adaptation of Brecht's work in very different locations in roughly the same time period.

Diana Taylor examines the reception of Brecht's ideas in Latin America, where, despite the prevalence of his influence, it is difficult to identify anything as specifically Brechtian. Brecht's ideas arrived in Latin America at roughly the same time as Latin American theatre practitioners began to turn away from European traditions in favor of indigenous performance forms. Brecht's work was not widely known in Latin America until the 1950s, by which time a dialectical historically situated theatre had already emerged there. Thus Brecht's theories reinforced directions already taken in Latin America where testimonies of violence were suppressed in a manner that made social truth and fiction, history and story, crucial subjects for theatres of social action. Latin American theatre had to provide the means for spectators to be skeptical witnesses to official history and Brecht's theories helped to achieve this goal.

Tadashi Uchino provides a longer historical view, outlining the history of Brecht as a "displaced political playwright and theorist" in Japan. Brecht's legacy in Japan remains inextricably linked with that of

Koreya Senda, the *shingeki* ("new theatre") practitioner who journeyed to Germany in 1927 to seek new ideas for a workers' theatre. In *The Threepenny Opera*, Senda saw a form of performance that could fulfill the popular and leftist needs of *shingeki*. Senda did not even wait for the publication of Brecht's script, but instead used the widely available Weill score and his own memory of the text to reconstruct his own freely-adapted version, *The Beggar's Play*, in Tokyo in 1932. In subsequent decades, Brecht's significance in Japan has risen and fallen along with *shingeki*.

The need to adapt Brecht's ideas to American theatre of the 1960s is unmistakable in Erika Munk's 1968 interview with Joseph Chaikin, the founding actor-director of the influential Open Theatre. Chaikin restates Brecht's concern with balancing entertainment and instruction in the theatre. Nevertheless, Chaikin saw some of Brecht's theatrical techniques as inappropriate for American audiences. As Chaikin saw it, the problem for American directors was to find a new way to direct Brecht's plays, while remaining true to their own American themes and intentions.

Karen Laughlin surveys the influence of Brecht's theories on American feminist theatre of the 1960s, 1970s, and 1980s. She describes how Brecht's concepts of *Gestus* and alienation and his insistence that dramatic events be "historicized" was crucial to the political aims of feminist theatre. Laughlin's article is part of an ongoing debate about the rejection, acceptance, or adaptation of theatrical realism for feminist theatre in the U.S.[9]

Finally, Carol Martin's essay on Brecht and Chinese theatre discusses theatrical innovations in China and Japan at the time Brecht saw Mei Lanfang perform in Moscow and American feminists' use of Brecht for a politically engaged theatre. Martin asks us to look at the history of the forms being used as well as the history of dramatic events when considering the implications of theatrical inventions.

In Latin America today, Brecht's theories are more important than his plays. In Japan, where Brecht's name was associated with the at first radical but then conservative *shingeki* (new theatre) of Koreya Senda, his plays are better known than his theories. In the U.S., mainstream venues produce his plays while Chicano and feminist theatre practitioners take up his theories to invent their own practices conducive to their own politics.

As the instability of local subjects and their global translations becomes evident the advent of an international style of theatre emerges. This does not necessarily negate particularity of knowledge and taste, but identifies shared techniques. Although an international style of theatre can make productions readable across cultures, it does not assure consistency of meaning in different contexts. The early twentieth century can be characterized by a new awareness of a multitude of local theatrical forms (often with a concomitant effort to preserve those forms). At the same time, the movement of individuals like Brecht accelerated the deterioration of artistic borders.

Taken together we hope the essays in this collection will provoke further thinking on Brecht's key aesthetic theories, the process of putting his theories into practice, and the complex diffusion of his ideas in varied contexts.

NOTES

1. John Fuegi, *Bertolt Brecht: Chaos According to Plan* (Cambridge: Cambridge University Press, 1987) 10.
2. Phyllis Rose, *Jazz Cleopatra: Josephine Baker in Her Time* (New York: Doubleday, 1989) 84–5.
3. When the German Parliament building caught fire, Nazi propaganda proposed that Communist arson was the cause; the Nazi's red-baiting helped them win 43.9 percent of the vote in the March elections. Hitler subsequently disqualified the 81 Communist members of the Reichstag giving the Nazis a clear majority.
4. Ann Daly, *Done Into Dance: Isadora Duncan in America* (Indiana University Press, 1995) 10.
5. The German title of the essay is "Verfremdungseffekte in deder chinesischen Schauspielkunst" hence another translation of the title is "Alienation Effects in Chinese Acting."
6. John Willett (ed. and tr.), *Brecht on Theatre: The Development of an Aesthetic* (New York: Hill and Wang, 1992) 99.
7. Ibid. 6.
8. Dorothy McCall, *The Theatre of Jean-Paul Sartre* (New York: Columbia University Press, 1969) 1–3.
9. Patricia R. Schroeder, *The Feminist Possibilities of Dramatic Realism* (Fairleigh Dickinson University Press, 1996). In the first chapter of her book Schroeder summarizes and argues with feminist critiques of theatrical realism.

Part I:
BRECHT'S AESTHETIC THEORIES

1

ON CHINESE ACTING

Bertolt Brecht

Translated by Eric Bentley

In the following paper something will be said about the use of "alienation" in Chinese acting. The "alienation effect" has been used in Germany in plays of a non-Aristotelian kind, that is, in plays which are not based on empathy (*einfuehlung*). I refer to various attempts to act in such a manner that the spectator is prevented from feeling his way into the characters. Acceptance or rejection of the characters' words is thus placed in the conscious realm, not, as hitherto, in the spectator's subconscious.

The attempt to "alienate" the events being presented from the audience was made in a primitive way in the theatrical and pictorial displays of old fairs. We also find it in the circus clown's manner of speech and in the way in which so-called "panoramas"[1] are painted. The reproduction of the painting *The Flight of Charles the Bold After the Battle of Murten*, often to be found on German fairgrounds, was always inadequately painted. Yet the copyist achieved an alienation effect not to be found in the original; and one can scarcely blame this on his inadequacy. The fleeing general, his horse, his retinue, and the landscape are quite consciously painted to give the impression of an *extra*-ordinary occasion, a forbidding catastrophe. Despite his inadequacy the painter admirably produces the effect of the unexpected; astonishment guides his brush. This *effect of estrangement* is also known to the Chinese actor, who uses it in a very subtle manner.

Everyone knows that the Chinese theatre makes use of many symbols. A general wears little ribbons on his shoulders, as many, in fact, as the regiments he commands. Poverty is indicated by sewing irregular patches onto silk robes, the patches being also of silk, though of a different color. The personages of a play are characterized by a particular kind of make-up, that is, simply by paint. Certain gestures with both hands represent the forcible opening of a door, and so forth. The stage stays unchanged though articles of furniture are brought on during the play. All this has been known for a long time and can scarcely be taken over by us *in toto*. And one is accustomed to regard an artistic phenomenon *in toto* – as a whole. However, if you want to study one particular effect among many you have to break with this custom.

In the Chinese theatre the "alienation effect" is achieved in the following way. The Chinese performer does not act as if, in addition to the three walls around him there were also a fourth wall. *He makes it clear that he knows he is being looked at.* Thus, one of the illusions of the European stage is set aside. The audience forfeits the illusion of being unseen spectators at an event which is really taking place. The European stage has worked out an elaborate technique by which the fact that scenes are so arranged as to be easily seen by the audience is concealed. The Chinese approach renders this technique superfluous. As openly as acrobats the actors can choose those positions which show them off to best advantage.

Another expedient is this: *the actor looks at himself.* Presenting, let us say, a cloud, its unsuspected appearance, its gentle yet strong development, its speedy yet gradual transformation; from time to time he looks at the spectator as if to say: Isn't it just like that? But he also looks at his own arms and legs, guiding them, examining them, in the end, perhaps praising them. If he glances at the floor or measures the space available for his act, he sees nothing in this procedure that could disturb the illusion. In this way the performer separates mimicry[2] (presenting the act of observation) from gesture[3] (presenting the cloud) but the latter loses nothing thereby, for the attitude of the body reacts back upon the face, gives to the face, as it were, its own expression. An expression now of complete reservation, now of utter triumph. The performer has used his face as an empty sheet of paper that can be written on by bodily movement.

The performer wishes to appear alien to the spectator. Alien to the point of arousing surprise. This he manages by seeing himself and his performance as alien. In this way the things he does on the stage become astonishing. By this craft everyday things are removed from the realm of the self-evident.

A young woman, a fisherman's daughter, is shown on the stage, rowing a boat. She stands up and steers the (non-existent) boat with a little oar that hardly comes down to her knees. The current runs faster. Now it is harder for her to keep her balance. Now she is in a bay and rows more quietly. Well, that's the way to row a boat. But this voyage has an historic quality, as if it had been sung in many songs, a most unusual voyage, known to everyone. Each of this famous girl's movements has been preserved in pictures. Every bend in the river was an adventure that one knows about. The bend she is now approaching is well-known. This feeling in the spectator is called forth by the performer's attitude. It is she who confers fame on the voyage. (The scene reminds us of the march to Budweis in Piscator's production of *The Good Soldier Schweik*. Schweik's three-day march under sun and moon to the front, which, curiously enough, he never reaches, was seen in a completely historical way, as something just as worth thinking about as Napoleon's journey to Russia in 1812.)

To look at himself is for the performer an artful and artistic act of self-estrangement. Any empathy on the spectator's part is thereby prevented from becoming total, that is, from being a complete self-surrender. An admirable distance from the events portrayed is achieved. This is not to say that the spectator experiences no empathy whatsoever. He feels his way into the actor as into an observer. In this manner an observing, watching attitude is cultivated.

In many ways the art of the Chinese actor seems to the western actor cold. Not that the Chinese theatre renounces the presentation of feelings! The actor presents events of considerable passionateness, but his delivery remains unimpassioned. At moments when the presented character is deeply excited, the performer takes a strand of hair between his lips and bites it. That is pretty much of a rite; there is nothing eruptive about it. Clearly it is a matter of the repetition of an event by another man, a *rendering* (artistic, certainly). The performer shows that *this man is beside himself* and he indicates the outward signs of such a state of mind. This is the proper way to express being beside oneself. (It may be improper too, but not for the stage.) Anyway a few special symptoms are chosen out of many – obviously with great deliberation. Anger is naturally distinguished from fury, hate from dislike, love from sympathy, but the various movements of feeling are sparingly presented. The pervading coolness arises from the fact that the individual is not so much the center of interest as in western theatre. True, the cult of the star has gone further in Asia than perhaps anywhere else. The spectator's eyes positively hang on the star. The other roles give him the cue to the star, place obstacles in his way, show him off. Nevertheless, the star places himself at a distance from the role he plays in the manner just described. He guards against making the audience feel exactly what the character is feeling. Nobody will be raped by the individual he presents. This individual is not the spectator but his neighbor.

The western performer does all he can to bring the spectator as close as possible to the events and the character being presented. To this end he gets him to feel his way into him, the actor. He spends all his strength on transforming himself as completely as possible into another type of person, the type being presented. When this complete transformation is achieved, his art is pretty much exhausted. Once he *is* the bank clerk, the doctor, the general, he needs just as little art as the bank clerk, the doctor or the general need in real life. The act of completely transforming oneself takes a lot of trouble to accomplish. Stanislavsky provides a whole list of devices, a whole *system* of devices, by means of which this "creative mood" can be produced afresh at each performance. Usually the actor does not succeed for long in really feeling like the other person. He soon begins, in his exhaustion, to copy certain external features of his carriage or tone of voice, and thereby the effect on the audience is appallingly weakened. Doubtless the reason is that the creation of the Other Man was an intuitive act taking place in the subconscious. The subconscious is very hard to regulate. It has, so to speak, a bad memory.

The Chinese performer knows nothing of these difficulties. He eschews complete transformation. He confines himself at the outset to merely *quoting* the character. But with how much art he does this! He requires only a minimum of illusion. What he shows is worth seeing even to those who are not out of their senses. What western actor, with the exception of a comedian or so, could do what the Chinese actor Mei Lanfang does – show the elements of his craft clad in evening dress in a room with no special lights before an audience of professionals? The scene of Lear's division of his kingdom, let us say, or Othello and the handkerchief? He'd be like a conjurer at a fairground showing his magical tricks, which no one would want to see a second time. He would merely show how one *dissembles*. The hypnosis would pass and there would remain a couple of pounds of badly beaten-up mimicry, a commodity quickly thrown together for sale in the dark to customers who are in a hurry. Naturally, no western actor would arrange such a performance. Isn't art sacrosanct? Isn't theatrical metamorphosis a mystical process? He lays store by the fact that what he does is unconscious; it has more value for him that way. A comparison with Asiatic acting shows how deeply parsonic our art still is.

Certainly it gets harder all the time for our actors to consummate the mystery of complete transformation. Their subconscious minds' memories are getting weaker all the time. And even when the actor is a genius it is hard to create truth out of the adulterated intuition of a member of a class society.

It is difficult for the actor to generate certain emotions and moods in himself every evening and comparatively easy to render the outward signs that accompany and denote these emotions. Certainly the transference of these emotions to the spectator, the emotional contagion, does not take place automatically. The "alienation effect" enters in at this point, not in the form of emotionlessness, but in the form of emotions which do not have to be identical with those of the presented character. The spectator can feel joy at the sight of sorrow, disgust at the sight of anger. We speak of rendering the outward signs of emotions as a way of effecting alienation. This procedure may, however, fail to do so. The actor can so render these signs and select these signs that, on the contrary, emotional contagion follows, because the actor *has*, while rendering the signs, generated in himself the emotions to be presented. The actor can easily stir up anger within himself by letting his voice swell and by holding his breath, also by drawing his throat muscles together so that the blood flows to his head. In this case, "alienation" is out of the question. On the other hand, "alienation" does occur when at a particular point and without transition the actor displays a deadly pale face which he has acquired artificially. (He held his face in his hands, and in his hands was some white grease paint.) If the actor exhibits at the same time an apparently undisturbed nature, his fright at this point in the play (occasioned by a piece of news or a discovery) will produce the "alienation effect." To act in this manner is more healthy and, it seems to us, more worthy of a thinking being. It calls for a considerable knowledge of men, a considerable general intelligence, and a keen grasp of what is socially important. Obviously a creative process is going on here too. And one of a higher sort, since it belongs to the sphere of consciousness.

Obviously the "alienation effect" in no way presupposes an unnatural style of acting. One must at all costs not think of what is called Stylization. On the contrary the success of the "alienation effect" is dependent on the lightness and naturalness of the whole procedure. And when the actor comes to examine the truth of this performance – a necessary operation, which gives Stanislavsky a lot of trouble – he is not merely thrown back on his natural sensibility. He can always be corrected by reference to reality. Does an angry man really speak like that? Does a guilty man sit like that? He can be corrected, that is, from without, by other people. His style is such that nearly every sentence could be *judged* by the audience. Nearly every gesture is submitted to the approval of the audience.

The Chinese actor is in no trance. He can be interrupted at any moment. There is no question of his "coming to." After an interruption he will take up his performance at the exact place where he was interrupted. We disturb him at no mystic moment of creation. He had finished "creating" before he came on the stage. If scene building is going on while he is acting, he doesn't mind. Stagehands hand him whatever he needs for his work quite openly. During a death scene played by Mei Lanfang a spectator sitting near me let out a startled cry at one of the actor's gestures. Several spectators in front of us turned indignantly around and hissed: *Sh*! They conducted themselves as at the death of some real girl. Perhaps their behavior was right for a European production, but it was unspeakably ridiculous in a Chinese theatre. The "alienation effect" had misfired.

It is not altogether easy to regard the "alienation effect" of Chinese acting as something that can be shaken loose from the Chinese theatre and exported. The Chinese theatre seems to us uncommonly precious, its presentation of human passions merely schematic, its conception of society rigid and false. At first sight nothing in this great art seems useful in a realistic and revolutionary theatre. The motives and aims of the "alienation effect" are alien and suspect.

In the first place it is difficult, when watching the Chinese act, to rid ourselves of the feeling of strangeness that they arouse in us because we are Europeans. One must be able to imagine they achieve the "alienation effect" also in their Chinese spectators. But, and this is more difficult, we must not allow ourselves to be disturbed at the fact that the Chinese performer creates an impression of mystery for a quite different purpose from any that we can envisage. If one has learned to think dialectically one can find it impossible that a technique which is taken from the realm of magic can be used to combat magic with. The Chinese performer may intend to use the "alienation effect" to make the events on stage mysterious, incomprehensible, and uncontrollable to the audience. And yet this effect can be used to make the events mundane, comprehensible, and controllable.

The attitude of the scientist, who at first views the object of his investigation with astonishment, may resemble the attitude of a magician. Yet these apparently identical attitudes have a precisely opposite function. Whoever finds the formula 2 × 2 = 4 obvious is no mathematician; neither is the man who doesn't know what the formula means. The man who viewed a lamp swinging on a rope with astonishment at first and found it not obvious but very remarkable that the lamp swung thus and not otherwise – such a man approached the understanding of the phenomenon and, with this, the mastery of the phenomenon. It won't do to exclaim that this attitude is appropriate to science alone and not to art. Why shouldn't art try (by its own means, of course) to contribute to the great social task of mastering life?

A technical feature like the "alienation effect" in Chinese acting can be studied with profit only by those who *need* such a feature for particular social purposes. As charm, novelty, finesse, and formalistic frivolity it could never become significant.

Moreover, in the experiments of the new German theatre, the "alienation effect" was developed quite independently. The influence of Asiatic acting was nil.

In the German epic theatre the "alienation effect" was employed not only through the actors but also through the music (choruses and solos) and the décor (placards, film, etc.). The aim was the *historification* of the events presented. Under this head the following is meant.

The bourgeois theatre (this is everything that we think of when we speak of theatre in general) sifts out from its materials the timeless element. The presentation of the human being stops with the so-called Eternally Human. By a certain ordering of the plot or fable, general situations are created in which Man – the man of all periods and every color – can express himself. Events on stage are all one long cue, the cue for the Eternal Answer, the inevitable, usual, natural, human answer. Here is an example. The black man loves in the same way as the white man. But only when the plot extorts the same reaction from him as the white man gives (the formula presumably works in reverse too) is the result called Art. The peculiar and distinct elements may have a place in the cue; the answer is the same for both; and in the answer there is nothing peculiar and distinct.

Such a philosophy may acknowledge the existence of history but it is an unhistorical philosophy. Certain circumstances may be changed;

milieux are transformed; but man does not change. History is valid for the milieu; but not for man. The milieu is so essentially unimportant, is understood just as the *occasion* for things. A variable quantity, and essentially inhuman, it really exists without man. It confronts him as a closed unity. And *he* is forever unchanged, a fixed quantity. To regard man as a variable which, moreover, controls the milieu, to conceive of the liquidation of the milieu in relationships between men – these notions spring from a new mode of thought, historical thought. An example will cut short this historical-philosophical excursion.

The following is to be presented on the stage. A girl leaves her family to take a job in a big city. (Dreiser's *American Tragedy*, which was adapted to the stage by Piscator.) For the bourgeois theatre the idea is a pretty limited one. It constitutes only the beginning of a story, the bit of information we must have if we are to understand or be excited by what follows. The actor's imagination can hardly be set in motion at all by this. In a way the event is general: girls do take jobs. And in this case one can be excited at the thought of what in particular will happen to her. The event is also peculiar: this girl leaves home; had she stayed, the following would not have occurred. The important thing is what kind of girl she is. What is her character? That her family lets her go is not a subject for investigation. It is credible. Motives are "credible."

For our history-making theatre it is otherwise. It seizes on the special, the particular, on what needs investigation in this everyday event. What? The family lets one of its members leave the paternal roof? To live quite independently and earn her living without assistance? Can she do it? Will what she has learned in the family help her to earn her living? Can families not keep their children any more? Are they a burden? Is this so in all families? Was it always so? Is this the way of the world and not to be affected? "When the fruit is ripe, it falls from the tree:" does the proverb apply? If children always and at all times make themselves independent, if this is something biological, does it always happen in the same way, for the same reason, with the same results?

These are the questions – or some of them – that the actors have to answer if they want to present the event as a unique historical one, if they want to point to it as a custom which provides a key to the whole social structure of a particular, transitory period. How can such an event be presented so that its historical character comes out? How can the confusion of our unhappy age be made to stand out while a mother, amid warnings and moral demands, packs her daughter's bag, which is a very small bag? So many demands and so little underwear? Warnings for a lifetime and bread for five hours? How is this to be put on the stage? When she hands the small bag to her daughter the mother says: "Well, I think that'll be enough." How can the actress playing the role speak this sentence so that it will be understood as an historical expression? It can only be done if the "alienation effect" is brought off. The actress must not make of this sentence an affair of her own. She must hand it over for criticism. She must make it possible for the audience to understand the motives behind it. She must make protest possible.

In the Artef Players Collective in New York (1935), I saw a stage version of Samuel Ornitz' *Haunch, Paunch and Jowl*, which showed how an east-side boy rose to be a corrupt lawyer. The theatre could not play the piece. And yet scenes like this were in it. Sitting in the street in front of his house, the young lawyer gives legal advice at very low prices. A young woman comes with the complaint that her leg had been damaged in a traffic accident. But the case was bungled. Her claim for compensation has not yet been handed in. In despair she points at her leg and shouts: "It's healing already!" Working without the "alienation effect," this theater could not adequately display the horror of a bloody age in this extraordinary scene. Few people in the auditorium paid any attention to it. Few of them, even if they read these lines, would remember the woman's cry. The actress spoke it as something obvious. But precisely the fact that such a complaint seems obvious to the poor woman the actress should have reported to the audience as an outraged messenger returning from the lowest of hells. In this she would have needed to be helped by a special technique to underline the historical nature of a given social condition. Only the "alienation effect" makes this possible.

In bringing forward new artistic principles and in working out new methods of presentation we must proceed from the imperative demands of an age of transition. It seems possible and necessary to rebuild society. All events in the human realm are being examined. Everything must be seen from the social standpoint. Among other effects, a new theatre will find the "alienation effect" necessary for the criticism of society and for historical reporting on changes already accomplished.

NOTES

1. A "panorama" is a series of pictures used by a ballad singer as an accompaniment to his songs.
2. *Mimik.*
3. *Gestik.*

THEATRE FOR LEARNING

Bertolt Brecht

Translated by Edith Anderson

When anyone spoke of modern theatre a few years ago, he mentioned the Moscow, the New York or the Berlin theatre. He may also have spoken of a particular production of Jouvet's in Paris, of Cochran's in London, or the Habima performance of *The Dybbuk*, which, in fact, belonged to Russian theatre since it was directed by Vakhtangov; but by and large, there were only three capitals so far as modern theatre was concerned.

The Russian, the American and the German theatres were very different from one another, but they were alike in being modern, i.e., in introducing technical and artistic innovations. In a certain sense they even developed stylistic similarities, probably because technique is international (not only the technique directly required for the stage, but also that which exerts an influence on it, the film, for example) and because the cities in question were great progressive cities in great industrial countries. Most recently, the Berlin theatre seemed to have taken the lead among the most advanced capitalist countries. What was common to modern theatre found there its strongest and, for the moment, most mature expression.

The last phase of the Berlin theatre, which as I said only revealed in its purest form the direction in which modern theatre was developing, was the so-called *epic theatre*. What was known as the *Zeitstueck*[1] or Piscator theatre or the didactic play all belonged to epic theatre.

EPIC THEATRE

The expression "epic theatre" seemed self-contradictory to many people, since according to the teachings of Aristotle the epic and the dramatic forms of presenting a story were considered basically different from one another. The difference between the two forms was by no means merely seen in the fact that one was performed by living people while the other made use of a book – epic works like those of Homer and the *minnesingers* of the Middle Ages were likewise theatrical performances, and dramas like Goethe's *Faust* or Byron's *Manfred* admittedly achieved their greatest effect as books. Aristotle's teachings themselves distinguished the dramatic from the epic form as a difference in construction, whose laws were dealt with under two different branches of aesthetics. This construction depended on the different way in which the works were presented to the public, either on the stage or through a book, but nevertheless, apart from that, "the dramatic" could also be found in epic works and "the epic" in dramatic works. The bourgeois novel in the last century considerably developed "the dramatic," which meant the strong centralization of plot and an organic interdependence of the separate parts. The dramatic is characterized by a certain passion in the tone of the exposition and a working out of the collision of forces. The epic writer, Döblin,[2] gave an excellent description when he said that the epic, in contrast to the dramatic, could practically be cut up with a scissors into single pieces, each of which could stand alone.

I do not wish to discuss here in what way the contrasts between epic and dramatic, long regarded as irreconcilable, lost their rigidity, but simply to point out that (other causes aside) technical achievements enabled the stage to include narrative elements in dramatic presentations. The potentialities of projection, the film, the greater facility in changing sets through machinery, completed the equipment of the stage and did so at a moment when the most important human events could no longer be so simply portrayed as through personification of the driving forces or through subordinating the characters to invisible, metaphysical powers. To make the events understandable, it had become necessary to play up the "bearing" of the *environment* upon the people living in it.

Of course this environment had been shown in plays before, not, however, as an independent element but only from the viewpoint of the main figure of the drama. It rose out of the hero's reaction to it. It was seen as a storm may be "seen" if you observe on the sea a ship spreading its sails and the sails bellying. But in the epic threatre it was now to appear as an independent element.

The stage began to narrate. The narrator no longer vanished with the fourth wall. Not only did the background make its own comment on stage happenings through large screens which evoked other events occurring at the same time in other places, documenting or contradicting statements by characters through quotations projected onto a screen, lending tangible, concrete statistics to abstract discussions, providing facts and figures for happenings which were plastic but unclear in their meaning; the actors no longer threw themselves completely into their roles but maintained a certain distance from the character performed by them, even distinctly inviting criticism.

• Nothing permitted the audience any more to lose itself through simple empathy, uncritically (and practically without any consequences) in the experiences of the characters on the stage. The presentation exposed the subject matter and the happenings to a process of de-familiarization.[3] De-familiarization was required to make things understood. When things are "self-evident," understanding is simply dispensed with. The "natural" had to be given an element of the *conspicuous*. Only in this way could the laws of cause and effect become plain. Characters had to behave as they *did* behave, and at the same time be capable of behaving otherwise.

These were great changes.

TWO OUTLINES

The following little outlines may indicate in what respect the function of the epic is distinguished from that of the dramatic theatre:

1

Dramatic Form	*Epic Form*
The stage "incarnates" an event.	It relates it.
Involves the audience in an action, uses up its activity.	Makes the audience an observer but arouses its activity.
Helps it to feel.	Compels it to make decisions.
Communicates experiences.	Communicates insights.
The audience is projected into an event.	Is confronted with it.
Suggestion is used.	Arguments are used.
Sensations are preserved.	Impelled to the level of perceptions.
The character is a known quantity.	The character is subjected to investigation.
Man unchangeable.	Man who can change and make changes.
His drives.	His motives.
Events move in a straight line.	In "irregular" curves.
Natura non facit saltus.	Facit saltus.
The world as it is.	The world as it is becoming.

2

The audience in the dramatic theatre says:

Yes, I have felt that too. – That's how I am. – That is only natural. – That will always be so. – This person's suffering shocks me because he has no way out. – This is great art: everything in it is self-evident. – I weep with the weeping, I laugh with the laughing.

The audience in the epic theatre says:

I wouldn't have thought that. – People shouldn't do things like that. – That's extremely odd, almost unbelievable. – This has to stop. – This person's suffering shocks me, because there might be a way out for him. – This is great art: nothing in it is self-evident. – I laugh over the weeping, I weep over the laughing.

DIDACTIC THEATRE

The stage began to instruct.

Oil, inflation, war, social struggles, the family, religion, wheat, the meat-packing industry, became subjects for theatrical portrayal. Choruses informed the audience about facts it did not know. In montage form, films showed events all over the world. Projections provided statistical data. As the "background" came to the fore, the actions of the characters became exposed to criticism. Wrong and right actions were exhibited. People were shown who knew what they were doing, and other people were shown who did not know. The theatre entered the province of the philosophers – at any rate, the sort of philosophers who wanted not only to explain the world but also to change it. Hence the theatre philosophisized; hence it instructed. And what became of entertainment? Were audiences put back in school, treated as illiterates? Were they to take examinations and be given marks?

It is the general opinion that a very decided difference exists between learning and being entertained. The former may be useful, but only the latter is pleasant. Thus we have to defend the epic theatre against a suspicion that it must be an extremely unpleasant, a joyless, indeed a wearying business.

Well, we can only say that the contrast between learning and being entertained does not necessarily exist in nature; it has not always existed and it need not always exist.

Undoubtedly, the kind of learning we experienced in school, in training for a profession, etc., is a laborious business. But consider under what circumstances and for what purpose it is done. It is, in fact, a purchase. Knowledge is simply a commodity. It is acquired for the purpose of being resold. All those who have grown too old for school have to pursue knowledge on the Q.T., so to speak, because anybody who admits he still has to study depreciates himself as one who knows too little. Apart from that, the utility of learning is very much limited by factors over which the student has no control. There is unemployment, against which no knowledge protects. There is the division of labor, which makes comprehensive knowledge unnecessary and impossible. Often, those who study do it only when they see no other possibility of getting ahead. There is not much knowledge that procures power, but much knowledge is only procured through power.

Learning means something very different to people in different strata of society. There are people who cannot conceive of any improvement in conditions; conditions seem good enough to them. Whatever may happen to petroleum, they make a profit out of it. And they feel, after all, that they are getting rather old. They can scarcely expect many more years of life. So why continue to learn? They have already spoken their "Ugh!"[4] But there are also people who have not yet "had their turn," who are discontented with the way things are, who have an immense practical interest in learning, who want orientation badly, who know they are lost without learning – these are the best and most ambitious learners. Such differences also exist among nations and peoples. Thus the lust for learning is dependent on various things; in short, there *is* thrilling learning, joyous and militant learning.

If learning could not be delightful, then the theatre, by its very nature, would not be in a position to instruct.

Theatre remains theatre, even when it is didactic theatre; and if it is good theatre it will entertain.

THEATRE AND SCIENCE

"But what has science to do with art? We know very well that science can be diverting, but not everything that diverts belongs in the theatre."

I have often been told when I pointed out the inestimable services that modern science, properly utilized, could render to art (especially to the theatre), that art and science were two admirable but completely different fields of human activity. This is a dreadful platitude, of course, and the best thing to do is admit at once that it is quite right, like most platitudes. Art and science operate in very different ways – agreed. Still, I must admit – bad as this may sound – that I cannot manage as an artist without making use of certain sciences. This may make many people seriously doubt my artistic ability. They are accustomed to regarding poets as unique, almost unnatural beings who unerringly, almost like gods, perceive things that others can only perceive through the greatest efforts and hard work. Naturally, it is unpleasant to have to admit not being one of those so endowed. But it must be admitted. It must also be denied that this application to science has anything to do with some pardonable avocation indulged in the evening after work is done. Everyone knows that Goethe also went in for natural science, Schiller for history, presumably – this is the charitable assumption – as a sort of hobby. I would not simply accuse these two of having needed the science for their poetic labors, nor would I use them to excuse myself, but I must say I need the sciences. And I must even admit that I regard suspiciously all sorts of people who I know do not keep abreast of science, who, in other words, sing as the birds sing, or as they imagine the birds sing. This does not mean that I would reject a nice poem about the taste of a flounder or the pleasure of a boating party just because the author had not studied gastronomy or navigation. But I think that unless every resource is employed towards understanding the great, complicated events in the world of man, they cannot be seen adequately for what they are.

Let us assume that we want to portray great passions or events which influence the fates of peoples. Such a passion today might be the drive for power. Supposing that a poet "felt" this drive and wanted to show someone striving for power – how could he absorb into his own experience the extremely complicated mechanism within which the struggle for power today takes place? If his hero is a political man, what are the workings of politics? If he is a business man, what are the workings of business? And then there are poets who are much less passionately interested in any individual's drive for power than in business affairs and politics as such! How are they to acquire the necessary knowledge? They will scarcely find out enough by going around and keeping their eyes open, although that is at least better than rolling their eyes in a fine frenzy. The establishment of a newspaper like the *Völkische Beobachter* or a business like Standard Oil is a rather complicated matter, and these things are not simply absorbed through the pores. Psychology is an important field for the dramatist. It is supposed that while an ordinary person may not be in a position to discover, without special instruction, what makes a man commit murder, certainly a writer ought to have the "inner resources" to be able to give a picture of a murderer's mental state. The assumption is that you only need look into yourself in such a case; after all, there is such a thing as imagination. . . . For a number of reasons I can no longer abandon myself to this amiable hope of managing so comfortably. I cannot find in myself alone all the motives which, as we learn from newspapers and scientific reports, are discovered in human beings. No more than any judge passing sentence am I able to imagine adequately, unaided, the mental state of a murderer. Modern psychology, from psychoanalysis to behaviorism, provides me with insights which help me to form a quite different judgment of the case, especially when I take into consideration the findings of sociology, and do not ignore economics or history. You may say: This is getting complicated. I must answer, it *is* complicated. Perhaps I can talk you into agreeing with me that a lot of literature is extremely primitive; yet you will ask in grave concern: Wouldn't such an evening in the theatre be a pretty alarming business? The answer to that is: No.

Whatever knowledge may be contained in a poetic work, it must be completely converted into poetry. In its transmuted form, it gives the same type of satisfaction as any poetic work. And although it does not provide that satisfaction found in science as such, a certain inclination to penetrate more deeply into the nature of things and a desire to make the world controllable, are necessary to ensure enjoyment of poetic works generated by this era of great discoveries and inventions.

IS THE EPIC THEATRE A SORT OF "MORAL INSTITUTION"?

According to Friedrich Schiller the theatre should be a moral institution. When Schiller posed this demand it scarcely occurred to him that by moralizing from the stage he might drive the audience out of the theatre. In his day the audience had no objection to moralizing. Only later on did Friedrich Nietzsche abuse him as the moral trumpeter of Säckingen.[5] To Nietzsche a concern with morality seemed a dismal affair; to Schiller it seemed completely gratifying. He knew of nothing more entertaining and satisfying than to propagate ideals. The bourgeoisie was just establishing the concept of the nation. To furnish your house, show off your new hat, present your bills for payment is highly gratifying. But to speak of the decay of your house, to have to sell your old hat and pay the bills yourself is a truly dismal affair, and that was how Nietzsche saw it a century later. It was no use talking to him about morality or, in consequence, about the other Friedrich. Many people also attacked the epic theatre, claiming it was too moralistic. Yet moral utterances were secondary in the epic theatre. Its intention was less to moralize than to study. And it did study; but then came the rub: the moral of the story. Naturally, we cannot claim that we began making studies just because studying was so much fun and not for any concrete reason, or that the results of our studies then took us completely by surprise. Undoubtedly there were painful discrepancies in the world around us, conditions that were hard to bear, conditions of a kind not only hard to bear for moral reasons. Hunger, cold and hardship are not only burdensome for moral reasons. And the purpose of our investigation was not merely to arouse moral misgivings about certin conditions (although such misgivings might easily be felt, if not by every member of the audience; such misgivings, for example, were seldom felt by those who profited by the conditions in question). The purpose of our investigation was to make visible the means by which those onerous conditions could be done away with. We were not speaking on behalf of morality but on behalf of the wronged. These are really two different things, for moral allusions are often used in telling the wronged that they must put up with their situation. For such moralists, people exist for morality, not morality for people.

Nevertheless it can be deduced from these remarks to what extent and in what sense the epic theatre is a moral institution.

CAN EPIC THEATRE BE PERFORMED ANYWHERE?

From the standpoint of style, the epic theatre is nothing especially new. In its character of show, of demonstration, and its emphasis on the artistic, it is related to the ancient Asian theatre. The medieval mystery play, and also the classical Spanish and Jesuit theatres, showed an instructive tendency.

Those theatre forms corresponded to certain tendencies of their time and disappeared with them. The modern epic theatre is also linked with definite tendencies. It can by no means be performed anywhere. Few of the great nations today are inclined to discuss their problems in the theatre. London, Paris, Tokyo and Rome maintain their theatres for quite different purposes. Only in a few places, and not for long, have circumstances been favorable to an epic, instructive theatre. In Berlin, fascism put a violent end to the development of such a theatre.[6]

Besides a certain technical standard, it presupposes a powerful social movement which has an interest in the free discussion of vital problems, the better to solve them, and can defend this interest against all opposing tendencies.

The epic theatre is the broadest and most far-reaching experiment in great modern theatre, and it has to overcome all the enormous difficulties that all vital forces in the area of politics, philosophy, science and art have to overcome.

NOTES

1. Play dealing with current problems (Trans.).
2. Alfred Döblin (1878–1957), German novelist and essayist, author of *Berlin Alexanderplatz*, etc.
3. *Entfremdung*: "alienation."
4. Reference to popular German literature about Red Indians, by the author Karl May, in which, after a chieftain had given his opinion at a pow-wow he would conclude, "I have spoken. Ugh!" (Trans.).
5. Nietzsche's quip referred to a banal verse tale by Viktor Scheffel, *Der Trompeter von Säckingen*, a standard favorite in Germany's "plush sofa kultur" – a parallel of Victorianism – in the second half of the nineteenth century (Trans.).
6. After the defeat of the Nazis in 1945, the German administrators of the then Soviet-occupied zone – later to become the German Democratic Republic [now part of the unified Federal German Republic] – invited Brecht to establish his own theatre in East Berlin. This theatre, the "Berliner Ensemble," is recognized today all over the world as a classical type of epic theatre (Trans.).

3

AN EPIC THEATRE CATECHISM

Mordecai Gorelik

By this time many of us have heard of the controversial doctrines of epic theatre. Some of us have been intrigued by epic theory; others have lost no time expressing their annoyance. In his lifetime Bertolt Brecht, epic's chief architect, encountered a full measure of both reactions. He accepted enthusiasms calmly and took rejections in the same spirit. In spite of all box-office accountants he insisted that the validity of a theatrical credo was not to be determined by a counting of heads. "Einstein's theory was understood at first by half a dozen people," he once told me. "Whether I am accepted by six people or six million is beside the point. The point is whether I am justified."

It must be admitted that the meaning of epic theatre is not quickly grasped. We may have learned that it originated in Germany in the 1920s with the plays of Brecht and the stage direction of Erwin Piscator. We may have seen one or two epic plays on stage in Europe, or at least have witnessed a local attempt at an epic production of one of Brecht's plays. We may have heard that epic aims at a stage form worthy of our age of science. We may have learned, in greater detail, that epic is anti-magical, anti-romantic, anti-naturalistic, anti-mystical and anti-Freudian, and that it rejects the Wagnerian concept of the synthesis of theatrical elements on stage.

The more we have learned, the worse the confusion. It may be helpful to consider some of the many misconceptions now current among theatre people concerning epic theatre.

Does a director's use of epic technique automatically prove he is talented?

Not necessarily. Not every "modernist" who paints in the style of Picasso or Bracque is an automatically gifted painter. Any dramatist, director, actor or designer who essays the epic method must give proof of his talent in the technique he has chosen.

Does epic believe in alienating an audience?

No. The idea is to get the audience to think, to reflect, as well as to feel;

to judge the characters and the action of a play rather than to sit on the edge of their chairs with excitement. This "alienation" should also be applied to the script, whose story should be offered with a certain reasonable detachment instead of with sheer emotionalism or metetricious excitement. If this treatment "alienates" an audience, so much the worse for the audience.

Is it a fact that Brecht was against suspense and climax in drama, and that he objected to the well-made play?

The "well-made play" to which this question refers is the kind developed by Sardou. Considered the ideal form in the contemporary theatre, it is tightly written and suspenseful, with a crisis in each act building to a shattering emotional climax and followed by a brief dénouement. Brecht was suspicious of this form on the ground that it is an instrument for "putting over" trivial, stereotyped or false ideas. I have never agreed with Brecht about this; it seems to me like throwing out the baby with the bath water. I see no reason why a play of real merit should not be well-organized in its presentation. In fact Brecht employs suspense in his plays, but it is usually a sense of reasonable expectation rather than one of nail-chewing apprehension. Brecht also has climax in his plays, but it is the weight of a cumulated experience rather than an explosion of feelings. This type of suspense and climax are typical of the chronicle form, which was the form that Brecht invariably used.

Is epic opposed to catharsis in drama?

It is opposed to catharsis as the *sole purpose* of drama. Believing, as it does, that the basic purpose of drama is to teach, it opposes the current notion that the basic purpose of drama is to purge the spectator and to do no more than that. Epic maintains that the spectator should not merely be relieved of his apprehensions but that he should be shown how to deal with his problems. Epic expects the playgoer not only to leave the theatre "feeling better" but to go away wiser and more capable. Current dramatic criticism, which makes so much of Aristotle's theory of catharsis, has forgotten all about Aristotle's theory of *anagnorisis* – the movement of a drama from the unknown to the known.

Is epic anti-emotional and addressed strictly to the intellect?

No. The contemporary theatre, which relies heavily on sex, sadism and sweetness, is overwhelmingly emotional in its appeal. Epic sees no reason why the spectator should be asked to check his intelligence along with his hat and coat when he enters the theatre. Brecht observed, "Our contemporary theatre is decapitated; we must put its head back on its shoulders." A healthy play should engage the mind as well as the emotions. Deep feeling combined with thoughtfulness is the ideal epic writing.

Are plays like Samuel Beckett's *Waiting for Godot* epic?

This notion is naive. Epic is opposed to naturalistic writing and the picture-frame, peep-box, proscenium-frame stage; the supposition is, therefore, that all non-naturalistic plays are epic. But in fact epic opposes all plays, whether naturalistic or not, which fail to create living characters, plausible motivations, or rational dilemmas. It has no use for virtuoso theatricalism and had equally small use for dim allegories which dress up some stereotyped philosophy or other or which give only a vivid impression of the dramatist's own complexes. Plays of this sort are as nearly anti-epic as is possible for any play to be. In this category fall such diverse efforts as Ionesco's *The Chairs*, Tennessee Williams' *Camino Real*, Saroyan's *The Time of Your Life*, Wilder's *The Skin of Our Teeth*, T. S, Eliot's *The Family Reunion*, Fry's *A Sleep of Prisoners*, Kafka's *The Trial*, Georg Kaiser's *Gas*, Strindberg's *Dream Play*, Ibsen's *The Master Builder*, or some of Brecht's earlier plays such as *Man is Man*.

Are Brecht's the only epic plays so far written?

To date, at least, there have been no examples of completely epic plays. Some plays are more epic than others, depending on how much they tell of the wider social background of their *personae*. Shakespeare, who could evoke the whole social matrix of his characters, was an epic dramatist long before Brecht. So was Molière. It is characteristic of better playwrights that their stories emerge out of the nexus of social relations. Arthur Miller's *The Crucible* is more epic than his *Death of a Salesman*. But even the cheapest boy-meets-girl concoction usually offers some fragments of epic information: boy-meets-girl in the French Revolution at least employs a few clichés of history in bringing on the aristocrats and the sanscoulottes, the tumbrils and the guillotine. Brecht considered his own plays to be first steps in the direction of a specifically epic drama.

Does the epic insistence on "learning-plays" turn theatre into a dull lecture?

It is a fallacy to suppose that a good play does not teach anything. Even the stupidest play teaches something – if only stupid banalities. Epic says healthy plays bring clarity to their audiences. Of course, no lecture has a right to be dull. Didactic theatre, especially, has the obligation to use all its colorful resources in order to make its teaching in the highest degree entertaining. Brecht's stage productions, while unorthodox in form, have always been fascinating experiences.

Are all "thesis" plays epic?

By no means. While epic dramaturgy calls for mind as well as for feelings, it does *not* call for debate instead of action. Especially if – as usually happens in thesis plays – the script does not contain real people. Hack propaganda plays are even more impoverished. Some of George Bernard Shaw's plays, including, for instance, *In Good King Charles's Golden Days*, must be set down as boring pieces of ratiocination rather than living, didactic drama. A play like *Widowers' Houses* comes much closer to epic.

How can epic expect a dramatist to deal with a great many more facts without making his play discursive?

This is not a matter of quantity but of quality. The ability to choose themes of large scope, and to compress large themes dramatically, are among the indications of a superior dramatic talent.

Is epic against the delineation of individual character in a play?

On the contrary, epic asks for more insight into the sources of individual character. Good dramatic writing (except in special cases such as that of the Living Newspaper) is, and must be, *interpersonal*. But it should describe individuals in relation to the social, historical, and political circumstances under which they live. Current dramatic writing too often presents individuals as though they existed in a vacuum or, at most, in an aura of local color.

Is epic opposed to all psychology in dramatic writing and acting?

Epic is opposed to the over-valuation of Freudianism and especially to the current emphasis on the sexual aspects of Freudian psychiatry. This preoccupation of the contemporary theatre tends strongly to limit the themes of its scripts and its acting. Epic does, in fact, lean towards Gestalt psychology in asking for a proper adjustment of foreground characters to background and in calling for an alert type of audience reaction (contact instead of confluent attention).

Is epic theatre anti-poetic?

There is no basis for such belief. Any play that looks at life with more than a casual glance, any dramatic inquiry that has height and depth, will express itself in poetic imagery. Brecht himself was a poet-dramatist. Epic is suspicious of plays with "built-in" poetry – plays which set themselves the task of being poetic and which usually wind up as adolescent efforts without real characters or events.

Does the epic stage form consist of half-curtains on a wire, projected titles, film sequences, fragmentary scenery and loudspeaker comment?

These have been Brecht's and Piscator's personal trade-marks, used in order to compel audience attention, to amplify the script with additional data, or to deliberately slow up audience excitement. The Living Newspaper productions of the Federal Theatre era made brilliant use of such elements in dramatizing statistics and other factual data. But the use of projections, etc., is *primitive* epic form, mere beginnings in the search for a classic stage method of the future. There have been too many local productions in which these novelties appeared as guarantees of epic staging. Epic staging does not consist in the use of novel "stunts," nor is it a pastime for snobbish intellectuals. No one, at present, knows exactly what the epic form is, or what it is likely to be in the future. Right now epic is a critique, a policy, a standard, rather than a stage form that makes use of projections or loudspeaker comment.

Is epic acting anti-Stanislavsky?

In some ways, yes; in other ways, no. Epic acting is classic rather than romantic or Freudian. It denies that the actor can "creep into the skin" of his character. It asks the actor to observe and imitate the actions of his character instead of trying to "feel into" the emotional makeup of his role. The epic character explains himself fully on stage and by means of his actions; it is not necessary to know his complexes, to guess at his childhood traumas, or even to know his past personal history. On the other hand, epic is not *opposed* to learning what it can of a character's history, emotions or complexes. Epic finds that all this data is subordinate to the character's actions in the course of the story. From this point of view epic supersedes rather than negates Stanislavsky.

Does epic make the actor self-conscious by expecting him to add his own comment to the role?

Every actor adds his own comment to the part he plays; he cannot do otherwise. A bad actor calls attention to himself instead of to the character. A good actor colors his part with his own personality. Thus, there have been many differing interpretations of Hamlet by actors of the first rank. Only a very mediocre actor can turn out a characterization so neutral as to be meaningless. On the other hand, a very fine actor makes us aware that we are in the presence of a superior personality, one who tells us much about himself in telling us about the character whom he is portraying.

Are epic settings negative and colorless?

No. It is true that the epic setting is totally without "atmosphere." No attempt is made to reproduce an environment. Only such properties are used as are required by the action, and the settings are so utilitarian that they may be regarded as larger-scale properties. The cyclorama or sky drop, with its suggestion of infinite space, is not employed, and the stage is a finite platform or box. At the same time the epic scenic elements are chosen with great care and are therefore evocative as well as utile. The epic designer is still required to be selective and to organize his scenic elements on stage; furthermore, these elements are used more dynamically than in contemporary staging. The epic setting, in the productions of both Brecht and Piscator, has been colorful, inventive, rich in detail and dynamic in function. New York recently saw an example of epic design in the settings for Dürrenmatt's *The Visit*, designed by the gifted Swiss artist, Teo Otto.

Even if the criticisms made by epic are justified, of what use are they if a contemporary audience won't accept them?

There are many contemporary audiences: the American audience of Broadway, of Off-Broadway, of the university and community theatres; the naive audience; the sophisticated audience; the coterie audience. There is the audience of Western Europe and the audience of Eastern Europe. Any one of these publics may be more willing to accept epic than another may be. Brecht sometimes spoke harshly to today's audience, which he called "primitive." It consists, he said, of couples who came to the theatre to be emotionally titillated – a crude, vitiated audience which needed to be verbally spanked and reconditioned. He knew, undoubtedly, that in order to teach an audience one must take account of its current limitations. But you do this by starting off from common ground with your audience, not by catering to its prejudices.

In view of the above answers, it looks as if there is nothing new about epic at all! If Shakespeare and Molière are epic playwrights; if a good actor is an epic actor; if a good designer is an epic designer; if there is no definite epic stage form – what need is there for epic theory?

Epic does not consider itself sprung fully grown from the forehead of Zeus. It claims honorable descent from the line of healthy theatre, and it has opened the perspective of a theatre that will have a strength and grandeur equal to our achievements in science and industry. Its program can expect less than a lukewarm response from the commercial producers. But it offer a first-rate challenge to the educational and community playhouses. These have experimented with technique long enough. Let them now turn to the building of an important American theatre.

4

ARE STANISLAVSKY AND BRECHT COMMENSURABLE?

Eric Bentley

"How does Brecht's system differ from Stanislavsky's?" I have often heard this question asked, sometimes in exactly these words, and probably we shall all live to see the question appear in much this form on college examination papers. I recall, too, that as a young admirer of Brecht's, nearly twenty years ago, I myself described an actor in one of his plays as having gone "beyond Stanislavsky." Will the acting profession soon be divided between Method actors and Brechtians?

Possibly it will, so far as nomenclature is concerned, and so far as the actors' declared allegiances are concerned. It is obviously possible for some actors to love Stanislavsky, others, Brecht. What I would question is whether there are indeed two systems, two ways of life, presenting the actor with an either-or choice.

At least some of the differences between what the two men said stem from the fact that they addressed themselves to different subjects; that they differed about the *same* subject remains to be proven. Take Stanislavsky's alleged preoccupation with subjective elements and Brecht's alleged preoccupation with objective elements. Brecht speaks of what is done in a finished performance. As a director, he tells actors to do what is presumably to be done "on the night." Some Method actors will protest that it is wrong of him to tell them this: he is "working in terms of results" instead of stimulating their subconscious. Some Brechtian actors will retort that theatre *is* results, that drama is action, that the notion of a subconscious is bourgeois and decadent . . . And so the issue is joined.

But it is an imaginary issue. We can side-step it by remembering that Brecht was a playwright, Stanislavsky an actor. For Brecht, actors were the means toward the full realization of his plays. Because he had the good luck to work in a highly professional environment and with actors of very great talent, he could with reason take it that the actor's craft was simply *there* to be used. At worst, it only needed adjusting to a new kind of playwriting. At best, it could give the new playwright ideas *on* playwriting. (Some of Brecht's "theories" are deductions from the work of particular actors.) In short, Brecht, who regarded his scripts as forever unfinished, forever transformable, and his dramaturgy as young and developing, tended to regard the actor's craft as given and as already there in finished form. Thus Brecht assumed that the actor in one of his shows *was* an actor, and had his training behind him, while he made a different assumption about playwriting: namely, that he was constantly giving himself an education in it. Hence, Brecht's rehearsals, while they trained the playwright, did not, in any such direct way, train the actor. This is but another way of saying that, in a playwright's theatre, the actor is there to do what the playwright says, and he better know how to do it pronto and not hold the playwright up: that's what he's paid for. For Stanislavsky, on the other hand, it was the play which was a *fait accompli*. We do not read of his reworking his scripts either in the manner of Brecht or of the Broadway directors. He was too busy re-working the actors. I suppose every director looks for clay to mold. For Stanislavsky, the clay consisted of actors; for Brecht, of his own collected writings.

I know that the antitheses I am using oversimplify. What antitheses don't? In his last years, Brecht was beginning to mold actors, beginning, in fact, to *learn* to mold actors, and beginning to talk of acting schools and the younger generation. And conversely, perhaps, examples could be given of Stanislavsky's editing and adapting plays. Such factors, however, imply only slight modifications of the point I have made. And by consequence what Brecht, in his theoretical pronouncements, is talking about is what actors, finally, can and should do, while what Stanislavsky is talking about is the question of how they may be brought to the point where they can do this or anything else. Brecht is talking about the end result; Stanislavsky about education, about the actor's training. To say this does not provide us with all the answers. Rather, it opens up new questions.

For example, did Brecht assume that the present-day actor can give him just the result he wants? Stanislavsky, it is well known, presupposes just the opposite. In his view, it is because the actors cannot produce the right results that the Method is needed and that the emphasis on education and training is justified. Hence, when the Brechtians protest that a director must not degenerate into an acting coach, the Stanislavsky-ites can retort: "Yes, he must – at a time when the actors are not perfected professionals but still need coaching." And indeed that our "professional" actors attend acting schools and the like until middle age testifies less to their modesty than to the fact that we do not have a profession any more. Was this not true in Brecht's Germany? Another hard and ambiguous question. I would say it was on the whole not true of the Germany of Brecht's youth and therefore that his reliance upon a realized professionality was justified. That he began to get interested in training young people after World War II represents not a change of heart on his part but a change of situation in his country. It was not to a land of well-trained Weigels, Homolkas, and Granachs that he returned, and so in his latter days Brecht acquired an interest in what had been Stanislavsky's lifelong concern: the development of young people into actors.

If the generalization still stands – that by and large Brecht is concerned with getting the play produced, Stanislavsky with training the actor to be in it – would it necessarily follow that an actor trained by Stanislavsky would be a bad actor for Brecht's plays? Were Stanislavsky alive today, one can be reasonably sure he would answer this question in the negative, for it was his aim to create an instrument which could be used for *any* honorable theatrical purpose. And it is clear that he regarded this aim as attainable.

The Brechtians have their doubts – or should, if they wish to tread in the Marxian steps of the *Meister*. Stanislavsky's notion of a universally valid training and a possibly omnicompetent kind of acting they will (or should) describe as bourgeois. And they will call for a more historical view of things, according to which Stanislavsky belongs to one class and one epoch, the Brechtian theatre to another class and another epoch.

Nonetheless the record indicates that while Brecht's efforts show a single direction, Stanislavsky, like Reinhardt, produced all kinds of plays, and could train actors to excel in each of them. In my view, this is only to repeat that he was a director (a director has to work with the whole repertoire) while Brecht was a writer concerned with writing (chiefly his own). It has been the tendency of the Berlin Ensemble to impose Brechtianism upon plays by other authors; but the results are unfortunate except when the other authors are quite Brechtian. Stanislavsky on the other hand was by no means the servant, let alone the prisoner, of one style or school. It is true that he created stage naturalism in Russia. But equally he might be said to have created stage symbolism there, by his productions of Maeterlinck and Andreyev. Given a few more years of life, would he have created a Brechtian theatre? The dangers of historical "If's" are notorious. And who would wish to overlook the obvious: that Stanislavsky and Brecht were such utterly different men – different personally, as well as in nationality? And though they both came of the upper bourgeois class – which is amusing – their relation to that class is different in quite an ironic way. Stanislavsky – prize exhibit of Stalin's Russia as he lived to be – remained genteel to the end. Acquiescent in the New Society, all that he was he brought from the old. He did not like the new Communist plays, and his theatre became a museum for the best in "bourgeois" drama. While Stanislavsky was not even a rebel against his own family background, Brecht was nothing if not just that; and his love of "the people" is pale indeed beside his rage against his own class. Hence, while it is ironic enough that Stanislavsky should be the darling of a terrorist regime, it is doubly ironic that supporters of that regime should champion him against an artist who had gone out of his way to praise Stanlinist terrorism.

That part of the story would be irrelevant to my present argument except that the Communists, for their own reasons, have so handsomely contributed to the confusion that reigns concerning this Stanislavsky–Brecht relationship. In 1953, a spokesman for the German Communist Party declared Brecht's theories to be "undeniably in opposition to everything the name Stanislavsky stands for. The two leaders of the Ensemble must surely be the last people to hide their heads in the sand when faced with these facts."[1] At that time the "two leaders" of the Berlin Ensemble were Brecht himself and his wife, Helene Weigel. Frau Weigel attended the Stanislavsky Conference of 1953 with the laudable aim of showing that Brecht and Stanislavsky were not as incompatible as all that. But if, as I gather, all she had to offer was a rehash of the Nine Points her husband had printed the year before in *Theaterarbeit*, she could only have made the confusion worse. For like the Party leaders, the Brechts identified the word "Stanislavsky" with the word "Soviet." And one notes that the New Society is as given as any American orator on Commencement Day to orotund platitude. Stanislavsky believed in Man, Brecht believed in Man; Stanislavsky regarded Truthfulness as a duty, Brecht regarded Truthfulness as a duty; Stanislavsky had a sense of responsibility to society, Brecht . . . Since only seeing is believing, I will reproduce Brecht's Nine Points at the foot of this article.

When Brecht was not busy blotting himself out (like his Young Comrade) in order to be Stalin's organization man, he was apt to express hostility to Stanislavsky, as in two passages which Mr. Willett rightly cites in *Brecht on Theatre* along with the Nine Points. In the first of these passages, the target is naturalism:

> What he [Stanislavsky] cared about was naturalness, and as a result everything in his theatre seemed far too natural for anyone to pause and go into it thoroughly. You don't normally examine your own home or your own feeding habits, do you?

In the second, the target is not only the strictly naturalistic theatre but any theatre that depends too heavily on empathy. Brecht finds in the hypnotic kind of theatre a soporific intention based on fear of the audience's intelligence: "The audience's sharp eye frightens him [Stanislavsky]. He shuts it." Such passages remind us that *Brecht knew very little about Stanislavsky* and, like the rest of the world, thought of him as the lackey of one style of theatre. If the word "Soviet" does not define Stanislavsky's general outlook, neither do words like "naturalistic" and "empathic" define his theatre as a whole.

To revert to the quetion of whether Stanislavsky, had his health been better and had he lived on, would have proceeded to create a Brechtian theatre, or at least to have achieved some authentically Brechtian productions, one would probably be wise to answer: No, he belonged too unalterably to the pre-1914 world. He would not have been any more at home with Brecht than he had been with the Russian Communist playwrights – or with his own rebellious sons, such as Meyerhold. The difference between generations is a difference of spirit and temper. *But this is not to say that Stanislavsky's approach to acting will have to be discarded if Brecht's plays are to be well performed.* First a man can become an actor – with the help of the Method. Then he can learn to adapt himself to different kinds of plays – including Brecht's. Is the difference between Brecht and all other playwrights greater after all than other differences which actors have already learned to confront – say, between Shaw and Shakespeare, Wilde and Arthur Miller? Brecht's assult upon the idea of empathy and his defense of "alienation" sound more threatening in their abstract theoretic grandeur than in practice they turn out to be. The "alienation effect" is not alien to the tradition of comic acting as Stanislavsky and everyone else know it – what Brecht is attacking is the tragic tradition in its attentuated form of domestic, psychological drama of pathos and suspense. But the Charlie Chaplins and Zero Mostels practice "alienation" as Monsieur Jourdain composed prose. Perhaps it takes a German intellectual to make such heavy weather of the thing.

Incidentally, Brecht never considered that "epic" acting had really been achieved either by the Berlin Ensemble or anyone else. So there is his own authority for saying: there are no Brechtian actors. Evidently *what he had was a vision of what acting might become*, given not only changes on stage, but also in the auditorium. Should that vision ever be realized, it is conceivable that Stanislavsky may prove to have been one of the contributors to it.

SOME OF THE THINGS THAT CAN BE LEARNT FROM STANISLAVSKY[2]

1. *The feeling for a play's poetry.* Even when S.'s theatre had to put on naturalistic plays to satisfy the taste of the time, the production endowed them with poetic features; it never descended to mere reportage. Whereas here in Germany even classical plays acquire no kind of splendor.
2. *The sense of responsibility to society.* S. showed the actors the social meaning of their craft. Art was not an end in itself to him, but he knew that no end is attained in the theatre except through art.
3. *The star's ensemble playing.* S.'s theatre consisted only of stars, great and small. He proved that individual playing only reaches full effectiveness by means of ensemble playing.
4. *Importance of the broad conception and of details.* In the Moscow Art Theatre every play acquired a carefully thought-out shape and a wealth of subtly elaborated detail. The one is useless without the other.

5. *Truthfulness as a duty.* S. taught that the actor must have exact knowledge of himself and of the men he sets out to portray. Nothing that is not taken from the actor's observation, or confirmed by observation, is fit to be observed by the audience.
6. *Unity of naturalness and style.* In S.'s theatre a splendid naturalness went arm-in-arm with deep significance. As a realist he never hesitated to portray ugliness, but he did so gracefully.
7. *Representation of reality as full of contradictions.* S. grasped the diversity and complexity of social life and knew how to represent it without getting entangled. All his productions make sense.
8. *The importance of man.* S. was a convinced humanist, and as such conducted his theatre along the road to socialism.
9. *The significance of art's further development.* The Moscow Art Theatre never rested on its laurels. S. invented new artistic methods for every production. From his theatre came such important artists as Vakhtangov, who in turn developed their teacher's art further in complete freedom.

NOTES

1. Martin Esslin, *Brecht: The Man and His Work* (New York: Doubleday, 1961), pp. 179–80.
2. From *Theaterarbeit* (Dresden, 1952), p. 413. Translated by John Willett, *Brecht on Theatre* (New York: Hill and Wang, 1964), pp. 236–7. Reprinted by permission of the publishers.

5

BRECHT'S CONCEPT OF *GESTUS* AND THE AMERICAN PERFORMANCE TRADITION

Carl Weber

Whenever Brecht's theory and practice of the theatre are discussed, the focus is mainly on the concept of Epic Theatre, on "alienation," "estrangement," "distancing," – whatever term is preferred – and the discussion yields vastly different opinions and often rather imaginative interpretations of what Brecht supposedly did, or intended, as a theorist and practitioner of the theatre. There is, of course, the other term coined by Brecht, *Gestus*. However, it seems to invite less attention and explication by Brecht scholars. It certainly is not very familiar to actors and directors in the American theatre. I would like to talk about Brecht's concept of *Gestus* and formative influence American performance traditions had on it.

The term "*Gestus*" appeared first in Brecht's writings in a theatre review he wrote in 1920 for a local Augsburg newspaper;[1] he used it then merely to signify body gesture as opposed to the spoken word. It was not until 1929, ten plays and several productions he directed later, that Brecht began to use *Gestus* and *Gestik* in the sense which made the concept one of the pillars of his paradigm for the new theatre, "Epic theatre." Eventually, *Gestus* became to be understood by Brecht, as far as the actor is concerned (there are other applications of the concept, but we are talking about the actor here), as the total process, the "ensemble" of all physical behavior the actor displays when showing us a "character" on stage by way of his/her social interactions. It is an ensemble of the body and its movements and gestures, the face and its mimetic expressions, the voice and its sounds and inflections, speech with its patterns and rhythms, costume, makeup, props, and whatever else the actor employs to achieve the complete image of the role he/she is performing. It was important to Brecht that such *Gestus* was memorable for an audience, and, consequently, quotable. Equally important was that *Gestus* defined a social position, the character's status and function in society, and that it yielded an image of a socially conditioned behavior that, in turn, conditions the functioning of society. Though he emphasized the social relevance of *Gestus*, Brecht always was aware of other agents that condition it.

Walter Benjamin explained in an essay on Brecht's Epic theatre, in 1939, why quotability is an essential property of *Gestus*, in Brecht's understanding of it. As a particular sentence or paragraph can be quoted to point out the thrust or message of a text, a particular gestural detail of an actor's performance should be quotable, demonstrating the social *Gestus* of his performance, of the scene, or even the play. In context, Benjamin uses an example derived from the "frozen frame" in cinematography, when the action is arrested at the moment of a particular gesture: for instance, a mother raising an object in order to hurl it at her daughter, while the father is opening the window to call for help. "At this instant, a stranger appears at the door. *Tableau* – as they used to say around 1900. This means: the stranger is confronted with the [family's] situation."[2] A moment frozen in this manner would establish a quotable *Gestus* that invites speculation, provokes critical thinking, and may result in a specific conclusion which then would activate the spectator as to forming an attitude or opinion and thus influence his future behavior versus society.

If we try to isolate sources from which Brecht derived specific ideas concerning *Gestus*, like quotability, we certainly must consider his practice as a playwright and director, specifically, during the 1920s at various theatres in Munich and Berlin, where he had the opportunity to observe many of the greatest German actors of his time in rehearsal and performance. There is also his fascination with spectator sports, like boxing and bicycle racing, and the new audience he discovered there. During the latter years of the decade, insights he gained from his studies of Marxist theory had their impact on his theatrical concepts. All these experiences are evident in his evolution of the concept of *Gestus*.

Several performers were specifically cited by Brecht in the context of *Gestus*. One of these was Karl Valentin, the popular Munich comedian, whose influence on the young Brecht has become almost proverbial by now. Peter Lorre was among them, the Viennese actor Brecht hired for a small part in *The Threepenny Opera* and, soon after, cast as Galy Gay in his own production of *Man is Man*. There was Carola Neher, for whom he wrote Polly in *Threepenny Opera*, sister Lilian in *Happy End* and Joanna Dark in *St Joan of the Stockyards*; or Helene Weigel, his second wife, who was his Widow Begbick in *Man is Man*, the Fly in *Happy End*, and Palegea Vlassova in *The Mother*. However, the one performer to whom Brecht devoted several essays and whom he mentioned more frequently than any of his German protagonists before 1930 – the year his concept of *Gestus* had become, more or less, definitive – was the British/American silent movie star Charlie Chaplin. His films *The Face on the Barroom Floor* and *Gold Rush* seemed to have impressed Brecht more than any other movie during the 1920s except Eisenstein's *Potemkin*.

Chaplin's character, the little tramp, seems to have been the first complete achievement of *Gestus* that Brecht observed. In 1926, he wrote about Chaplin: "This artist is a document that is effective with the power of historical events."[3] As early as 1920, he had described the little tramp's face: "Chaplin's face always is motionless as if it were made of wax. One single mimetic flicker rips it open, quite simply, with power and with effort. A pale clown's face with a thick moustache, the curls of an artist, the tricks of a clown."[4] This sounds like a perfect illustration of Brecht's later postulate that the actor's face should be an empty face written on by the body's *Gestus*.

In 1929, Brecht wrote in an essay, *About a Modern Type of Actress*: "The type represented by Duse or Bernhardt, for instance, has been made obsolete by the, so far, most recent type of actress: the 'girl' type. This 'girl' type represents a substantial advance: it was more classical, so to speak, and showed instead of a mannered expression no expression at all – if you consider the expression of Lilian Gish, for instance, not quite as an expression but rather as an accidental side-effect of a pretty and weak personality that has nothing to do with the (real) expression of the beggar girl at Pont des Arts, for example."[5] Again, the face appears here without any expression, a page to be written on. Three more quotes may serve as evidence for how much Brecht's thinking about epic theatre and "gestic" acting was influenced by the art of Chaplin and American silent movies. In 1931, commenting on his own production of *Man is Man*, Brecht noted: "The spectator is asked to assume an attitude which equals the comparable way a reader turns the pages of a book. The actor of the epic theatre needs an artistic economy totally different from that of the dramatic actor. In a way , the actor Chaplin would serve the demands of the epic theatre better than those of the dramatic theatre."[6] One reason for this conclusion was given in Brecht's notes on the *Threepenny Trial*: "The great American humoresques [Brecht's term for slapstick comedies] present man as an object and would appeal to an audience of behaviorists."[7] Brecht seems to anticipate here the concept of "the children of the scientific age," the audience he wanted to address with his theatre in his later years. And in 1936, he emphasized: "The epic mode of acting owes much to the silent film. Elements of it were taken back into the art of acting. Chaplin, the former clown, didn't have the tradition of the theatre and approached the presentation of human behavior in a new way."[8]

In the same year, he began an article, "Theatre for Entertainment or Theatre for Instruction,"[9] with the statement: "When some years ago there was talk of a modern theatre, the theatre in Moscow, New York, and Berlin was cited." And he pointed out: "There were only three capitals of the theatre, as far as modern art was concerned . . . The Russian, American, and German theatres were very different, but they were comparable in that they were modern, that is they introduced technical and artistic innovations" [see "Theatre for Learning", this volume]. In writing this Brecht didn't have just Chaplin in mind, and other American actors he had watched in movies, but also theatre performance he had seen during his stay in New York, 1935–6. He was impressed by *Waiting for Lefty*, the Clifford Odets play about a cab driver strike, by two performances of *Green Pastures*, with an all black cast, and by Rouben Mamoulian's production of *Porgy and Bess*. He also responded positively to some *Living Newspaper* productions by Jospeh Losey.

Above all things, however, he seems to have like watching gangster movies, which he regarded as the most realistic representations of American life. It probably was the quotability of the performances he saw there that corresponded to Brecht's concept of *Gestus*. The frequently observed habit of young spectators, who begin to swagger like the actor-hero of the film they just watched, when they leave the theatre, offers an example of the *Gestus* that is being quoted. It used to be the hallmark of movie stars that they possessed or created a quotable personal *Gestus* for their characters, as such actors as Chaplin, Buster Keaton, W.C. Fields, the Marx Brothers, Gary Cooper, Lilian Gish, Mae West or Greta Garbo, to name only a few, had demonstrated. Of course, what Brecht demanded of a quotable *Gestus* went far beyond the effect a gunslinger's strut might have on his juvenile fans. It rather had to do with what Charles Laughton expressed when, ten years later, he told Brecht that he became an actor, "because people don't know what they are like but I believe I'm able to show them."[10] Brecht demanded a performance that offered the character's behavior to critical inspection by the audience. Chaplin and the other American actors seemed to have achieved this to Brecht's satisfaction.

After Brecht had settled in Santa Monica in 1941, for more than six years of exile, he soon discovered that most of the American theatre was a far cry from the vanguard position in modern art he had assigned to it in his 1936 article. Already in 1935, he had expressed his disappointment with the unfortunate production of his play *The Mother* by New York's Theatre Union, and stated that in three instances only a correct mode of delivery was achieved during the performance, when sentences were spoken as though by a witness "in court, talking for the record," and in a case where "the *Gestus* can be retained in [the spectator's] memory."[11] He probably saw such elements of epic acting in Helen Henry's performance as Pelegea Vlassova; Henry was an actress with experience in vaudeville.

In 1944, Brecht explained in a short treatise, *Kleines Privatissimum fr meinen Frenund Max Gorelik*, to his American stage designer friend: "The manner in which Broadway or Hollywood create certain thrills and emotions may be artful, but it serves merely to fight the awful boredom which a perennial repetition of falsehoods and stupidities evoke in every audience. This 'technique' is employed and developed to elicit interest in matters and ideas which are not the audience's interest."[12] Obviously, such a technique was aimed at the opposite of what *Gestus* was meant to achieve. In American movies, where he once had discovered the first example of gestic acting, he now found mostly naturalism and mediocrity. He observed, for example: "While the audiences of the Globe Theatre still shared the experiences of the extraordinary Hamlet, our audiences share merely the extraordinary experiences of Mr. Clark Gable. [. . .] The American film has not transcended the phase of situation comedy and situation tragedy. The average lover, villain, hero, or mastermind is moved across certain situational fields."[13] And he concluded that the American people who are so proud of their individualism didn't see individualities in their movies, with the exception, maybe, of Orson Welles' films, "where damaged individuals appear."[14] Eventually, he arrived at the opinion that the better traditions of the American theatre were surviving only in Broadway musicals.

Brecht made some determined efforts to write for Broadway, and he was involved in several projects which were aimed at a Broadway production. However, only one of them ever made it to Broadway, the Auden/Brecht adaptation of Webster's *Duchess of Malfi*. When it arrived, Brecht's name had been withdrawn from the credits, and the production, with Elisabeth Bergner in the lead role, closed after 39 performances, ostensibly a flop. In his notes on the hapless venture, Brecht wrote in 1946 that the production, which had been directed by George Rylands from Great Britain in an old-fashioned English style, should better have followed the model of a Broadway musical that "has been evolved to the true expression of everything that is American. Stage designers and choreographers use V-effects ["alienating effects"] to a great degree, the latter ones such [effects] that have been culled from folklore. The painted backdrops, the most important part of the sets, show the influence of modern painting among other good surrealist concepts. In the dance numbers, which are sometimes intelligently devised pantomimes, the gestic elements of epic theatre appear."[15]

Brecht had seen several musicals in New York, among them, *Oklahoma*, in 1946. One performance he liked so much that it is the only Broadway production approvingly mentioned in his journal: Thornton Wilder's *Our Town*, directed by Jed Harris. Brecht called it "a progressive production."[16] Wilder's play certainly corresponds in its structure to some ideas immanent in Brecht's paradigm of epic theatre. However, when he saw *The Glass Menagerie*, he noted in his journal that the play was "idiotic," yet, called Laurette Taylor who played the mother "a totally modern actress. She plays epic theatre."[17]

Many years later, when Brecht commented on his own production of the *Caucasian Chalk Circle* at the Berliner Ensemble, he stated: "The play owes much of its structure to disgust with the commercialized drama of Broadway; yet, it also employs certain elements of the older American theatre that excelled in burlesque and show. In these imaginative presentations, which remind us of films by the exceptional

Chaplin, the audience's attention was not merely focused on the advancement of the plot, except in a much cruder and larger manner than today, it was more concerned with the 'how.' Today the joy of story telling is stifled by the fear of achieving no impact."[18] (The concluding remark certainly seems to aim also at the prevailing mode of drama in East Germany during the mid-1950s.)

In 1942, when Brecht told Clifford Odets how much he had liked his *Waiting for Lefty*, he baffled the playwright with the observation: "This little play employed the only form which has a tradition here, namely the form of vaudeville."[19] Brecht's esteem for this American heritage wasn't all too widely shared, as he discovered. But it was children of vaudeville, like Chaplin or the Marx Brothers, who had built and improved on this tradition and who had demonstrated to him in their films the potential of *Gestus* for a new kind of theatre. Returned to Germany, where Brecht had his own company, he applied in his directorial work much of what he had seen in American films and, maybe, on New York stages.

For him, entertainment was as indispensable to the theatre as his concept of *Gestus*, but both were never ends in themselves. *Gestus* was subsumed in the encompassing paradigm of epic and, later dialectic theatre, as he renamed and redefined it in his last years. The *Gestus* of the performer and the *Gestus* of the performed were to interact in a dialectic that reveals their social function while creating the *Gestus* of the performance. And the *Gestus* of the performance was to take sides in the social struggles of our age. Brecht noted in his journal, August 1943: "American actors [when asked why they act] say: to express themselves, to use their creative potential. [. . .] Tsiang [an American-Chinese actor Brecht befriended in Hollywood] acts because he loves people and he hates people, thus he recommends or discredits them."[20] It is obvious which of these two answers Brecht preferred.

NOTES

1. Bertolt Brecht, *Gesammelte Werke*, vol. 15 (Frankfurt: Suhrkamp, 1967) 29.
2. Walter Benjamin, *Versuche ber Brecht* (Frankfurt: Suhrkamp, 1966) 26.
3. Bertolt Brecht, *GW*, vol. 18: 138.
4. Bertolt Brecht, *Tagebucher 1990-22* (Frankfurt: Suhrkamp, 1966) 171.
5. Bertolt Brecht, *GW*, vol. 15: 187.
6. *GW*, vol. 17: 987.
7. *GW*, vol. 18: 171.
8. *GW*, vol. 15: 238.
9. Ibid. 262.
10. *GW*, 118
11. Ibid. 1052
12. *GW*, vol. 15: 469.
13. Ibid. 274 & 494.

14. Ibid. 494.
15. Bertolt Brecht, *Schriften zum Theater* (Frankfurt: Suhrkamp, 1963), vol. 4: 196.
16. Bertolt Brecht, *Arbeitsjournal 1942–55* (Frankfurt: Suhrkamp, 1973) 645.
17. Ibid. 744.
18. *GW*, vol. 17: 1204.
19. Bertolt Brecht, *Arbeitsjournal*, 456.
20. Ibid. 606.

6

BEYOND BOURGEOIS THEATRE[1]

Jean-Paul Sartre

Translated by Rima Drell Reck

The bourgeoisie has been in control of the theatre for about 150 years now. First of all, it controls it by the price of land, which rose so sharply in the nineteenth century that, as you know, the workers left the city, resulting in buildings and entire quarters belonging to the bourgeois; the theatres are almost all located in the center of the city. The bourgeoisie controls the theatre by the price of thickets which rose steadily in order to make the theatre a profit-making enterprise. In France it also controls it by centralization, so that in just those cities where contact with a varied audience would be possible, plays do not come or come much later, on tour. Finally, it controls it through the critics. It is an error to contrast the newspaper critic with the public. The critic is the mirror of his public. If he writes nonsense, it is because the public which reads the newspaper will speak nonsense too; therefore, it would be futile to oppose one to the other . . .

. . . One deals here with an absolute control, the more because this same bourgeoisie, to scuttle a play, has merely to do one thing – namely, not to come. It is evident then that the dictatorship of the bourgeoisie has created a bourgeois theatre. Is this simply dangerous, this introduction of a too particular content, or has this dictatorship destroyed the very foundations of what the theatre should be? This is what we shall attempt to discover.

. . . A question immediately arises: why do men live surrounded by their own images? After all, they could very well not have any images. You remember that Baudelaire used to speak of the "tyranny of human passion." Sometimes it is so tiring to submit to this tyranny all day. My God, why must we also have portraits in our room, why must we see representations of ourselves in the theatre, why must we walk in the midst of statues which represent us, why must we go to the movies and always see ourselves again? There is a kind of endless repetition of oneself by people, by all of you and by myself, which is rather surprising. If one reflects on it, however, it is not so difficult to explain. I think that people live in the midst of their own images because they do not succeed in being real objects for themselves. Men are objects for others but they are not completely objects for themselves. Take an individual example, be it in the form of the experiment of the mirror which is so important in all of early childhood, be it in the errors of an animal who looks into a mirror, be it in the mistake of an adult who, in a dark room, suddenly sees someone in a mirror and does not notice that it is he. One comes to oneself as to an object, because one comes to oneself as to another. That is objectivity. As soon as you recognize yourself, you are no longer an object. In fact, one does not see one's own face as one sees that of others. One sees it with privileged elements because one has a profound interest in the one who is there; it is impossible to seize him with this absolutely cold and formal bond which is simple sight. One seizes him by a kind of participation.

. . . What I say about the individual is valid for any social group as well. Men cannot see themselves from the outside, and the real reason for this is that in order truly to seize a man as object, one would both have, at the same time and contradictorily, to understand and not to understand his actions. For you evidently cannot consider that you have before you a truly objectified man, someone of whom you can say, he's really someone I know, if you don't know him through an understanding of what he seeks, what he wants, beginning with his future, with his most personal efforts to attain his ends. But if you know him by understanding him, this also means that, whatever disapprobations you may feel with regard to his conduct on other levels, you share his aims, you are in a completely closed world or rather, if you wish, not closed but limited, limited by itself and from which you can never escape . . . If, on the other hand, you cease to understand his aims and if he becomes, at that moment, a being who is uniquely comprehensible, or at least explicable by the order of things, at that very moment you have lost the man, you have the insect. So that between this understanding of man in which man is never wholly an object but rather a quasi-object for other men, and this refusal to understand, there is no place for men to know one another completely, as objects. One might be a total object for the ants or for the angels, but not as a man for men.

. . . The theatre being an image, gestures are the image of action, and (here is something never said since the advent of bourgeois theatre and which must nevertheless be said) dramatic action is the action of characters. People always think that dramatic action means great gestures, bustle. No, that's not action, that's noise and tumult. Action, in the true sense of the word, is that of the character; there are no images in the theatre but the image of the act, and if one seeks the definition of theatre, one must ask what an act is, because the theatre can represent nothing but the act. Sculpture represents the form of the body, the theatre the act of this body. Consequently, what we want to recover when we go to the theatre is evidently ourselves, but ourselves not as we are, more or less poor, more or less proud of our youth and our beauty; rather to recover ourselves as we act, as we work, as we meet difficulties, as we are men who have rules and who establish rules for these actions. Unfortunately, as you see, we are very far at this moment from the bourgeois theatre; if what I say to you in no way resembles what has been playing on the stage for the last 150 years, except, of course, for a few exceptions, it is because the bourgeois theatre does not want any dramatic action. It desires, more precisely, neo-dramatic action; but it does not want the action of man to be represented, it wants the action of the author constructing events. In truth the bourgeoisie wants to have an image of itself represented, but – and here one understands why Brecht created his epic theatre, why we went completely in the other direction – an image which is pure participation; it absolutely does not want to be represented as a quasi-object. When it is totally object, that's not very agreeable . . . The bourgeois theatre is therefore subjective, not because it shows what is going on inside the head of the character (often one does not see this at all), but because the bourgeoisie wants a representation of itself which is subjective. That is to say, it wants produced in the theatre an image of man according to its own ideology and not man seeking through this sort of world of individuals who see one another, of groups which form judgments about one another, because then, the bourgeoisie would be contested.

One recognizes what is human in the bourgeoisie by what is bad, since the reasoning usually is: it's human when someone has just committed a knavery, a cowardice; therefore, it is necessary that this nature be bad and it is necessary that it be immutable. I don't insist on that point, and you can see why: if man is bad, then that which counts is order, any order at all . . . Besides, if human nature is bad and eternal, isn't it evident that no effort is necessary to achieve some progress . . . But, to act, which is precisely the object of the theatre, is to change the world and in changing it, of necessity to change oneself. Fine. The bourgeoisie has changed the world profoundly, and now it no longer has any desire to be changed itself, above all from without. If it changes, it is in order to adapt itself, to keep what it has, and in this position what it asks of the theatre is not to be disturbed by the idea of action . . . There can be no action, because in these plays the moving element, as in the philosophy of Aristotle, must be a rapid disturbance between two moments of calm . . . In effect, in its plays the bourgeois theatre has replaced action with passion, and action such as it is known today in the theatre simply means a practical construction.

. . . Brecht felt that the distance between actors and audience was not great enough, that one tried much too much to *move* the audience, to touch them, and not enough to *show* them; in other words, too many participational relationships, too many images, not enough objectivity. In my opinion the bourgeois public is foolish not because it participates, but because it participates in an image which is the image of a fool.

. . . We have a number of plays today which, in good faith, use the expressionist themes again without realizing it. For example, the theme of Beckett, in *Waiting for Godot*, is a very remarkable thing. I find it the best play since 1945, but one must admit that it is expressionist and that it is at the same time pessimist . . . But it is a play which, at bottom, has a content pleasing to the bourgeois. In the same way, another recent play, Ionesco's *Rhinoceros*, is an expressionist play, since you have a man who becomes "a rhinoceros . . ." What does it mean to become a rhinoceros? Is it to become a fascist or a communist, or both? It is evident that if the bourgeois public is delighted with it, it must be both. Do you follow me? It is absolutely impossible to derive any meaning from Ionesco's play except that a great misfortune, a great peril of annihilation menaces the world and that, good heavens, the danger of contagion is very grave . . . And why is there one man who resists? At least we could learn why, but no, we learn not even that. He resists because he is there. He resists because he is *Ionesco*: he represents Ionesco, he says I resist, and there he remains in the midst of the rhinoceroses, the only one to defend man without our being very sure if it might not be better to be a rhinoceros. Nothing has been proved to the contrary . . .

. . . I only mean to say that you always have the right to speak ill of the bourgeois as a man, but not as bourgeois. That's the heart of the matter. The pessimism must be a total pessimism, a pessimism of inaction, it must be a pessimism which condemns all possibilities, all hopes, individuals. But if it is a moderate pessimism which simply says: the situation is not good, our ruling classes could do better that they do, etc. . . . Then that's no longer theatre, is it? That's subversion. I don't want you to think that pessimistic theatre is not bourgeois theatre. All the theatre I have just mentioned, of passivity, of permissiveness, of dead end and of evil, is bourgeois theatre . . . If, on the contrary, we want to know what true theatre is, we must look in the opposite direction. This means that dramatic action is the narration of an action, is the staging of an action, one or several, of a few individuals or of a whole group – some people find themselves at the point of wanting something and they try to realize this desire. It makes no difference whether they succeed or fail; what is clear is that they must realize an attempt on the stage and that this is what we demand to see.

. . . From this arises a problem: the accessories are of no use. The settings are never of any use. One can never illuminate a place by some thing. That is not the director's role; these are merely bits of bravura. The only manner in which objects are born, is in the gestures: the gesture of stabbing gives birth to the knife.

. . . The real problem is to know how to create real contradictions and a real dialectic of the object, the act and the man in the theatre. This is one of the most difficult things, precisely because the object comes after the action. In the films the object engenders the action, in the theatre it comes after, is engendered by it. Thus the whole problem of the dialectic of work is a real problem. In a film you can very easily recount the life of a mechanic in a documentary without boring anyone. Can you imagine this in the theatre? With a cardboard locomotive! With fireworks to move it! This is impossible, and yet what is the theatre to speak of if not of work, for in the final analysis action and work are the same thing. Here is the true inner contradiction of the theatre, and here is why it has not yet been resolved; because it is not enough, as the epic theatre shows us, to show contradictions which engender actions, actions which are not quite action because they bear too strongly the mark of their former maledictions. What we must find out is how to convey work in the theatre without having someone say, "Ah! You have worked hard, my friend." This has never been resolved . . . There is a language particular to the theatre: it must be as irreversible as action; that is to say, not in a single sentence nor a single piece of dramatic prose spoken by an actor, must one be able to change the order of sentences at will . . . The meaning of action is that it always radicalizes itself, unless the person acting dies or there is some brusque interference . . . The action itself always goes to the end, it is irreversible, and if it is irreversible, the story too must be irreversible. But then you will ask me, "Is there nothing but action? Aren't there passions? Don't people love, and don't they hate? The theatre you describe is indeed hard and cold!" My answer is that, on the contrary, we will have only characters who are passionate, but only in the good sense of the word and not in the bad. The bad sense of the word passion means: blindly sufficient unto yourself and to others, so that you accomplish only foolishness and finally you wander away from your interests by massacring everyone around you; but you have understood nothing of what is happening to you: a fit of passion, people say, meaning a fit of foolishness. I have never met people who were like that. I have met people who were foolish, but foolishness and passion didn't necessarily go together and usually, when they were passionate, they were less foolish.

. . . Today it is impossible to distinguish in a general way the individual man from the social man in us, and the social man is, of necessity, at the base of all of our passions. Envy is an exigency, an extremely unfortunate passion but at the same time a feeling of right . . . Passion is a way of sensing that one is right, of relating oneself to a social world of exigencies and values. To justify wanting to keep something, to take, destroy, construct something, passionate men do nothing but reason . . . They are frequently very tiresome and Pirandello saw this: in Pirandello, every time a man comes to grips with a passion, he speaks endlessly, because the passion expresses itself through words, through calculation, through researches . . . Vailland has said, "Italians are jurists," and I think passionate men are also jurists. In these conditions, passion appears when a right is infringed; the passion is a reciprocal phenomenon, in the sense that it is a social claim an individual makes when he decides to go to any length to realize it. From the moment, he must judge himself wronged by another and the other must judge himself wronged by this right. In effect, passion exists only in the form of contradictory demands.

. . . There is no need for psychology in the theatre. Psychology is a waste of time; because plays are long, the public has only a brief span of attention, and nuances have absolutely no interest. A play is something which hurls people into an undertaking. There is no need for psychology. Instead, there is need of delimiting very precisely what position, what situation each character can take, as a function of the causes and the anterior contradictions produced with respect to the principal action. In this way we will have a certain number of secondary or primary characters who will define themselves in the course of the action itself, and this action must be a common enterprise containing the contradictions of each and of all. For example, the very contradictions of war are marked by the contradictions of *Mother Courage* by Brecht, for she is a woman who detests war but thrives on it. War hurts her in every possible way but she cannot live without it, she is happy when it begins again and she is miserable when it continues – an admirable choice, to have taken the contradictions of war in order to see war . . . Up to that point all goes smoothly. We all agree; the real problem arises in a different way, it arises the moment we ask ourselves: is it necessary that the object created thus, which is the play, be represented before the audience *qua* object or *qua* image? I mean: is it really necessary, under the pretext that the bourgeoisie used it as a weapon, to reject participation, which is the profound essence of the theatre? And if one does not suppress, must one at least reduce it so as to give a greater place to application and to understanding? Or must one consider the whole problem from a different angle, by refusing precisely to suppress this participation? The epic theatre aims to show us the individual adventure in the measure that it expresses the social adventure, and it aims at the same time, in a non-didactic way but based on didactic plays, to show us the implications and the reciprocal corrections beginning with a larger system, for example, modern capitalistic society.

There is a choice in Brecht. The proof is that in *The Caucasian Chalk Circle* he distinguishes levels of reality and levels of characters. One may debate whether there are political or moral judgments (or whatever you wish) made about these, but why declare *a priori* that certain characters, namely the bad ones, for example the brutes who are palace guards and who play cards all day and kill people as if they were nothing, why declare that they are to wear masks while the two or three characters from the people are not to wear any? At that moment, therefore, in the name of social contradictions we establish people who are actually empty bodies, who are eaten away inside and whom we need only represent with masks. Then another category which will be further away from the mask but still not quite human, and finally the serving girl and her fiancé who are a true woman and a true man almost without makeup and acting in a natural manner because they have a kind of plenitude. But what gives them more dimension, under the pretext that they do things in the direction of social utility, in the direction of their nature and their reality, than these guards? The latter are people no more or less dimensional, they are men. This way of conceiving things is too simple. It consists in saying that man is transformed into an abstract – it is a way of understanding Marxism which is not the good way. To put various realities into perspective indicates an extremely dubious ideological position. Such a thing must not be accepted. Reality cannot be put into perspective because it is not *in* perspective. It *is*, on other levels, but a man is a man, whatever he be, and there are no men who must be conceived more or less fully. If this is an esthetic point of view, it must be based on something and there it is founded on nothing. In my opinion, therefore, hierarchies are constructed and perspectives established which are not suitable. Besides, who proves to us that this way of suppressing the participation we seek is staked on a true philosophy? That Marx is the great philosopher of the nineteenth century, there is no doubt; that Brecht read Marx and that he knew him well, about this too there is no doubt. But there is also no doubt that there are 500 interpretations of Marx. Therefore, why declare that the theatre will be demonstrative if it is uncertain what is to be demonstrated? And if the theatre must limit itself to a few reflections, to carrying out certain very rudimentary thoughts found in Marx, the simplest, I see no need to create distanciation for this. If the theatre should go further, let it be revealed how, and what is to be shown us . . . Which proves that there will not be a great number of epic theatres which will have varying meanings, for the difference between the epic and the dramatic theatre is that the author who creates dramatic theatre speaks in his own name, tells a story with his own interpretation, while the other is demonstrative and does not speak in his own words. He effaces himself at the same time that he effaces the audience before the play he presents. At this level, that's fine when it concerns a society which is in the process of disappearing and when one takes the point of view of one of the classes, for example the class which is rising or which wants to rise, and which is doing so on the shoulders of the others. It's fine in a period when, for example, Brecht can consider himself the spokesman of the oppressed classes and "judge-explicator" of the bourgeoisie to those classes. But now let us suppose that in East Germany, for example, Brecht had had the opportunity of speaking of East Germany as well . . . Let us suppose that Brecht had wanted to explain, for himself or for his public, in what ways there are also contradictions in socialist society. Would he have used the same method? Would one have seen functionaries guilty of a little negligence or of a total lack of imagination, would they have worn masks? Would one have seen them from outside and in the absudity of their contradictions or, on the contrary, at that moment *with* their contradictions – for Brecht was honest, but from the inside, in sympathy with them. To explain another way, if we imagine the history of a functionary who has committed faults, errors which manifest the contradictions of socialism, I am convinced that this character would have been treated by Brecht taking his aims into consideration, considering that he is a man who was defined from the outset by aims which must be understood, the same aims as Brecht, to accomplish the Revolution. When one does not share the aims of a social group one is defining, one can create a kind of distanciation and, as a result, show people from the outside. But when one is in a society whose principles one shares, this becomes more difficult and therefore one must say, "Yes, he is guilty, but the poor boy, you don't realize the problems there are . . . Here are the contradictions . . .," etc. At that moment we are dealing with another theatre, a theatre which tries to understand. This is precisely the difference between the epic and the dramatic theatre: that in the dramatic one can try to understand, and in the epic as it now exists, one explains what one doesn't understand. I am not speaking of Brecht himself, but in a general way. Thus, if you wish, we shall say that if there is a clear insufficiency in the epic theatre, this is due to the fact that Brecht never resolved (and he never had any reason to do so), in the framework of Marxism, the problem of subjectivity and objectivity. And therefore he was never able to make a meaningful place in his work for subjectivity as it should be.

. . . The serious flaw in dramatic theatre is that it has sprung, all the same, from the bourgeois theatre, that it has sprung from means created by its individualism and is still poorly adapted to speaking of work. The other cannot do this either, but it is quite evident that it would be a pity to renounce one or the other of these branches and say that each author may not seek, if he wishes, to create an epic or a truly dramatic drama. In these conditions it seems that all the forces which the young theatre can martial against the bourgeois plays which we have now, must be united, and that there is, in short, no true antagonism between the dramatic form and the epic form, except that one of them draws toward the quasi-objectivity of the object, which is man. The error here lies in believing that one can present a society-object to the audience, while the other form, if uncorrected, would go too far in the direction of sympathy with the aim of objectivity, and thus would risk falling to the bourgeois side. Therefore, I believe that today the problem can be pinpointed between these two forms of theatre.

NOTE

1. Excerpts of a lecture given by M.Sartre at the Sorbonne in the Spring of 1960.

Part II:
BRECHT'S THEORIES IN PRACTICE

7

GESTUS[1] IN MUSIC

Kurt Weill

Translated by Erich Albrecht

In my attempts to arrive at a basic form for the musical theatre, I noticed several things which at first seemed to me to constitute entirely new insights but which after a closer look were revealed as but logical parts of the whole historical situation. While working on my own compositions, I constantly forced myself to answer the question: What occasions for music does the theatre offer? But as soon as I looked back at the operas written by myself and others, another question arose: What is the nature of music which is found in the theatre, and does such music have definite characteristics which label it music of the theatre? After all it has often been stated that a number of important composers have either never paid any attention to the stage or that they have tried in vain to conquer the stage. There surely must be definite qualities which make a particular kind of music seem suitable for the theatre, and I believe they can be resumed under a single head, which I call music's gestic character.

In doing so I postulate a form of theatre which constitutes the only possible foundation for opera in our time. The theatre of the past epoch was written for sensual enjoyment. It aimed at titillating, exciting, inciting, and upsetting the spectator. It gave first place to the story, and to convey a story it had recourse to every theatrical accessory, from real grass to the treadmill stage. And whatever it granted the spectator, it could not deny its creator; he too felt sensual enjoyment when he wrote his work, for he experienced the "intoxication of the creative moment," the ecstasy of the creative impulse of the artist, and other sensations of pleasure. The other type of the theatre which is in the process of being established, presupposes a spectator who follows the action with the composure of a thinking man and who – since he wishes to think – considers demands made on his sensory apparatus an intrusion. This type of theatre aims to show what a man does. It is interested in material things only up to the point at which they furnish the frame of or the pretext for human relations. It places greater value upon the actors than upon the trappings of the stage. It denies its creator the sensuality its audience chooses to do without. This theatre is unromantic to the highest degree, for the "romantic" in art excludes the process of thinking: it works with narcotic devices, it shows man in an exceptional state and during its flowering (in the case of Wagner) it had no image of the human being.

If one applies the two ideas of the theatre to the opera, it appears that the composer of today may no longer approach his text from a position of sensual enjoyment. As far as the opera of the nineteenth and the beginning twentieth century is concerned, the task of music was to create atmosphere, to underscore situations, and to accentuate the dramatic. Even that type of musical theatre which used the text merely as an excuse for free and uninhibited composition is in the final analysis only the logical consequence of the romantic ideal of the opera, because in it the music participated even less in the carrying-out of the dramatic idea than in the music-drama.

The structure of an opera is faulty if a dominant place is not given to the music in its total structure and the execution of its smallest part. The music of an opera may not leave to the libretto and to the stage-setting the whole task of carrying the dramatic action and its idea; it must be actively involved in the presentation of the individual episode.

And since to represent human beings is the main task of the theatre of today the music too must be related solely to man. However, it is well known that music lacks all psychological or characterizing capabilities. On the other hand, music has one faculty which is of decisive importance for the presentation of man in the theatre: it can reproduce the *Gestus* which illustrates the action on stage, it can even create a kind of basic *Gestus* which forces the actor into a definite attitude which precludes every doubt and every misunderstanding concerning the relevant action. In an ideal situation it can fix this *Gestus* so clearly that a wrong representation of the action concerned is impossible. Every observant spectator knows how often even the most simple and the most natural human actions are represented on the stage by wrong sounds and by misleading movements.

Music can set down the basic tone and the basic *Gestus* of an action to the extent that a wrong interpretation can be avoided, while still affording the actor ample opportunities to display his individual style. *Naturally gestic music is by no means* limited to the setting of texts and if we accept Mozart's music in every form, even his non-operatic music, as dramatic we do so because it never surrenders its gestic character.

Music is gestic wherever an action relating human beings to each other is represented in a naïve manner – most strikingly in the recitatives of Bach's Passions, in the operas of Mozart, in *Fidelio*, and in the work of Offenbach and Bizet. In "This picture is bewitchingly beautiful" ["*Dies Bildnis ist bezaubernd schön*" – an aria from *The Magic Flute*] the attitude of a person who looks at a picture is completely fixed by the music. He can hold the picture in his right or left hand, he can hold it up or lower it, he can be set off by a spotlight or he might stand in the dark – his basic attitude will be right because the music will have dictated it.

What gestic means does music have at its disposal? First of all, there is the rhythmic fixing of the text. Music has the power of recording in written form the accents of speech, the distribution of short and long syllables, and most important – pauses. In this manner most sources for a wrong treatment of the libretto on the stage are eliminated. One can – to say this in passing – interpret a passage rhythmically in various ways, and even the same *Gestus* can be expressed in various rhythms; the decisive point is, whether the *Gestus* is correct. This setting of the rhythms on the basis of the text constitutes no more than the foundation of music that is gestic. The really productive work of the composer begins when he uses all the other means of musical expression to make contact between the word itself and what it is trying to express. The melody likewise contains the *Gestus* of the action which is to be presented but since the stage action is already rhythmically saturated, there exists far more elbow-room for formal, melodic and harmonic invention than in purely descriptive music or in music which merely runs parallel to the action and which is in constant danger of being drowned out. The rhythmic restriction imposed by the text is therefore no greater a limitation than the formal scheme imposed by the *Fugue*, the *Sonata*, the *Rondo* is for the classical master. Within the framework of such rhythmically predetermined music all devices of melodic elaboration, of harmonic and rhythmic differentiation are possible, if only the overall musical tensions correspond to the gestic development. Thus, a coloratura-type lingering on one syllable is justified by a gestic lingering at the same point [in the story].

I shall give an example taken from my own practice. Brecht formerly printed tunes to some of his poems because he felt the need to make the *Gestus* clear. Here a basic *Gestus* is being rhythmically defined in the simplest way, while the melody catches that wholly personal and inimitable way of singing which Brecht adopted when performing his songs. In this version the "Alabama Song" looks as follows [see Figure 1]:

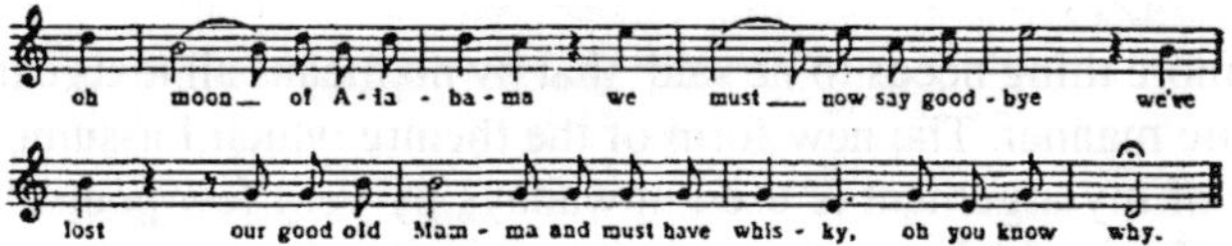

Figure 1

One can see that this is merely a recording of the rhythm of speech and cannot be used as music. In my own setting of the same text the same basic *Gestus* has been established, only it has – in my case – really been "composed" by the far ampler means of the composer. The song has – in my case – a much broader basis, extends much farther afield melodically speaking, and has a very different rhythmic foundation – but the gestic character has been preserved, although it appears in a totally different form [see Figure 2]:

Figure 2

One more thing needs to be said: that by no means all texts can be set in a gestic manner. The new form of the theatre which I assume for the purpose of my argument is used nowadays by very few poets, but it is only this form which permits and allows gestic language. The problem which I have touched upon in this essay is thus essentially a problem of modern drama. But the type of theatre which aims at presenting human beings finds music indispensable because of its ability to clarify the action by gestic means. *And only a type of drama which finds music indispensable can be completely adapted to the needs of that purely musical work of art which we know as "opera."*

NOTE

1. This word has been left in German because its most natural English equivalent – the word "gesture" – is so misleading. John Willett in his book on Brecht says, "there is no single word by which *Gestus* can be translated. It is at once gesture and gist, attitude and point: one aspect of the relation between two people, studied singly, cut to essentials and physically or verbally expressed . . ."

8

COMPOSING FOR BB: SOME COMMENTS

Paul Dessau

Translated by Hella Freud Bernays

I had already heard a good deal about Brecht as far back as the twenties, and *Der Jasager*, Brecht and Weill's school opera, made a tremendous impression on me when it was performed at the Karl Marx School in Berlin. Not long after, in the Kroll Opera House under the direction of Otto Klemperer, I went to a concert performance of Brecht and Weill's (and Hindemith's) *Der Flug der Lindberghs*. And, of course, there was the *Dreigroschenoper*. But I knew at that time it was too early for me to talk to Brecht about collaborating – the libretto for my *Children's Cantata*, which I had written myself, demonstrated both my lack of independent ideas and the great influence Brecht then had on me.

The first text of Brecht's for which I did the music was the series of scenes later called *Fear and Misery of the Third Reich*; I wrote 99 percent of the songs. Brecht himself considered the work relatively "Aristotelean" (and to my mind it is uncharacteristic, *Mother Courage* being characteristic). We used only seven musicians, and the *Gestus* of the music was purely political. The first performance using my songs was in Paris in 1938. Helene Weigel was in the cast, Slatan Dudow directed.

Our close work together began after we had both emigrated to America, during World War II. At "An Evening with Brecht," in a large auditorium in New York City, 1942 (Elizabeth Bergner and Peter Lorre were there), a young Italian singer was to sing the music I had written for the "Song of the Black Straw Hats," from *St Joan of the Stockyards*. At the very last minute, the singer didn't appear. Brecht, who particularly liked the song, urged me to take her place – "Eisler sometimes sings his own songs himself, too!" Later that evening we set a date for our first working conference, and he suggested that I set to music his poem, "Oh, Germany, Pale Mother," which later became the introduction to the choral work, *German Miserere*; we worked on the *Miserere* for a long time, and it wasn't completed until shortly before we returned to Germany.

I recall that Brecht would give me texts almost as an aside, as though he was somewhat embarrassed. For example, he handed me the poem "Song of a German Mother" one day as we were walking on Broadway, with the words, "I've already composed one line myself." He then sang for me the few notes which he had composed, right then and there, loudly:

"Had I known then what now I know"

Obviously, it's hard to incorporate into your own song a phrase by someone else, with nothing preceding or following it, but I liked these two bars very much and was especially pleased with the way Brecht sang them, so I put a lot of effort into it, and thought and hummed continuously to myself, trying to make eight bars out of Brecht's two (for the lines called for eight bars). Pretty soon I was able to play the whole song for Brecht, and he was very happy about it.

Before he left New York, Brecht said to me, "Why don't you come along to Hollywood too? We'd be able to work together better there." Easier said than done. Where would I get the money for the trip? What would I live on once I got there? Fortunately, a solution came out of the blue: a young director, with whom I had already worked in Paris, commissioned me to write some music for a film short. At that time I was earning my living as a worker on a chicken farm in New Jersey, but I had enough spare time for composing. So my work on the movie score provided travel funds to California.

I visited Brecht in his little white house in Santa Monica, and our work proceeded as though there had been no interruption. One day he said, "Here's a play that you really ought to read one of these days, because there's got to be some music in it." He immediately began to read the verses aloud to me, quietly, delicately, and in a manner wholly dedicated to the meaning, as musically as any poet had ever read aloud before. Then he gave me the little book, bound in black – an offset copy of the text of *Mother Courage*.

Earlier, Brecht had showed me a melody which was printed among the songs appended to *Hauspostille*. It was called the "Ballad of the Pirates," and the melody supposedly stemmed from the French, "L'Etandard de la Pitié." [See p. 259 of Eric Bentley's translation of *Hauspostille*, Grove Press, 1966]

I was quite taken aback by the banality of this melody, and by Brecht's suggestion, which he made quite politely, that he would like to use it as the model for the opening song of *Mother Courage*. I told him, "It would require a great deal to enable such a theme to carry an important song," and he agreed. That is how the song came into being in its present form:

This sort of plagiarism was quite unknown, and somewhat shocking to me at that time. Today it seems not only perfectly legitimate, but natural and productive.

It was always a great delight to observe Brecht when he listened to music, and I learned from watching him. So he wouldn't be diverted by anything extraneous, he used to close his eyes, and he never was satisfied by listening to something just once. Brecht always first acquainted himself thoroughly with the vocal line alone; only then would he listen to a song with its accompaniment. He had the memory of an elephant. He was very sparing in his judgments, and sometimes I'd learn only months later what his opinion was: a happy contrast to the general run of professional critics. He took his time, which is just as important for prescribing as for producing.

Brecht had the highest regard for Bach and Mozart. As for Beethoven, Hanns Eisler had reported Brecht's opinion: he thought it insulting to have to listen to Napoleon's lost battles set to music. Oddly enough, he most liked music in which nothing counts but the sounds themselves, and despised program music. The music in his plays does not illustrate the text, though it may comment on it. Incidentally, we never used the real music of a period as direct source material. Though the songs in *Mother Courage* have a folk, archaic feeling, they, like the language he used, create Brecht's world of the 30-years-war, not history's.

Most modern composers aroused Brecht's scepticism, and he particularly disliked Strauss, Hindemith, and Honegger. As for Schoenberg, the kind of poetry he used in his vocal work disturbed Brecht. Stravinsky, however, was asked by Brecht in California to work in making an opera from *The Trial of Lucullus*, but Stravinsky said he was overwhelmed with work and wouldn't be able to get to the project for two years, so the idea was dropped.

As for me, I found that the limitations imposed by writing for actors rather than trained singers were a positive advantage because of the discipline imposed. Also, the dialectic between the actor/song and accompaniment/comment was a pleasure – for example, in *The Trial of Lucullus* (which I composed for Brecht finally), when the general sings about the famous family he comes from, the accompanying music caricatures him, and, as he goes on and on, the orchestra ends up making a fool of him. The direct involvement with stagecraft and Brecht's meticulous rehearsing was also helpful and fascinating for me; to take just one case, the Eilif Song in *Mother Courage* was entirely developed during the 1948 rehearsals at the Deutsches Theatre, finally going through five or six versions.

ABOUT THE MUSIC FOR *THE CHALK CIRCLE*

The richness and diversity of *The Caucasian Chalk Circle*'s music were created at Brecht's direction. The importance he attached to the music for this particular play is indicated by that fact that at the very beginning he calls for a "singer" who is further assisted by two "musicians." There are nine instrumentalists called for ideally – an unusually large number for what is not, after all, an opera. If necessary, the piano part can be taken by the gong player; if one does without guitar, mandolin, and accordion, the music can be, for better or worse, performed by five players. It will be very much for the worse. Yet Brecht always happily reminded us that we must think of performances at schools, colleges, and other small theatres.

There are several versions of the score, and I would like to emphasize that one should not shrink from varying a piece of stage music; it *must* be adaptable to the specific performers. When I look at the score today, it is imaginable, for example, that the first passages of the singer could be done *a capella*. In the Berlin performance, #6 (Singer: "Forever, my great lord!") was omitted – since there is a total of 45 musical numbers, a few can be left out.

In #8 ("As she stood between the door and the gate"), the pantomime of Gruscha with the child is portrayed by the singer. This very important number has its difficulties, and, if it cannot be handled either instrumentally or vocally, it must at least be spoken, with Gruscha performing what the singer describes. This is an adaptation from the Chinese theatre of which Brecht made frequent use. An ambitious and talented player can learn an enormous amount about how to do this pantomime through studying the polyrhythms of the music.

From #10 on, alternating songs begin between the male singer and his two assistants. In our original Berlin production, the short duets were done by two female voices. In Cracow, however, they followed my original directions and used two male singers – which convinced me of the correctness and beauty of my original idea. What's more, much of the music in Cracow was done by heart – a pleasant surprise, which I mention only to say that there is nothing wrong with having the singer and his assistants sing from notes.

To illustrate the contradictory relation that often is present between the music and the text: at the point when the Ironshirts are just about to take over the Palace, there is a place where the guitars are gently overtaken by the piano. The duet is to be rendered (despite the indicated "Cantabile") very lightly, in contrast to the text, not the least bit hurried or anxiously, but with a veritably bewildering cheerfulness, that is, a "quasi leggiero con anima."

#17 (Gruscha: "As one wants to take you") should be sung *a capella*. For #19 (Gruscha: "Those that go together will hang together") I would like to suggest a new version. The words "Mitgegangen" to "nicht unsern Weg" are to be spoken, then (one bar before #20) begin with the male singer. #20 itself (Gruscha: "Your father is a robber") could if necessary be sung *a capella*.

Beginning with #22 ("In the northern mountains") the quality of the music changes. The source was a book of Azerbaijanian folk dances, though for the most part I took only segments of the melodies, and did not always adhere strictly to the notes. Only one piece is directly and entirely "quoted" – an Agachanym folk tune which Katchaturian also used, in his ballet *Gajaneh*.

In the original, there is an additional section, from which I took only one item, a four-part tune in 16th notes, and transplanted it:

This motif, with its intervals changed but the characteristic four-part time preserved, is carried through all the story-telling songs, which form a commentary, as a rhythmic ostinato. In these songs the folk tune also appears, partly in its original form, partly in variations – for example, this one, which is in songs #23, #25, and #28:

Through the thematic relationship a complete entity is formed, linking words, music, and the play's overall structure.

The final dance (#45) is in eight sections, the basis of which is a reminiscence of the Agachanym folk dance which recurs throughout. Unfortunately, Brecht never put this final dance on the stage, and a "Polonaise," in which the principal characters in the play, as well as the little horse and its "little apples," appear once more, the way they would in a revue, was omitted. The original intention was that the music of the final dance would be played, and danced, until the public leaves the theatre. It would get softer and softer, and would stop only when the lights in the auditorium were lowered.

9

ACTORS ON BRECHT: THE MUNICH YEARS

W. Stuart McDowell

> Brecht . . . somehow wanted a narrative theatre rather than one of illusion. He didn't want the actor to awaken the illusion that he suffered or was in agony and – to a certain extent – he didn't want the actor to "sink into a role" . . . And that's what I find remarkable: that he completely accepted me as an actor, while I have been my whole life long an actor who becomes the role, who immerses himself in the part, in pain, or in agony, or whatever there is to present. It's remarkable that I never played in the manner he wanted, and yet he accepted me entirely in my acting method.
>
> **Erwin Faber**

> Brecht loved the actor above all else. He went so far as to say that in an age where there are no longer great actors, there are no good dramatists. When he wrote a play, he wrote it for the talent that was then in Germany.
>
> **Käthie Reichel**

Between September 1922 and March 1924, Bertolt Brecht worked in Munich on the original productions of three of his four plays, *Drums in the Night*, *In the Jungle* (later called *Jungle* and finally, *In the Jungle of Cities*), and *Edward II*. During this brief span of a year and a half, Brecht also made a short film, *Mysteries of a Barber Shop*, with many of the same actors from the three play productions. Unlike Brecht's later theatre work, which is thoroughly documented with many photographs and extensive production notes, these earliest productions remain relatively obscure. In an attempt to add to the information we do have, interviews were conducted with the three surviving actors in those first productions of Brecht's work: Hans Schweikart, who played a significant supporting role in *Edward II*; Blandine Ebinger, who played the comic-romantic lead in *Mysteries of a Barber Shop* (as well as several leading roles in other Brecht productions outside of Munich), and Erwin Faber, whose portrayals of lead roles in each of the four productions forms a veritable through-line of Brecht's professional work in his Munich years. Since the subject of the interviews was some fifty years past, many of the details of the productions had been forgotten; yet the amount of information recalled by these actors is probably due to the fact that all three still actively participate in theatre production today. (Information in the following conversations has been extracted from as many as three different interviews over a period of up to a year.)

I. *DRUMS IN THE NIGHT*

By the time that Otto Falckenberg began to cast *Drums in the Night* in late spring of 1922, the Kammerspiele (literally: the "chamber plays") was internationally reknowned for its many avant-garde productions and was well suited for the naturalistic-expressionistic character of Brecht's "comedy." On their intimate stage of "barely twenty-five feet in width and no depth" the Kammerspiele had premiered plays by the naturalists Hauptmann and Ibsen as well as by the expressionists Wedekind, Strindberg and Kaiser. Falckenberg had firmly established his reputation as the "matrix of Munich expressionism" with his productions of Strindberg's *Ghost Sonata* (1 May 1915) and Kaiser's *From Morning till Midnight* (28 April 1917). As artistic director of the Kammerspiele from 1917 on, he had gathered an ensemble of young actors who could perform his productions. The casting of *Drums in the Night* reflected the "Falckenberg style" in the variety of extreme character types and the robustness of the lead actor, Erwin Faber. Although Faber had been "discovered" by Falckenberg and had joined the Kammerspiele in 1916 to act in many of Falckenberg's productions, in 1920 he became the leading actor at the National Theatre and had to be "borrowed" to play the role of Andreas Kragler in *Drums in the Night*. (Faber was still acting with the National Theatre at the age of 86.)

MCDOWELL: My first questions concern *Drums in the Night* . . .

FABER: That premiered in September of 1922.

MCDOWELL: How did you come to be cast in the role of Andreas Kragler?

FABER: Brecht was then dramaturg at the Kammerspiele and requested that I play the lead in *Drums in the Night* . . . so Falckenberg in turn asked the director of the National Theatre (Carl Zeiss) who released me for the production.

MCDOWELL: Had you known Brecht before that?

FABER: Yes. We would sometimes go for walks in the woods and he'd play his guitar and sing – in a somewhat raspy voice – his "Ballad of the Drowned Girl" and "The Ballad of the Dead Soldier" . . .

MCDOWELL: Do you know why Brecht recommended you to Falckenberg?

FABER: Who can say what was on his mind? . . . I only know that he had seen me in several lead roles and must have been struck by something he saw . . .

McDOWELL: Falckenberg rehearsed *Drums in the Night* for nearly four and a half weeks. Wasn't that unusually long for productions at the Kammerspiele at that time?

FABER: Falckenberg was still the master of the theatre, and although it's true that he had to bring out a production every three or four weeks . . . when he directed, he wouldn't produce the play until he was satisfied. We had rehearsed *The Conspiracy of Fiesco of Genua* (11 March 1920) for almost six weeks, and for those times that was quite a lot. Then I played Hamlet under Erich Engel's direction (9 March 1922) and rehearsals lasted nearly six weeks as well.

McDOWELL: How much did Brecht participate in rehearsals for *Drums in the Night*?

FABER: He would just sit in the auditorium and observe. He didn't yet take an active part . . .

McDOWELL: Not at all?

FABER: Hardly at all. Just conversations on the stage after rehearsals, but he didn't yet get very involved.

McDOWELL: Did he change the text of *Drums in the Night* during those rehearsals?

FABER: No. In *Drums in the Night*, he didn't change a thing . . . There were a few cuts, to clarify the text, but he did not write any new text.

McDOWELL: Looking at the photographs of the production gives the impression that the acting was extremely stylized, with the actors in grotesque and exaggerated postures – the ensemble always gathered around you at center stage. To what extent does this reflect Falckenberg's style of the production?

FABER: The photographs were not "staged" photographs but were made during the course of one of the final dress rehearsals . . . Our acting style was perhaps not quite so grotesque as the pictures indicate, but the drama was played realist-expressionistically, as you can see by our realistic costumes and expressionistic setting by (Otto) Reigbert.

McDOWELL: Reviews of your work before *Drums in the Night* had characterized you as an "intuitive expressionistic actor." To what extent was your portrayal of Kragler expressionistic?

FABER: Falckenberg had wanted us to play the whole thing expressionistically, and I was against it . . .

MCDOWELL: And Brecht?

FABER: He was against it, too. But still, the play was already expressionistic, that is, realistic-expressionistic. It was born of the times, and I played Kragler as such . . . By the time Brecht arrived, the period of expressionism in Munich had already passed . . . This play was perhaps one of the last to be played expressionistically.

MCDOWELL: Could you characterize expressionism as you played it?

FABER: Expressionism means a forced, vexed acting method . . . with great trumpeted means of expression . . . to speak with agony towards an audience, formally . . . to yell out the thing that disturbs you, loud and with large gestures. Of course it could also be played quietly, but then it would have to be done with such an intensity that was still an outcry. For example, (Fritz) Kortner rode down those enormous steps crying out like a child, "A horse, a horse . . ." in *Richard III* in such an exaggerated, overdone manner.

MCDOWELL: Is this to arouse the feeling of the audience?

FABER: Of course. The audience wanted to get excited . . . The heyday of expressionism came in the aftermath of World War I, when we were all exhausted by the war: hunger, suffering, and grief was in every family who had lost a loved one. There was a tension that could only be resolved by an outcry.

MCDOWELL: Do you feel that you "became" Kragler as you played him?

FABER: Yes, of course! It came from my very nature . . . What I first read in Brecht's script – that was me. It was easy, very easy, to play that role and "become" the character while playing it.

MCDOWELL: Could you describe your acting method that you then used?

FABER: I always found something that let me "slip into" a role, to lose myself in ecstasy or in agony or in pain; truly acting and not just indicating.

MCDOWELL: How did you portray Kragler?

FABER: Aggressively! . . . but that came naturally because *Drums in the Night* was like a fresh piece of meat: It was the truth. Someone had finally understood and expressed the whole chaotic world that grew out of World War I. For us, it was clear what kind of world we were born into, what kind of chaotic world . . .

MCDOWELL: But Kragler eventually rejected this chaotic world . . .

FABER: You mean, he rejected the (Spartakus) Revolution. He thinks to himself "What should I do? Let myself get shot for these idiots?" He comes home, and his girlfriend has been stolen by a pimp, so he steals her back and thinks to himself: "You can lick my ass with your revolution. I'm going to bed!"

MCDOWELL: In the final scene of the play, Kragler appears over the "wooden bridge" beneath the moon that glows red with his every entrance. He finds Anna, his lover, and rejects the Spartakus Revolution.

FABER: . . . and I hauled off and threw [the drum of a nickelodeon] at the moon . . . which was just a red balloon . . . [Brecht] had found it all laughable, that everything was so incompetent – the whole Revolution here in Munich, just as in Berlin – and he turned it around and made it cynically laughable. He had had no intention of writing a deadly serious revolutionary play. On the contrary, he wanted to show what kind of idiots they were . . . And at the same time it's a joke on theatre: Away with every kind of blood earnestness!

II. *MYSTERIES OF A BARBER SHOP*

In February of 1923, a month delay in beginning rehearsals for *In the Jungle* gave the director, Erich Engel, and Brecht their first chance to make a film: a half-hour, slapstick, melodramatic romance entitled *Mysteries of a Barber Shop*. The eleven actors Engel and Brecht brought together were a cross-section of the acting talent then in Munich: comic character-actors, music-hall comedians, cabaret singers and lead actors of serious dramas. The film, however, reveals a coherent though complicated plot, while it presents a visual collage of German acting styles of the early 1920s. One of the only mentions of the film by Brecht was in a letter to Herbert Ihering (who had given Brecht the Kleist Prize for his production of *Drums in the Night*). In February of 1923, Brecht wrote, "By the way, I'm making a little film with Engel, Ebinger, Valentin, Leibelt, Faber."

FABER: I was called for about two days of shooting, and the others too . . . Brecht had said to Engel, "Let's make a film with Karl Valentin. You'll direct and I'll write the script." – which he never did. You see, Valentin had made films earlier, grotesque films, and had a studio in Schwabing that he had rented to make those films, and that's where we made it . . . and Blandine Ebinger played a role, as did Hans Leibelt and Otto Wernicke. Just about everyone that had a name played in the film . . .

MCDOWELL: How long did you rehearse?

FABER: We didn't rehearse at all. They started shooting right away. [Faber laughs] whatever came into our heads.

McDOWELL: What exactly did Engel and Brecht do for the film?

FABER: Hardly anything . . . Engel said to Brecht, "Where is the manuscript for today?" and Brecht searched through his pockets for maybe something he'd written . . . So Engel said to us, "He enters and then he gets [Faber slams the table] 'pow!' And then there's some noise and then . . ." It was all completely improvised without any manuscript, without any goal, without any clear concept at all. And that's how we made it.

McDOWELL: In the film you play a hair specialist, Dr. Moras, and are accidentally shaved to resemble a Chinese by an absent-minded barber played by Karl Valentin; then you get into a duel with saber-wielding Kurt Horwitz (whose head had already been cut off and taped back on by Valentin) and you slice off his head and win the heroine of the film, Blandine Ebinger. Isn't your fight as a Chinese with an Occidental similar to the conflict of Schlink and Garga in *In the Jungle*, especially considering that the film was made during a rehearsal delay for *In the Jungle*?

FABER: No, not at all; but some things are carried over (in the film), like the battle between a white and a Chinese . . . not the way it's fought, just the notion of the fight . . . but it's difficult to remember many of the details about the film, because we just improvised our parts and right afterwards forgot what we'd done. [Faber even failed to recognize himself when shown photos from the film.] I do remember Valentin cutting off Horwitz's head, which begins to move around the room on its own . . .

McDOWELL: Was that an idea of Brecht's?

FABER: Of course!

McDOWELL: Karl Valentin was renowned for his comic improvisation. Did his work influence your own in the film?

FABER: Mine? No. But Brecht . . . he wanted us to improvise the whole thing, because he loved the improvisations of Valentin and Chaplin. He must have thought, "Those are similar comics, aren't they?" So he made this film.

McDOWELL: While you were filming, did you make use of much dialog?

FABER: It was a silent film! But still, everyone improvised whatever came into their heads. It was the beginning of the silent films then. The greatest Chaplin films weren't yet there, but rather his first films struck us more like a circus . . .

McDOWELL: Was it a problem that Brecht hadn't written a manuscript at all and relied so much upon mere improvisation?

FABER: Yes and no. You could say that Brecht had taken the film a bit too lightly – that he imagined it to be a little easier than it turned out . . . We were supposed to become a great film company, and ended up . . . an impoverished one.

McDOWELL: Yet it's surprising that Brecht, who had already written three complete film scripts (*Three In a Tower*, *The Brillantenfresser*, and *Mysteries of the Jamaika Bar*) in the hopes of making quite a bit of money from film-making, didn't even try with *Mysteries of a Barber Shop* . . .

FABER: Well, it was begun frivolously and so it ended. Erich Engel eventually wanted to make films and obviously had hoped to make something out of this one. But after it was over, he pleaded with me, "Erwin, I implore you: Never tell a soul I've already made a film!"

Other evidence suggests that Karl Valentin, the "frustrated Chaplin of Germany," had also hoped to make money from the film and that his disappointment with its outcome had been one of the darkest moments in his career. This is substantiated by Valentin's refusal to let the film be released. But if Valentin was unhappy with the film, he didn't hold it against Brecht, as his participation at Brecht's rehearsals of *Edward II* later demonstrated. The comic heroine of the film, Blandine Ebinger, whose remarks support those of Faber, recalls that there was neither talk of "serious film making" nor of becoming a financially successful film industry:

> I never heard anything about getting any money out of the film . . . we didn't ask for any. Valentin just cut off Horwitz's head, handed it to me, and I danced around like a little Salomé . . . it was all done just for fun and laughs.

Refreshed from his experiment with actors' improvisation in film, Brecht wrote his friend Arnold Bronnen: "Tomorrow the little film will be finished, and we're going to take a bath" (Arnold Bronnen, *Tage mit Brecht*).

III. *IN THE JUNGLE*

Erich Engel's production of *In the Jungle* finally had its premiere on 9 May 1923, but only after it had met numerous problems. Brecht's radical depiction of brutal survival-of-the-fittest existence in Chicago had been chosen to be produced in one of the more conservative theatres in Germany – one that had an audience that included growing numbers of the newly formed Nazi party. Engel's complicated staging of the play, making use of the Residenz-Theater's enormous revolving stage, had prolonged rehearsals to an unheard of six-week length – a fact that critics later pointed out when they lambasted the premiere. Brecht's frequent changes in the text had further complicated the production. They included rewrites of the conflict between the two main characters, Garga and Schlink – originally cast with Otto Wernicke and Erwin Faber.

FABER: [Brecht] had seen me in the Kammerspiele's production of a rather unimportant play by [Melchoir] Lengyel, titled *Taifun*, in which I played a Japanese . . . there was a conflict in court between the Japanese and a writer, and this particular role, so [Brecht] said, had impressed him while he wrote the role of the Malaysian in *In the Jungle*.

McDOWELL: Schlink?

FABER: Yes, Schlink . . . Brecht told me he had written Schlink with me in mind.

McDOWELL: Then how did you come to be cast as Garga?

FABER: Because I preferred the role of Garga: It's more dramatic. Right in the first scene, Garga is continually harpooned by [Schlink], but I react to it, which appealed to me.

McDOWELL: And Brecht did not object?

FABER: He immediately agreed. But Engel and I eventually had quite a few arguments. Both he and I . . . realized that the audience would sit there and have no idea what was happening on the stage, because [Brecht] had intended that Garga's and Schlink's conflict be completely non-physical and that we attack each other only with words . . . he wanted to produce an effect like that of reading a book. And so it happened . . . and so it happened . . . And that was the way we were asked to play. It happened that this one collided with the other but didn't really collide. We were just like fish in an aquarium.

McDOWELL: Did the conflict with Engel concern the overall concept of the play?

FABER: No. It was more a question of style, acting style.

McDOWELL: How did you want to play it?

FABER: Because of my theatre instinct, I was in favor of playing the drama so that the audience would be drawn up into the plot – that they would be moved and suddenly interested in what's happening. But in *In the Jungle* that is extremely hard, because it's not written that way. It's an atmospheric play, and somehow you've got to understand the atmosphere to be moved by it. Whereas, if you want a clear, tangible action you can follow to figure out its meaning, then you've got yourself the wrong play.

MCDOWELL: What kind of atmosphere did Brecht and Engel attempt to create?

FABER: In *In the Jungle* Brecht somehow got the idea that without schnapps there wouldn't be much left. So there was quit a lot of drinking . . .

MCDOWELL: Real alcohol on the stage?

FABER: No, not real alcohol – just in the play, just as there was music in just about every scene. Brecht had bought himself a 25-mark tin gramophone and used to play American rhythm songs and such, just to get into the mood to write the play, while he was visualizing his own world, his own Chicago . . . consequently the drama plays like a ballad.

MCDOWELL: In the pictures of the production, your portrayal of Garga appears quite defensive and distressed, with your hands forever in your pockets, slouched forward, in unkempt clothes, solemn-faced – especially when compared with the aggressive appearance of Schlink. Wasn't your portrayal of Garga contrary to your usually "aggressive" characterizations up till then?

FABER: Yes, but Garga becomes ever more aggressive in the course of the play. Still, the conflict lies in the speeches, so that while we fought each other like boxers, we only harpooned each other with words . . . But to make it a great success, you'd have to rewrite the whole play, and that's exactly what [Brecht] didn't want. It was his experiment, as if reading a book or a story.

MCDOWELL: Did Engel agree with Brecht's idea?

FABER: Not entirely. That's why we fought so much. The arguments became so intense that one day the rehearsals had to be stopped. Then, together with the theatre director (Carl Zeiss), and the dramaturg (Jakob Greis), Brecht, Engel and I went to the dramaturg's office and talked over the conflict within the play, and still weren't able to reach an agreement when we broke for lunch. By four we were finally able to resume the rehearsals . . .

MCDOWELL: But Brecht won.

FABER: In what way?

MCDOWELL: That you should play it like "fishes in an aquarium."

FABER: That's right, but he still had to change a lot. I eventually had five different manuscripts . . .

MCDOWELL: Yet, despite the general praise of the reviews for your and Wernicke's acting in the production, the production had to be closed after only six performances . . .

FABER: Of course! I've never seen such pandemonium on opening night. It was the time that the *Voelkischer Beobachter* – the Nazi newspaper – first came out – only six months before the Hitler Putsch in Munich . . . The audience threw rotten eggs and stink-bombs onto the stage, and the performance had to be stopped, the theatre aired out, and even at the premiere of the play the police had to come, where they sat in every row of the theatre, while we played on with a half-lit house. It was the same with later performances. The audience fought with each other, and it was a sight . . .

IV. *EDWARD II*

FABER: Brecht had a contract to direct a Shakespeare at the Kammerspiele; *Macbeth*, *Coriolanus* came to mind, as did *King Lear*. So after my performance we would meet every evening in the Amalkasten (a café across from the Kammerspiele) and make plans . . . At that time [Albert] Ehrenstein, a noted translator of Chinese literature and friend of mine, sent me a play from Berlin. . . . I was supposed to play it in Berlin with Elisabeth Bergner, but as I read it I felt that its writer was very much akin to Brecht . . . So I brought the play to Brecht, who took it with him and returned the next day with all the poetry reworked, and I told him, "That is no longer *Edward II* from Marlowe but *Wenzelaus XIV* from Brecht!"

Brecht's first work as director began in mid-January of 1924 with rehearsals for his own version of Marlowe's *Edward II*. The next eight weeks of rehearsals at the Kammerspiele (the longest in that theatre's history up till then) have been well-documented in the memoirs of Bernhard Reich and Rudolf Frank and were characterized by extensive rewriting of the text by Brecht – often during the rehearsals – and by a demand for exactitude from the actors on the part of Brecht that verged on the fanatical. For his cast, Brecht had chosen Erwin Faber to play the lead supported by an unusual assortment of actors that included Hans Schweikart, the romantic-lead actor, in the role of Baldock, the betrayer of Edward.

MCDOWELL: Had you ever played a part like Baldock before?

SCHWEIKART: Actually, no. I had always played the great lovers: Tasso, Lysander, and that type. Baldock was one of my first character roles.

MCDOWELL: Were the rehearsals for *Edward II* so long because Brecht was so matter-of-fact?

SCHWEIKART: Yes. He was a fanatic. He paid complete attention [to the details] and we were far too esthetic and too playful and too pretty-colored, and he wanted everything very exact and matter-of-fact.

McDOWELL: Was he in this way more dictatorial than Falckenberg?

SCHWEIKART: Yes. That he was. Brecht was very dictatorial, and the discussions with Brecht always led to the point that he was right, and we would do as he wanted.

McDOWELL: Would you describe Baldock as you portrayed him?

SCHWEIKART: He was a traitor, and what interested me was that eventually he had a moral breakdown. I knew that a moralist was always tearful or in agony for what he had done. And that pleased Brecht very much.

McDOWELL: That you cried on the stage?

SCHWEIKART: Yes, that I feared what I had done, what I had seen.

McDOWELL: Was it his idea for you to cry?

SCHWEIKART: No. He saw me do it and approved.

McDOWELL: In this way, did Brecht want an emotional production?

SCHWEIKART: He didn't like emotional situations. He seldom had need for them. Rather he usually played direct feelings indirectly. He let the feelings be stated, so that the same feeling is presented from a standpoint critical to the feeling . . . As Brecht said in his Augsburg dialect, "You've always got to play 'thin and mean.'"

McDOWELL: What else did you learn from Brecht as director?

SCHWEIKART: Not to be pathetic and emotional but clear, sober, sharp, exact.

McDOWELL: But wasn't Baldock emotional for having cried on the stage?

SCHWEIKART: No. He only cried once; otherwise he remained cool. He talked *about* his feeling, of his relation to the king, while the same feeling flowed from his soul.

Bernhard Reich recounts one episode during rehearsals for the scene in *Edward II* in which Baldock surrenders his friend, Edward the King, to the enemy by handing him a handkerchief. After lengthy rehearsals, Brecht yelled out at Schweikart, "Not that way!" referring to Schweikart's hasty and direct way of performing the relatively simple action. Brecht then explained:

> "Baldock is a traitor . . . You must demonstrate the behavior of a traitor. Baldock goes about the betrayal with friendly outstretched arms, tenderly and submissively handing [Edward] the cloth with broad, projecting

> gestures . . . The public should note the behavior of a traitor and thereby pay attention!" (Bernhard Reich, *Im Wettlauf mit der Zeit).*

When questioned about this episode, Schweikart replied: "Brecht depended very much upon the moralistic judgments of his characters: It was important for him that we played them as such."

On the small stage of the Kammerspiele, Brecht made extensive use of smaller, more precise gestures as well as quieter, more intensive vocal control. Faber recalls an example of the results of this kind of work and the way in which it contrasted to that of Juergen Fehling's later production of Brecht's *Edward II* at the large Staatstheater in Berlin (4 December 1924).

FABER: In the Brecht production . . . they lead me in chains through England, the two murderers, and then one murderer asks me, "Isn't that right?" and he pulls my head down from behind [Faber flings his head back to one side], but I was already exhausted and said [faint and weak] "Yes." Then the other one pulls my head backwards [Faber twists his head to the other side – his body remaining otherwise motionless]. You see: It was so small, not a big to-do. But then I played it under the direction of Fehling in Berlin . . . He had me wrapped in chains and . . . I stood in the middle of the stage with one murderer at the far end of the stage and one at the other, and then they questioned me. The one who asked the question pulled me over to him, and then I collapsed, and then the other asked a question and dragged me over to him, and I collapsed . . . Brecht [who was present at many of the Berlin rehearsals] found that hardly necessary but instead had made it private, like a person really is. The smallest little thing can really hurt you, wound you . . . Brecht drew upon factual reality, so that things became tangible. For example, Edward, if he'd lived today, would be a poor dog – not a great classic figure. Brecht is primarily a naturalist. He works with the smaller, more natural form, to make things clear.

MCDOWELL: Can you recall another example of Brecht's use of small gestures?

FABER: Yes. Earlier in the play, Brecht simply had the three prisoners bound with one piece of cord, and suddenly they were prisoners. It was plastic, like Barlach. Simple, succinct, and clear.

MCDOWELL: Did this smallness of gesture imply that you played *Edward II* in a naturalistic style, without the tendency towards expressionism that characterized the Berlin production?

FABER: We played naturalistically from the first scene on, but now and then during Edward's long tirades there would be moments of expressionism – it was an exaggerated form of expressionism but it arose directly from the text . . .

MCDOWELL: How did you portray Edward after his decline, while he was in captivity?

FABER: I used the walls of the set as if I were hunted . . . and when I felt the net [the metal screen that separated the audience from the stage, which rang out with a clang when Edward touched it] I was filled with horror and, feeling something behind me, I quickly jerked around . . .

MCDOWELL: To what extent did the smallness of the Kammerspiele stage effect the smallness of gestures in the production?

FABER: Quite a bit . . . Brecht used the small stage effectively with his creation of the street scene in London, where many heads crammed through the small shuttered windows to suggest a crowded city as well as the battle scene, in which lighting streaked the actors from the side, so that only a few "extras" who marched around a drop – behind and then in front – on a raked platford created the impressions that there were thousands. They also carried enormous battle knives that sparkled in the light and produced a gruesome clang. It was during this that I called to Gaveston [in a mere whisper] "Gaveston," and he called back to me from the distance in like fashion. All that took place on the smallest stage. On a larger stage it would hardly have been possible, because you wouldn't have to have been so creative.

MCDOWELL: We spoke of the atmosphere of *In the Jungle*. How would you describe the atmosphere Brecht tried to create in *Edward II*?

FABER: Balladesque . . . Brecht in his first works is very balladesque, and that atmosphere was something he could depict superbly . . . His plastic use of language and of staging – that's what's new with Brecht.

Despite the lengthy, detailed work of Brecht with the actors up till the last moment before the premiere, the success of the production was denied through the foibles of a single actor:

FABER: The production would have been a tremendous success, if only [Oskar] Homolka had not been completely drunk as Mortimer . . . so that at the end of the play, when I was tied up with a cloth over my head, he was supposed to have this tense dialog with me, and nothing came. Suddenly, I noticed his head under mine, and he began talking to me with "Glaggarlh." I said, "Horrible, the play is through . . ." Thank God, it first happened in the last third of the play, because he was unable to play anymore but could only stammer, "Nrmaggargh."

10

BERTOLT BRECHT'S *J.B.*[1]

Lee Baxandall

Bertolt Brecht's Baden play for learning – *Das Badener Lehrstück vom Einverständnis* – is so named for having been first performed at the Baden-Baden music festival in 1929, and because it falls among his early Marxist plays with an explicitly didactic function. *Einverständnis* means agreement or acceptance. The piece was given at Baden-Baden accompanied by a score written by Hindemith, and in a shorter form than the version published in Brecht's *Stücke*. Hermann Scherchen conducted. The premier created a great scandal, marked especially by the exit of Gerhar Hauptmann in the middle of the Clown Scene.

I believe that of Brecht's plays this is the most unclear in conception and yet the most revelatory of the author's personal conflicts in relation to his thought and politics. It also happens to contain one of the most viciously funny scenes ever written. I want to set forth in this essay some tentative ideas regarding the play. There can be no certainty regarding all aspects of its interpretation until more is known of Brecht's life and thought during this period; yet it seems feasible to point out how such varied and powerful influences upon Brecht as Luther's Bible, the first Atlantic flights, Buddha's parables, and Marx are revealed within it. I shall attempt to view the work from several of these aspects.

The play opens with a "Report on Flying" which is, in effect, Brecht's paean of praise to the twentieth century. For the first time in all of history, nature's brute forces are being overcome by men's science and technology. "We have arisen." Ours is a new Golden Age, Brecht implies when he refers to the twentieth-century's "steel simplicity," an allusion surely meant to remind us of Winckelmann's opinion that the Golden Age of Greece possessed a "noble simplicity." The airplane symbolizes modern man's rise to domination over nature; it serves the same function in Brecht's preceding and first *Lehrstück, The Flight of the Lindberghs*.

Having characterized our age positively as one of conquest over the restraints of nature, Brecht turns to the negative aspects of contemporary culture. Technology has far outstripped morality, and a society possessing the science to destroy itself has little idea of how men must live together if they are to live in friendliness. This is a despair familiar to us ever since the First World War put an end to all unquestioning faith in the march of science. Brecht makes of it an allegory of four Flyers who had flown higher and higher, caught up in the excitement of progress so that they forgot who they were and what the purpose of their progress was, so that they crash and are near death when the play begins. The Flyers are confronted by Death in a vivid fashion; they suddenly show concern for their manner of living, are instructed by spokesmen for a Universal Purpose in what is right, are examined as to their correctness, and then are received with praises into the Body of the Elect, their minds at peace and again purposeful, with all existential fears allayed by their acceptance of the Universal Purpose.

The similarity to Christian morality plays of the fifteenth to seventeenth centuries is unmistakable. The language alone would cause us to suspect this source. In place of a King, Everyman, or Mankind, we have as subject of the great struggle between Death and Salvation, four Flyers, which is understandable enough considering Brecht's insistence that man's fate is largely collective. The Flyers win Salvation in the traditional manner, by agreement in creed and deed.

I would suggest that Brecht also wishes his Flyers to symbolize modern man in terms of a parallel to the biblical Job. Several passages seem to have too much in common with the Book of Job to be accidental. The probability is increased by Brecht's confessed familiarity with the Bible. When he was once asked what was his favorite book, he replied, "You will laugh. The Bible." Whether the parallel can be proven to be conscious or not, it is fascinating to compare the careers of Job and the Flyers. Job was a rich man brought low by impoverishment, bereavement and disease; the four Flyers have "flown high in the air and fallen to the earth." Job was seized with dread at suffering and death, as are the Flyers when shown pictures of it. Both Job and the Flyers seek help first and then, when help is not forthcoming, they seek to understand their condition. Conventional explanations are rejected. Both Job and the Flyers accept ultimately a doctrine on faith which, they are told, accords with the Purpose of the universe. Neither is promised an end to suffering and death, but "only an attitude." Nevertheless a reward follows: Job recovers his worldly estate, and the Flyers, apart from the one who is too proud, are granted social recognition and usefulness. From both the Book of Job and the Baden *Lehrstück* arises a cry of outrage at man's condition; in both there is the search for an explanation, a way out.

Job receives his answer from the Whirlwind only at the last of his Book, so that the answer plays very little part in the action. The Flyers, on the other hand, have hardly crashed when the Learned Chorus of Marxists appears by the wreckage to instruct them. By means of three Investigations, the Chorus talks the crowd (the audience) into agreeing that the Flyers' sufferings should not be alleviated, since help never really helps anyway, not as society presently exists. So the Chorus explains to Flyers and Crowd the means one uses to "give up" such things as poverty. The Flyers are examined then as to the correctness of their learning; one of their number, an inveterate individualist, is expelled and expropriated; the remaining men are congratulated and set to work at changing the world. This is Brecht's way out of the terrible misery which must not be accepted.

We may well inquire as to the nature of this Learned Chorus which plays so important a role. As the espouser of a collectivist doctrine, we expect it to be a collective vehicle. But why "learned"? There comes to mind Schiller's theory of a German populace which must not revolt but rather must become *gelehrt*. Did Brecht take Schiller his idea of *gelehrt*, but as a means to achieve rather than avoid revolution? It appears very likely. Both used choruses in a similar fashion:

> The Chorus is itself no individual but a general concept, but this concept is represented by a tangibly huge mass which impresses the senses with its substantiating presence. The Chorus goes beyond the narrow circle of the action to enlarge upon past and future, on distant times and peoples, on the Human in General, thus extracting the great inferences of living and articulating the teachings of wisdom.

Either Brecht or Schiller might have written this passage on his own work. It happens that the latter moralist did, in *On the Use of the Chorus*.

The revolutionary purposes of the Learned Chorus' teachings require no comment. Much more enigmatic and subjective is what Brecht has to say about methods a man must use to bring his life into line with his acceptance of social change. This teaching is epitomized in the "Commentary" which is read to the Flyers, explaining how everything eventually must be given up. Just as one's life will pass away, they are told, so poverty will some day disappear; one should accustom oneself to giving things up, accepting the alterations of all things. Whether the results are good or bad for oneself is of no moment. One must, indeed, adopt an attitude of active relinquishment, so that one will be free to bring the new into being. One cannot be with the flux of things when one clings to things. One "overcomes" something, be it death or poverty or a storm, by agreeing to the conditions of its process. One's "smallest size" is best for this.

Such doctrines certainly partake of the ascetic renunciation taught by the Church Fathers, the Jesuits, the "Imitation of Christ," etc. The psychological explanation perhaps is to be found in a line from the Book of Job, "He that riseth up hath no assurance of life." But other elements bespeak a Buddhist origin: as when the Speaker is made to seat himself among the fallen Flyers to teach, as Buddha had done; the parables involving a Thoughtful One (Buddha is the Enlightened One); and the essential agreement between Buddha and the Brecht of this play that misery originates in caring too much for the things of this world, and that wisdom begins in escape from the Wheel of Desire. But whether Christian or Buddhist, the tenor of the "Commentary" is distinctly mystical. For the sake of a principle of unseen Cosmic Process, everything tangible, from possessions to ideas to life itself, is to be given up. Being basically a materialist, Brecht of course hopes to get a better world of tangibles in return. But the emphasis is too much on abnegation, on "dying," and too little on increased life. For this reason the play has been severely criticized by such Marxists as Ernst Schumacher, who blames Brecht's zealotism on the difficulty he had in shedding his bourgeois upbringing. The play grows out of its author's personal conflicts rather than analytically observed social conflict, and therefore it remains a personal rather than a social statement, Schumacher says. I must agree as regards Brecht's instruction on attaining "agreement," although I feel that the opening sections state man's condition quite forcefully and impersonally.

One of those early sections deserves to be examined more closely; it is the Clown Scene. In an exaggerated manner two small men are shown to take advantage of a third, Mr. Smith, much larger than themselves but dull, obtuse, too obliging. Smith is vaguely unhappy and pays no attention to the two men he is with, preferring to direct his gaze off into the sky. Meanwhile his afflictors "crawl into his ass," that is, they sympathize with him over his minor pains while taking bold steps to incapacitate him. At last he lies quartered and helpless. "Unpleasant ideas" concerning his tormentors rise in his mind but he rejects them; he will not rebel, but only asks that such thoughts be put from him. The implication seems to be that Smith is the proletariat, vast in potential power but victimized again and again until it is helpless. I think also that Smith may be meant to suggest Job – not as mankind fallen, but as the example of a suicidal attitude toward reality. The Marxist point of view cannot, of course, accept Job's behavior as noble and tragic, for the reason that Job turned his face to God while living men brought him to ruin. The Clown Scene presents this process of affliction at length, so that we may see what the Bible passes over in a few words. Mr. Smith seems to be the Brechtian idea of a Jobian attitude regarding affliction. Even though Job is portrayed in the Bible as noble, and Smith is ignoble, Brecht appears to judge both cases of suffering as ignoble and ludicrous, because endured without comprehension of its causes.

Brecht's idea of how man must behave towards the real world is couched in words John Dewey might have used. It is an active, striving, relating process:

> When he is called for, he comes into being.
> If he is changed, then he exists.
> Whoever needs him, knows him.
> He who finds him useful magnifies him.

The Book of Job rejects such difficult living, in language which I believe Brecht consciously echoed:

> What is man, that thou shouldst magnify him,
> And that thou shouldst set thy mind upon him,
> And that thou shouldst visit him every morning,
> And try him every moment?

During his exile years Brecht kept a motto over his work desk: "The truth is concrete." One suspects he did not have it before his eyes when he wrote his Baden *Lehrstück*. And yet, the play reveals perhaps better than any other the essential Brecht, man and method, which remained vital if better concealed in his later work. *Das Badener Lehrstück vom Einverständnis* is for this reason an important play.

NOTE

1. *J. B.* refers to the play *J. B.* by Archibald Macleish which won the 1959 Pulitzer prize for drama.

BADEN LEHRSTÜCK

Bertolt Brecht

Translated by Lee Baxandall

CHARACTERS

The Flyer
The Speaker
The Three Mechanics
The Learned Chorus[1]
Three Clowns
Leader of Chorus

On a podium which corresponds in its dimensions to the number of participants, THE LEARNED CHORUS *stands in the background. The orchestra is located on the left; in the left foreground is a table at which are seated the conductor of the singers and musicians,* THE CHORUS LEADER, *and* THE SPEAKER. *The singers of* THE FOUR WHO ARE FALLEN *sit at a desk in the right foreground. For purposes of elucidating the scene, the wreckage of an airplane can lie on or near the podium.*

I. REPORT ON FLYING

THE FOUR FLYERS *report*:

In the era when mankind
Began to know itself
We have made airplanes
Of wood, iron and glass
And have flown through the air
And with a rapidity double that
Of the hurricane. Indeed,
Our motor was stronger
Than a hundred horses, although
Smaller than one horse.
For thousands of years, all things fell downwards

Except for the birds.
We have found no drawing
Even on the oldest stones
Of any human being
Who had flown through the air.
But we have arisen.
Late in the second millennium, as we count time
Our steel simplicity
Arose
Showing what is possible,
Without causing us to forget: the
Not yet achieved.

II. THE FALL

THE LEADER OF THE LEARNED CHORUS *addresses* THE FALLEN ONES:
Fly now no longer.
You no longer need to go faster.
The low earth
Is now
High enough for you.
That you lie motionless
Is enough.
Not far ahead of us
Not on your course
But motionless,
Tell us who you are.

THE FALLEN REPLY:
We took part in the work of our companions.
Our airplanes grew better
We flew higher and higher
The ocean was overcome
And the mountains made low.
The fever had seized us,
Of oil and city-building.
We thought only of machines
And, setting out to go faster
In our efforts we forgot
Our names and our features
And, setting out to go faster
Forgot the goal we set out for.
But we ask you
To come to us
And give us some water
And a pillow under the head

And to help us, for
We do not want to die.

THE CHORUS *turns to* THE CROWD:
Do you hear, four men
Ask you to help them.
They have
Flown in the air
And fallen to the earth
And do not want to die.
Therefore they ask you
To help them.
Here we have
A cup of water
And a pillow.
But you must tell us
Whether we are to help them.

THE CROWD *replies to* THE CHORUS:
Yes.

THE CHORUS *to* THE CROWD:
Have they helped you?

THE CROWD:
No.

THE SPEAKER *turns to* THE CROWD:
Over these bodies growing cold is inquired
Whether it is the custom for man to help man.

III. INVESTIGATIONS: DOES MAN HELP MAN?

(*First Investigation*)

THE LEADER OF THE LEARNED CHORUS *steps forward*:
One of us has crossed the ocean
And has found a new continent.
Many, however, after him
Have built up great cities there,
With much hard work and intelligence.

THE LEARNED CHORUS *replies*:
Yes, and our bread was no cheaper.

THE LEADER OF THE LEARNED CHORUS:
One of us has invented a machine
Which turns a wheel by steam, and this
Was the mother of many machines.

Many, however, must work them
Day after day.

THE LEARNED CHORUS *replies*:
Yes, and our bread was no cheaper.

THE LEADER OF THE LEARNED CHORUS:
Many of us have pondered
The movement of the earth round the sun,
The inner life of man, the laws
Of all things, the composition of air
And the fish of the deep sea.
And they have discovered great things.

THE LEARNED CHORUS *replies*:
Yes, and our bread was no cheaper.
Instead
The poverty has increased in our cities
And for a long time nobody has known
Just what a man is.
For example, while you flew
One just like you crawled the earth,
And not like a man!

THE LEADER OF THE LEARNED CHORUS *turns to* THE CROWD:
So. Does man help man?

THE CROWD *replies*:
No.

(*Second Investigation*)

THE LEADER OF THE LEARNED CHORUS *turns to* THE CROWD:
Observe our pictures and then see
If you can say that man helps man!

(*Twenty photographs are shown which demonstrate how, in our time, men are slaughtered by men.*)

THE CROWD *shouts*:
Man does *not* help man!

(*Third Investigation*)

THE LEADER OF THE LEARNED CHORUS *turns to* THE CROWD:
Observe our Clown Act,
In which men help a man!

(*Three circus clowns climb onto the podium. One, called* MR. SMITH, *is a giant. They speak very loudly.*)

FIRST: This is a very fine evening, Mr. Smith.

SECOND: What's that about the evening, Mr. Smith?

SMITH: I don't think it's so fine.

FIRST: Won't you sit down, Mr. Smith?

SECOND: Here's a chair, Mr. Smith, now why don't you answer us?

FIRST: Can't you see – Mr. Smith wishes to observe the moon.

SECOND: You, tell me, why do you always crawl into Mr. Smith's ass? It annoys Mr. Smith.

FIRST: Because Mr. Smith is so strong, that's why I crawl into Mr. Smith's ass.

SECOND: Me too.

FIRST: Ask Mr. Smith to sit down with us.

SMITH: This day does not please me.

FIRST: You must cheer up, Mr. Smith.

SMITH: I don't think I can ever cheer up again.

(*Pause.*)

What color is my face?

FIRST: Rosy, Mr. Smith, always rosy.

SMITH: You see, and I thought my face was pale.

FIRST: But that's queer, you say, you think, your face is pale? Do you know that when I look at you now just so, then I must admit it, I think so too now, your face *is* pale.

SECOND: If I were in your place I'd sit down, Mr. Smith, looking the way you do.

SMITH: I do not wish to sit today.

FIRST: Oh no no, don't sit, on no account sit down, rather remain standing.

SMITH: And why do you think I should remain standing?

FIRST *to* SECOND: He can't sit down today, 'cause if he does perhaps he can't ever get up again.

SMITH: My gosh!

FIRST: Do you hear, he already notices it himself. Mr. Smith would rather remain standing.

SMITH: Do you know, I almost believe my left foot hurts me a bit.

FIRST: Much?

SMITH, *in pain*: What?

FIRST: Does it hurt you much?

SMITH: Yes, already it hurts me much.

SECOND: That comes from standing.

SMITH: You're right, do you think I should sit down?

FIRST: No, on no account, we must avoid that.

SECOND: If your left foot hurts you, then there's only one thing to be done – off with the left foot.

FIRST: And the quicker the better.

SMITH: Well, if you think so . . .

SECOND: Of course.

(*They saw off his left foot.*)

SMITH: A cane, please.

(*They give him a cane.*)

FIRST: Well, can you stand any better now, Mr. Smith?

SMITH: Yes, on the left. But you must give me back my foot, I wouldn't like to lose it.

FIRST: Please, if you have suspicions . . .

SECOND: We can leave, you know . . .

SMITH: No no, you must stay now, you know I can't get around alone any more.

FIRST: Here is your foot.

(SMITH *tucks the foot under his arm.*)

SMITH: Now I've gone and dropped my cane.

SECOND: Yes, but you've got your foot back again.

(*Both roar with laughter.*)

SMITH: Now I really can't stand any longer. Because now naturally the other leg has begun to hurt too.

FIRST: There's nothing easier to imagine.

SMITH: I don't wish to trouble you more than is necessary, but without my cane I can scarcely get about.

SECOND: Rather than pick up the cane we can just as well saw off the other leg, which as you say hurts very much.

SMITH: Yes, perhaps it will be better that way.

(*They saw off the other leg.* SMITH *falls down.*)

SMITH: Now I can't stand up anymore.

FIRST: How horrible, and that's just what we absolutely wanted to avoid – that you should sit down.

SMITH: What?!

SECOND: No longer can you stand up, Mr. Smith.

SMITH: Don't say that to me, it hurts.

SECOND: What shouldn't I say anymore?

SMITH: That . . .

SECOND: That you can no longer stand up?

SMITH: Can you not keep your mouth shut?

SECOND: No, Mr. Smith; but I can twist off your left ear, then you won't hear me say anymore that you can no longer stand up.

SMITH: Yes, perhaps that is better.

(*They twist off his left ear.*)

SMITH *to the* FIRST: Now I can hear only you.

(SECOND *goes over to that side.*)

My ear please!

(*Becomes enraged.*)

And my missing second leg too, please. This is no way for you to treat a sick man. Give me back at once those now useless limbs, they belong to me.

(*They put the other leg under his arm, and lay the ear in his lap.*)

Really, if it's been your idea to play a little joke on me here, then you have just – now what's wrong with my arm?

SECOND: What's wrong is that you're dragging around all this useless junk.

SMITH, *softly*: Of course. Couldn't you perhaps take it from me?

SECOND: But we could take off the entire arm, it would be much better that way.

SMITH: Yes, please do if you think so . . .

SECOND: Certainly.

(*They saw off his left arm.*)

SMITH: Thank you, you take much too much trouble over me.

FIRST: There, Mr. Smith; there you have everything which belongs to you, and no one can take it away from you any longer.

(*They lay all the amputated limbs in his lap.* MR. SMITH *observes them.*)

SMITH: Funny, but I have such unpleasant ideas in my head. (*To* FIRST.) I ask you to say something pleasant to me.

FIRST: Gladly, Mr. Smith; would you like to hear a story? Two men come out of a tavern. There they get into a terrible quarrel and plaster each other with horseapples. The first hits the second with a horseapple in the mouth – whereupon the second says: All right, now I'm just going to leave it there until the police come.

(SECOND *laughs*; MR. SMITH *doesn't.*)

SMITH: That's not a very fine story. Can't you tell me something finer – I have, as I said, unpleasant ideas in my head.

FIRST: No; I am sorry, Mr. Smith, but except for this story I know of nothing more to say.

SECOND: But we can *saw* off your head, if you have such stupid ideas in it.

SMITH: Yes, please do; perhaps that will help.

(*They saw off the top half of his head.*)

FIRST: How's that, Mr. Smith; does that ease the weight on your mind?

SMITH: Yes. I feel quite lightheaded now. Only, my head is freezing.

SECOND: In that case you must put on your hat. (*Bellows.*) Put on your hat!

SMITH: But I can't reach down.

SECOND: Do you want your cane?

SMITH: Yes, please. (*He fishes for his hat.*) Now I've dropped my cane again, and I can't get to my hat. I'm very, very cold.

SECOND: How about if we twisted your head off entirely?

SMITH: Well, I don't know . . .

FIRST: Oh yes you do . . .

SMITH: No, truly, I don't know a thing anymore.

SECOND: For that very reason.

(*They twist off his head.* SMITH *tumbles over backwards.*)

SMITH: Wait! Will one of you just put your hand on my forehead?

FIRST: Where?

SMITH: Will one of you just hold my hand?

FIRST: Where?

SECOND: Is your mind lightened any now, Mr. Smith?

SMITH: No. What I mean is, I'm lying with a stone pressing into my back.

SECOND: You know how it is, Mr. Smith; you can't have everything.

(*Both roar with laughter. End of Clown Act.*)

THE CROWD *shouts*:
Man does *not* help man.

THE LEADER OF THE LEARNED CHORUS:
Shall we tear up the pillow?

THE CROWD:
Yes.

THE LEADER OF THE LEARNED CHORUS:
Shall we pour out the water?

THE CROWD:
Yes.

IV. THE REFUSAL OF HELP

THE LEARNED CHORUS:
Thus they shall not be helped.
We tear up the pillow, we
Pour out the water.

(THE SPEAKER *now tears up the pillow and pours out the water.*)

THE CROWD *reads for itself*:
No doubt you have seen
Help in many a place
Of many kinds, begotten by the condition
Of not yet to be renounced
Power.
Nevertheless, we advise you to confront
Grim reality more grimly

And with the condition
Which begot your demand
To give up the demand. Therefore,
Not to count upon help:
To refuse to give help, power is needed
To obtain help, power is also needed.
So long as power rules, help can be refused
If power no longer rules, help is no longer needed.
Therefore you are not to demand help, but do away with power.
Help and power are two sides of a whole
And the whole must be changed.

V. THE CONSULTATION

THE FALLEN FLYER:
Comrades, we
Are going to die.

THE THREE FALLEN MECHANICS:
We know that we are going to die, but
Do you know it?
Then listen:
You will certainly die.
Your life will be taken from you
Your achievement will be erased
You will die for yourself
Without any regarding it.
You will sure die
And so also must we.

VI. OBSERVING THE DEAD

THE SPEAKER:
Observe the dead!

(*Ten photographs are shown of the dead, very large, then* THE SPEAKER *says: "Second observing of the dead," and the photographs are again shown.*)

After the observing of the dead, THE FALLEN ONES *begin to cry out*:
We cannot die!

VII. THE READING OF THE COMMENTARY

THE LEARNED CHORUS *turns to* THE FALLEN ONES:
We cannot help you.
Only advice

Only an attitude
Can we give you.
Die, but learn
Learn, but learn rightly.

THE FALLEN ONES:
We have not much time
We can no longer learn much.

THE LEARNED CHORUS:
You have little time
You have time enough
For that which is right is easy.

(*From* THE LEARNED CHORUS *steps* THE SPEAKER *with a book. He joins* THE FALLEN ONES, *sits and reads from the Commentary.*)

THE SPEAKER: 1. He who takes a thing will hold fast to it. And he from whom a thing is taken will also hold fast to it. And from him who holds fast to a thing, something is taken.

Whoever among us dies, what does he give up? He does not give up merely his bed and board! Whoever among us dies, knows also that I give up whatever there is, more than I have I give away. Whoever among us dies, gives up the road which he knows and also the one which he does not know. The riches which he has and which he does not have. Poverty itself. His own hand.

Now how is he to raise a stone who has not trained for it? How is he to raise a great stone? How is he, untrained in giving things up, to give up his bed – or to give up all that he has and does not have? The road which he knows and also the one which he does not know? The riches which he has and which he does not have? Poverty itself? His own hand?

2. When the Thoughtful One got into a great storm, he was sitting in a large vessel and took up much space. The first thing he did was to alight from his vessel, secondly he took off his coat, thirdly he lay down upon the earth. Thus he overcame the storm in his smallest size.

THE FALLEN ONES *make inquiry of* THE SPEAKER:
That is how he weathered the storm?

THE SPEAKER:
In his smallest size he weathered the storm.

THE FALLEN ONES:
In his smallest size he weathered the storm.

THE SPEAKER: 3. To give a man courage to die, the Thoughtful One intervened to ask that he give up all his goods. When he had given up everything, only his life remained. Give up more, said the Thoughtful One.

4. When the Thoughtful One overcame the storm, he overcame it because he knew the storm, and agreed with the storm. Therefore, if you want to overcome dying, you will overcome it when you know what dying is, and agree with dying. But whoever desires to be in agreement, that one will hold to poverty. He does not hold onto things! Things can be taken, and then there is no agreement. Nor does he hold onto life. Life will be taken, and then there is no agreement. Nor does he hold onto ideas, ideas can also be taken, and then also there is no agreement.

VIII. THE EXAMINATION

1.

(THE LEARNED CHORUS *examines* THE FALLEN ONES *in view of* THE CROWD.)

THE LEARNED CHORUS: How high have you flown?

THE THREE FALLEN MECHANICS: We have flown tremendously high.

THE LEARNED CHORUS: How high have you flown?

THE FALLEN MECHANICS: We have flown as high as 13,000 feet.

THE LEARNED CHORUS: How high have you flown?

THE FALLEN MECHANICS: We have flown fairly high.

THE LEARNED CHORUS: How high have you flown?

THE FALLEN MECHANICS: We have risen a little above the earth.

THE LEADER OF THE LEARNED CHORUS *turns to* THE CROWD: They have risen a little above the earth.

THE FALLEN FLYER: I have flown tremendously high.

THE LEARNED CHORUS: And he has flown tremendously high.

2.

THE LEARNED CHORUS: Were you praised?

THE FALLEN MECHANICS: We were not praised enough.

THE LEARNED CHORUS: Were you praised?

THE FALLEN MECHANICS: We were praised?

THE LEARNED CHORUS: Were you praised?

THE FALLEN MECHANICS: We were praised enough.

THE LEARNED CHORUS: Were you praised?

THE FALLEN MECHANICS: We were tremendously praised.

THE LEADER OF THE LEARNED CHORUS *to* THE CROWD: They were tremendously praised.

THE FALLEN FLYER: I was not praised enough.

THE LEARNED CHORUS: And he was not praised enough.

3.

THE LEARNED CHORUS: Who are you?

THE FALLEN MECHANICS: We are the ones who flew over the ocean.

THE LEARNED CHORUS: Who are you?

THE FALLEN MECHANICS: We are some of you.

THE LEARNED CHORUS: Who are you?

THE FALLEN MECHANICS: We are nobody.

THE LEADER OF THE LEARNED CHORUS *to* THE CROWD: They are nobody.

THE FALLEN FLYER: I am Charles Nungesser.

THE LEARNED CHORUS: And he is Charles Nungesser.

4.

THE LEARNED CHORUS: Who waits for you?

THE FALLEN MECHANICS: Many people across the ocean wait for us.

THE LEARNED CHORUS: Who waits for you?

THE FALLEN MECHANICS: Our father and our mother wait for us.

THE LEARNED CHORUS: Who waits for you?

THE FALLEN MECHANICS: Nobody waits for us.

THE LEADER OF THE LEARNED CHORUS *to* THE CROWD: Nobody waits for them.

5.

THE LEARNED CHORUS: Who dies then, when you die?

THE FALLEN MECHANICS: Those who were too much praised.

THE LEARNED CHORUS: Who dies then, when you die?

THE FALLEN MECHANICS: Those who rose a little above the earth.

THE LEARNED CHORUS: Who dies then, when you die?

THE FALLEN MECHANICS: Those for whom nobody waits.

THE LEARNED CHORUS: Who dies then, when you die?

THE FALLEN MECHANICS: Nobody.

THE LEARNED CHORUS:
Now you know:
Nobody
Dies, when you die.
Now you have achieved
Your smallest size.

THE FALLEN FLYER:
But I, with my flying,
Have achieved my greatest size.
Higher than I have flown,
Nobody has flown.
I was not enough praised, I
Cannot be praised enough
I have flown for nothing and nobody.
I have flown for flying's sake.
Nobody waits for me, I
Do not fly toward you, I
Fly away from you, I
Shall never die.

IX. PRAISE AND EXPROPRIATION

THE LEARNED CHORUS:
Yes, but now
Show us what you have achieved.
For only
That which is achieved is real.
So give us now the motor
Wings and undercarriage, all
That enabled you to fly and
Was made by some of us.
Give it up!

THE FALLEN FLYER:
I'll not give it up.
What is
The airplane without the flyer?

THE LEADER OF THE LEARNED CHORUS:
Take it!

(*The airplane is carried off to the other corner of the podium by* THE FALLEN ONES.)

THE LEARNED CHORUS, *during the Expropriation, praises* THE FALLEN ONES:
Arise, flyers, you have changed the laws of the earth.
For thousands of years, all things fell downwards
Except for the birds.
We have found no drawing
Even on the oldest stones
Of any human being
Who had flown through the air.
But you have arisen
Late in the second Millennium, as we count time.

THE THREE FALLEN MECHANICS *point suddenly at* THE FALLEN FLYER:
Look here, what is this!

THE LEADER *to* THE LEARNED CHORUS, *quickly*:
Sing "Beyond Recognition."

THE LEARNED CHORUS, *encircling* THE FALLEN FLYER:
Beyond recognition
Are now his features
Begot by him and us, for
A man who used us
And whom we needed:
Such was he.

THE LEADER OF THE LEARNED CHORUS:
This man
Possessor of a public task
Even if usurped
Took from us what he could use,
And refused us what we needed.
Therefore his features
Faded with his task:
He had but one!

(FOUR *from* THE LEARNED CHORUS *discuss him.*)

THE FIRST: If he existed . . .

THE SECOND: He existed.

THE FIRST: What was he?

THE SECOND: He was nobody.

THE THIRD: If he was someone . . .

THE FOURTH: He was nobody.

THE THIRD: How did he become recognized?

THE FOURTH: By being employed.

ALL FOUR:
When he is called for, he comes into being.
If he is changed, then he exists.
Whoever needs him, knows him.
He who finds him useful magnifies him.

THE SECOND: But still he is nobody.

THE LEARNED CHORUS, *together with* THE CROWD:
What lies here, without a task
Is no longer any human thing.
Die now, you human-no-longer!

THE FALLEN FLYER:
I cannot die.

THE FALLEN MECHANICS:
O human being, you have fallen from the flux.
O human being, you have not been in the flux.
You are too great, you are too rich.
You are too much of yourself alone.
Therefore you cannot die.

THE LEARNED CHORUS:
However
He who cannot die
Also dies.
He who cannot swim
Also swims.

X. THE EXPULSION

THE LEARNED CHORUS:
One of us
In features, form and thought
Just like us
Must leave us, for
He has been branded overnight
And his breath has stunk since morning.
His form falls apart, his features
Once familiar, are already unknown.
Man, speak with us, we await
Your voice in the accustomed place. Speak!
He does not speak. His voice

Comes not. But not alarmed, man, but
Now you must depart. Leave quickly!
Do not look about, go
Away from us.

(*The Singer of* THE FALLEN FLYER *leaves the podium.*)

XI. THE AGREEMENT

THE LEARNED CHORUS *addresses* THE THREE FALLEN MECHANICS:
But you, you who agree to the flux of things
Do not sink back into nothingness.
Do not dissolve like salt in water, rather
Arise
Dying your death
As you have worked at your work
Altering what is altering.
And thus, although dying,
Be not governed by death.
Instead undertake for us the task
Of building our airplane.
Begin!
So you may fly for us
To the place where we can use you
And at the necessary time.
For we ask you
To march with us and with us
To change not only
One law of the earth, but
The fundamental law.
Agreeing that all will be changed
The world and mankind
Above all, the disorder
Of human classes while there are two kinds of men,
Exploiters and the unknowing.

THE FALLEN MECHANICS:
We agree to the change.

THE LEARNED CHORUS:
And we ask you
To change our motor and improve it
Also to increase its safety and speed
Also to not forget your goal in setting out to go faster.

THE FALLEN MECHANICS:
We will improve the motors, their safety and speed.

THE LEARNED CHORUS:
Give them up!

THE LEADER OF THE CHORUS:
Forward march!

THE LEARNED CHORUS:
If you have improved the world,
Then improve the world you have improved.
Give it up!

THE LEADER of THE LEARNED CHORUS:
Forward march!

THE LEARNED CHORUS:
If, improving the world, you have perfected truth,
Then perfect the truth you have perfected.
Give it up!

THE LEADER of THE LEARNED CHORUS:
Forward march!

THE LEARNED CHORUS:
If, perfecting truth, you have changed mankind,
Then change the mankind you have changed.
Give it up!

THE LEADER of THE LEARNED CHORUS:
Forward march!

THE LEARNED CHORUS:
Changing the world, change yourselves!
Give yourselves up!

THE LEADER of THE LEARNED CHORUS:
Forward march!

NOTE

1. This Chorus has at times been described in English as the "skilled," "trained," or "practiced" Chorus. I think "learned," pronounced in two syllables, is much closer to Brecht's meaning. Brecht would often use such scholarly terms when referring to the teachings of the Marxist–Leninist classics. It was part of his fight to give Marx an authority for this age comparable to the authority once held by Aristotle.

THE BEGGAR OR *THE DEAD DOG* (1919)

Bertolt Brecht

Translated by Michael Hamburger

CHARACTERS

The Emperor
The Beggar
Soldiers

A gate. To the right of it crouches a BEGGAR, *a great ragged fellow with a white forehead. He has a small barrel organ which he keeps concealed under his rags. It is early morning. A cannon shot is heard. The* EMPEROR *arrives, escorted by* SOLDIERS; *he has long reddish hair, uncovered. He wears a purple woollen garment. Bells are ringing.*

EMPEROR: At the very moment that I go to celebrate my victory over my worst enemy and the country blends my name with black incense a beggar sits in front of my gate, stinking of misery. But between these great events it seems fitting for me to converse with nothingness.

(*The* SOLDIERS *step back.*)

Do you know why the bells are ringing, man?

BEGGAR: Yes. My dog has died.

EMPEROR: Was that a piece of insolence?

BEGGAR: No. It was old age. He struggled on to the end. I wondered, why do his legs tremble so? He had laid his front legs over my chest. Like that we lay all night, even when it turned cold. But by the morning he had been dead a long time, and I pushed him off me. Now I can't go home because he's beginning to putrify, and stinks.

EMPEROR: Why don't you throw him out?

BEGGAR: That's none of your business. Now you have a hollow in your chest, like a hole in a drain; because you've asked a stupid question.

Everyone asks stupid questions. Just to ask questions is stupid.

EMPEROR: And yet I shall ask another: Who looks after you? Because if no one looks after you, you'll have to remove yourself. This is a place where no carrion may rot and no outcry may rend the air.

BEGGAR: Am I crying out?

EMPEROR: Now it's you that is asking, though there is mockery in your question, and I do not understand the mockery.

BEGGAR: Well, I don't know about that, and I'm the person involved.

EMPEROR: I take no account of what you say. But who looks after you?

BEGGAR: Sometimes it's a boy whom his mother got from an angel while she was digging potatoes.

EMPEROR: Do you have no sons?

BEGGAR: They've gone.

EMPEROR: Like the Emperor Ta Li's army, buried by the desert sand?

BEGGAR: He marched through the desert, and his people said: It's too far. Turn back, Ta Li. To that he replied every time: This territory must be conquered. They marched on each day, till their shoe leather was worn away, then their skin began to tear, and they used their knees to move on. Once the whirlwind caught a camel on the flank. That camel died in front of their eyes. Once they came to an oasis and said: That's what our homes are like. Then the Emperor's little son fell into a cistern and drowned. They mourned for seven days, feeling an infinite grief. Once they saw their horses die. Once their women could go no farther. Once came the wind and the sand that buried them, and then it was all over and quiet again, and the territory belonged to them, and I forgot its name.

EMPEROR: How do you know all that? Not a word of it is true. It was quite different.

BEGGAR: When he got so strong that I was like his child, I crawled away, for I allow no one to dominate me.

EMPEROR: What you are talking about?

BEGGAR: Clouds drifted. Towards midnight, stars broke through. Then there was silence.

EMPEROR: Do clouds make a noise?

BEGGAR: Many, it's true, died in those filthy hovels by the river that flooded its banks last week, but they didn't get through.

EMPEROR: Since you know that much – do you never sleep?

BEGGAR: When I lie back on the stones the child that was born cries. And then a new wind rises.

EMPEROR: Last night the stars were out, nobody died by the river, no child was born, there was no wind here.

BEGGAR: In that case you must be blind, deaf and ignorant. Or else it's malice on your part.

(*Pause.*)

EMPEROR: What do you do all the time? I've never seen you before. Out of what egg did you creep?

BEGGAR: Today I noticed that the maize is poor this year, because the rain hasn't come. There's such a dark warm wind blowing in from the fields.

EMPEROR: That's correct. The maize is poor.

BEGGAR: That's what it was like thirty-eight years ago. The maize perished in the sun, and before it was done for the rain came down so thick that rats sprang up and devastated all the other fields. Then they came into the villages and took bites out of people. That food was the death of them.

EMPEROR: I know nothing of that. It must be a fabrication like the rest. There's nothing about it in history.

BEGGAR: There's no such thing as history.

EMPEROR: And what about Alexander? And Caesar? And Napoleon?

BEGGAR: Stories! Fairy tales! What Napoleon are you talking about?

EMPEROR: The one who conquered half the world and was undone because he overreached himself.

BEGGAR: Only two can believe that: He and the world. It is wrong. In reality Napoleon was a man who rowed in a galley and had such a fat head that everybody said: We can't row, because we haven't enough elbow room. When the ship went down, because they didn't row, he pumped his head full of air and kept alive, he alone, and because he was fettered he had to row on – he couldn't see where to from down there, and all had drowned. So he shook his head over the world, and since it was too heavy, it fell off.

EMPEROR: That's the silliest thing I have ever heard. You have greatly disappointed me by telling me that yarn. The others were at least well told. But what do you think of the Emperor?

BEGGAR: There is no such person as the Emperor. Only the nation thinks there is such a person, and one individual thinks that he is the one.

Later, when too many military vehicles are being made and the drummers are well rehearsed, there is war and an opponent is looked for.

EMPEROR: But now the Emperor has defeated his opponent.

BEGGAR: He has killed him, not defeated him. One idiot has killed another.

EMPEROR, *with an effort*: He was a strong opponent, believe me.

BEGGAR: There is a man who puts stones into my rice. That man is my enemy. He bragged, because he has a strong hand. But he died of cancer, and when they closed the coffin they caught his hand under the lid and didn't notice it when they carried the coffin away, so that the hand hung out of it, limp, helpless and empty.

EMPEROR: Don't you ever get bored then, with lying about like this?

BEGGAR: In the past clouds used to drift down, along the sky, endlessly. I look at those. There is no end to them.

EMPEROR: Now there are no clouds moving in the sky. So your talk makes no sense. That's as clear as the sun.

BEGGAR: There is no such thing as the sun.

EMPEROR: Perhaps you are even dangerous, a paranoiac, a raving madman.

BEGGAR: He was a good dog, not just an ordinary one. He deserves a good deal of praise. He even brought me meat, and at night he slept in my rags. Once there was a great uproar in town, they all had something against me because I don't give anyone anything worth talking about, and even soldiers were brought in. But the dog drove them off.

EMPEROR: Why do you tell me that?

BEGGAR: Because I consider you stupid.

EMPEROR: What else do you think of me?

BEGGAR: You have a feeble voice, therefore you are timid; you ask too many questions, therefore you're a flunkey; you try to set traps for me, therefore you're not sure of anything, even the surest thing; you don't believe me but listen to me all the same, therefore you're a weak man, and finally you believe that the whole world revolves around you, when there are people far more important, myself for instance. Beside, you are blind, deaf and ignorant. As for your other vices, I don't know them yet.

EMPEROR: That doesn't look good. Don't you see any virtues in me?

BEGGAR: You speak softly, therefore you are humble; you ask many questions, therefore you seek knowledge; you weigh up everything, therefore you are sceptical; you listen to what you believe to be lies, therefore you are tolerant; you believe that everything revolves around yourself, therefore you are no worse than other men and believe nothing more stupid than they do. Besides, you are not confused by too much seeing, don't bother with things that don't concern you, are not made inactive by knowledge. As for your other virtues, you know them better than I do, or anyone else.

EMPEROR: You are witty.

BEGGAR: Every bit of flattery is worthy of its reward. But I am not going to pay you now for paying me.

EMPEROR: I reward all services done me.

BEGGAR: That goes without saying. That you expect approval reveals your vulgar soul.

EMPEROR: I hold nothing against you. Is that vulgar too?

BEGGAR: Yes. For there is nothing you can do to me.

EMPEROR: I can have you thrown into a dungeon.

BEGGAR: Is it cool down there?

EMPEROR: The sun doesn't penetrate there.

BEGGAR: The sun? There's no such thing. You must have a bad memory.

EMPEROR: And I could have you killed.

BEGGAR: Then the rain will no longer fall on my head, the vermin will disperse, my stomach will no longer grumble, and there will be the greatest quiet that I've ever enjoyed.

(A MESSENGER *comes and speaks softly to the* EMPEROR.)

EMPEROR: Tell them I shan't be long. (*Exit* MESSENGER.) I shall do none of those things to you. I am considering what I shall do.

BEGGAR: You shouldn't tell anyone that. Or he will draw conclusions when he sees what your actions are.

EMPEROR: I do not find that I am despised.

BEGGAR: Everyone bows to me. But it means nothing to me. Only important people trouble me with their chatter and questions.

EMPEROR: Am I troubling you?

BEGGAR: That's the stupidest question you have asked today. You're an impudent man! You do not respect a human being's essential privacy.

You do not know solitude, therefore you want the approval of a stranger like myself. You are dependent on every man's respect.

EMPEROR: I rule men. Hence the respect.

BEGGAR: The bridle too thinks that it rules the horse, the swallow's beak thinks that it steers the swallow, and the palm tree's topmost spike thinks that it pulls the tree after it up to heaven!

EMPEROR: You are a malicious man. I should have you destroyed if I wouldn't then have to believe that it was out of injured vanity.

(BEGGAR *takes out the barrel organ and plays.* A MAN *passes quickly and bows.*)

BEGGAR *puts away the barrel organ*: This man has a wife who steals from him. At night she bends over him to take money from him. At times he wakes up and sees her above him. Then he thinks that she loves him so much that she can no longer resist the impulse to gaze at him at night. For that reason he forgives her the little deceptions which he detects.

EMPEROR: Are you at it again? Not a word of it is true.

BEGGAR: You can go now. You're becoming coarse.

EMPEROR: That's unheard of – incredible!

(BEGGAR *plays on the barrel organ.*)

EMPEROR: Is the audience over now?

BEGGAR: Once again now they all see the sky beautified and the earth more fruitful because of this bit of music, and prolong their lives and forgive themselves and their neighbours, because of this bit of sound.

EMPEROR: Well, at least tell me why you simply cannot bear me and have yet told me so much?

BEGGAR, *nonchalantly*: Because you were not too proud to listen to my chit-chat, which I only used to forget my dead dog.

EMPEROR: Now I am going. You have spoilt the best day of my life. I should never have stopped here. Pity is no good. The only thing in your favour is the courage to speak to me as you have done. And for that I've kept everyone waiting for me! (*He leaves, escorted by the* SOLDIERS. *The bell rings again.*)

BEGGAR: *One sees that he is blind*: Now he's gone. It must be before noon, the air is so warm. The boy won't be coming today. There's a celebration in town. That idiot just now is going there too. Now I have to think again of my dog.

13

THE DIALECTICS OF *GALILEO*

Ernst Schumacher

Translated by Joachim Neugroschel

In the early 1950s, Brecht wanted to change from "epic" theatre to "dialectical" theatre. The latter was to keep the "narrative element" of the former, but had a distinct aim: ". . . *deliberately* to develop features – dialectical vestiges – from earlier forms of theatre and make them enjoyable" (*Schriften zum Theatre*, vol. 7, p. 316[1]). "Developmental laws" were to be worked out by means of "the dialectic of the classical writers of socialism, so that we could perceive and enjoy the alterability of the world." To this end, it would be necessary to make perceptible the "imperceptible contradictions" in all things, people, processes. Alienation techniques were to be used to depict the "contradictions and development of human co-existence," and to make dialectic "a source of learning and enjoyment." In line with this, Brecht wrote in an addendum to the *Kleines Organon*:

> The theatre of the scientific age will make dialectic enjoyable. The surprises of development – whether logically progressing or leaping – the instability of all conditions, the inherent humor of contradiction, etc., all let one enjoy the vividness of men, objects, and actions, and intensify *joie de vivre*. All arts contribute to the greatest art of all: *Lebenskunst*, the art of getting through life. (*SzT*, 7, p. 65)

In rehearsing for *Katzgraben* at the Berlin Ensemble, Brecht was intent on working out the desultory, transitory, intermittant, antithetical, on bringing "phenomena to their crises in order to grasp them," on working out "conflicts of a social nature (and naturally others as well)" (*SzT*, 7, pp. 113–14). He wanted an attractive and lucid structuring of scenes and characters. "The theatre of the dialectic urgently needs images that stick to the memory, because such plays develop, and the spectator must have the earlier stages at his fingertips in order to juxtapose and compare them with the newer phases" (*SzT*, 7, p. 103). By working out the contradictions and conflicts the plot can develop "in caracols and leaps . . . and avoid banality, idealization (the two go together) and the trite forcing of purely subordinate parts towards a conclusion satisfactory to all sides" (*SzT*, 7, pp. 71–2).

Brecht regarded *Galileo* as a play with "restricted" alienation effects, but its extremely powerful dialectic shaped its internal structure, the arrangement and interrelation of the scenes, the characterization, and the language. The later theory of a "dialectical theatre" included certain ideas that had been formulated in his 1931 essay *Dialectical Dramatics* (*SzT*, 3, pp. 195–6) and in his theses on *Dialectic and Alienation* [late 1930s or early 1940s] – ideas on the necessity of dialectics in modern theatre for modern purposes. *Galileo* reveals the great extent to which Brecht used these ideas in his art; furthermore, the play shows that the dialectic can be a major factor in the aesthetic value of any play. The overall structure of the play demonstrates this; it expresses not only antitheses but their coherence as well. It makes possible the illustration of contradiction rather than of contrast. It is not content with merely an "either-or," but must include the "this-as-well-as-that;" not merely a "this-is-the-way," but also "this-is-not-the-way," an "otherwise." It does not merely set negative against positive, but also shows their unity.

In *Galileo*, there are the antitheses of: scene 2, in which Galileo demonstrates his telescope to the Venetian Senate and is highly honored by the very men who make it impossible for him to engage in research, and scene 4, in which Galileo encounters disbelief and contempt at the very court on which he had set his hopes as a research scientist; the scene in which the Jesuits declare Galileo's theories to be correct and the scene in which the Inquisition puts the Copernican doctrine on the Index; the scene showing how Galileo's teachings spread among the common people and the (next) scene, which tells how Galileo is abandoned by the Grand Duke, on whom he relied more than on the common people. Antithesis also determines the internal composition of the scenes, and is complemented by their language. For example, the "reversal" scene in which Galileo decides to take up his research again, and the scene in which he recants.

Brecht jotted down elements of this kind in his early drafts. At one point he noted:

> The plague doesn't stop [Galileo].
> He resists the plague, he does not resist the Inquisition.
> A Cardinal in Rome: "He lives in Ravenna, doesn't he? The plague is raging there, isn't it? Why should we take his telescope away, everyone will claim the curia is afraid of what Galileo may see or not see in Heaven through his telescope. He lives in Ravenna, the plague is raging there."
> *The Conversations:*
> Bribery through flattery.
> Bribery with money.
> Bribery with respect.
> The Curia announces that Galileo's recantation will be read from the

> pulpits at early mass. The students are already covering their ears. The recantation is not read. Triumph. They explain why [it is] so important. Overwhelming joy. The recantation is read at vespers. Galileo is reviled. He comes back, *they all snub him*. His eyesight is poor. He needs them. I cannot see you. I cannot tell from your faces what you think of me. Let me tell you what I think of you.
>
> [. . .]
>
> Student who disapproves of recantation comes to get book, not to nurse Galileo. Takes book and plague along. Pope interrupts interview (recognizes disease), is disinfected.
>
> (*Brecht Archive, mappe 426*, pp. 48–9)

In rehearsals, as soon as Brecht pointed out these antitheses, he would stress their dialectical connection.

The theorem that a new age has dawned is integrated into the dramatic action as thesis/antithesis/synthesis. The new age seems agile and nimble, the old age shuffles along. And yet how weak the new age turns out to be! But the plot advances, the new age manages to survive. The discoveries have been made, the new knowledge remains, the old view of the universe will never again appear unshakeable. Reason is given a chance. Galileo seeks reason in the common people. By denying reason, he damages its chances. But even he ultimately realizes that reason is only just starting out and not ending.

The harbingers and champions of the new age have been disoriented and demoralized by their leader's betrayal. But they remain positive figures, precursors of followers capable of employing their knowledge better.

The play's symmetry helps this balance of the parts and the whole. A longhand sketch by Brecht of the scenes is revealing:

> *Game with the stone*
> in 3 before Sagredo
> in 6 among the riffraff
> in 12 before Andrea
>
> (*Brecht Archive, mappe 426*, p. 2)

Equally clear is an English-language sketch for the American version of the play:

> similia [sic] in 1) and 12)
> there is a morning in 1), and an evening in 12)
> there is a gift of an astronomical model in 1), of a goose in 12)
> there is a lecture for Andrea, the boy in 1), and a lecture for Andrea, the man in 12)
> there is a woman going around the [sic] watching in 1), and a woman going around watching in 12)
>
> (*Brecht Archive, mappe 976*, p. 33)

Symmetry is an essential aspect of classical drama. In *Galileo*, symmetry as a dramatic structural element underlines the "conservative" nature of the play, which I have discussed elsewhere. But analysis shows that it also helps express the dialectics immanent in the protagonist's life.

In the first scene, Galileo connects the new way of playing chess across the squares with the enormous perspectives made possible by new discoveries and knowledge. But when he repeats his simile to Cardinal Bellarmin's secretaries, we sense how restricted these perspectives are: the chess player's moves will be modest.

In the recantation scene, Andrea repeats the argument Galileo used with Mucius: the man who knows the truth and yet calls it a lie is a criminal. This not only ties an internal thread, it also tightens Galileo's noose, and reveals the good and bad in a single person.

The argument that one must creep into a position favorable to the dissemination of truth is used by Galileo in the third scene to rationalize his moving from Florence, and in the eighth to justify his remaining there. In both cases he has illusions: nevertheless, such "boot-licking" can be useful and necessary.

The doctrine that earthly disorder can be supported only by a metaphysical order taught by Aristotle and the Church ties together the seventh, eighth, and ninth scenes and lies at the center of the play. Yet Bellarmin, the Little Monk, and Ludovico offer it as a rationalization, while Galileo uses it as a reproach. It is an argument employed by the highest and the lowest in the social hierarchy, an ideological touchstone of decision.

The mardi gras of 1632 is a counterpart to the carnival in Bellarmin's home in 1666. But in the earlier scene, the aristocracy is amusing itself; in the later, the common people. The enjoyment is diametric. First the Inquisition refers to Galileo's support by the north Italian cities, then Vanni does – but the ultimate reversal is latent in both comments.

In the same manner the link between the first and the next-to-last scene is strengthened by events whose very similarity makes their dissimilarity apparent, as well as their intimate connection. In the opening scene, it is morning, the dawn of not only a new day but a new era, and in Galileo's room the bed is being made. In the penultimate scene, it is the evening not just of a day but of a life and its ideals, and the bed is being prepared for the night. In the first scene Galileo "sings" an "aria" to the new age. In the later scene he laboriously expresses his conviction that the new age has begun even if it looks like the old. But the theme recurs: at the end Andrea assures us that we are actually only at the beginning.

In the opening scene, Andrea is taught a lesson about nature; in the penultimate scene, a lesson on society. The teacher is the same man, yet totally different each time. The pupil has become a different person and yet remained the same.

In the second scene, Virginia asks Galileo what the night before was like. He answers, "It was bright." In the next-to-last scene, Galileo asks Virginia what the night is like. He receives the same reply. The first time, "bright"' refers to nature; the second time, not only to "nature" but to the nature of mankind and history.

Thus symmetry proves crucial, an integral part of the dialectic in the composition. It is much more significant than ending each scene with a statement or an event alluding to the next scene – a practice that *Galileo* shares with many other Aristotelian and non-Aristotelian dramas.

Scene 13 (Galileo's recantation) shows how Brecht used images that require the spectator to compare a present event with earlier ones. Brecht doesn't bother with a sensational trial scene. Instead of letting us watch what would have been an extremely illustrative act of recantation – in church before an ecclesiastical hierarchy – he shows the event in terms of the play's basic "gesture," the scientist's responsibility to society, relating this to the internal action of the play rather than to external history. After showing, in the ninth scene, how Galileo's decision to resume research in forbidden areas affected his students, Brecht demonstrates the effect of Galileo's recantation on them. He presents substance rather than accident.

This scene (like the ninth, to which it refers) is on two levels: in the foreground, Virginia praying for her father's salvation; in the middleground, the students filled with anxiety about their master's actions. The characters all act "according to the circumstances" which have molded them. Virginia has concentrated on saving her father's soul from eternal damnation. Andrea is equally passionate about adjuring his idol and ideal. The Little Monk sustains himself with beautiful logic and the logic of beauty, the things that so greatly impressed him about his master. And Federzoni stands among them, hopeful but worried, and a realist at the very moment the others so blatantly give in to their emotions. The scene shows the students' relationship to their teacher (an important component of the plot), confronts the scientist with his daughter, and demonstrates the different meanings of the event for the various characters.

To heighten the dramatic tension, Brecht slows the tempo in two ways. First, he brings on stage the man who announces Galileo's imminent recantation and thereby precipitates Andrea's open avowal of his belief in Copernicus. Next, the author lets the fifth hour pass with no sign of recantation, so that all the students, not just an enthusiastic Andrea, say a prayer of thanksgiving for the birth of the age of knowledge. These retardations are followed by the peripetia: the tolling of bells and the public reading of the recantation formula. But the meaning, drawn from constant variations on the basic constellation – the relationship between Galileo and his pupils – would be incomplete if it were not for the dramatic confrontation between the teacher, changed beyond recognition, and the pupils, who obviously can't understand him. Now the scene reveals its true sense, shedding light on the basic problem of the play. A "final word" seems to have been spoken: "Unhappy the land that needs a hero." Yet it is final only for this scene, not for the total structure, though the scene itself can be understood only in terms of the end, whose meaning it unravels. Its power comes from the dialectical reversals, which are an image of the growth and reversals of play *in toto*. The scene is essential to clarify the theme of the scientist's responsibility in the use of knowledge for or against society.

A form of dialectic also determines *Galileo*'s characterization; it is manifested as a relation in each person between the individual and the typical. As Brecht wrote:

> If a character is historicized and responds in accordance to his period but would respond otherwise in different periods, isn't that character *Everyman*? A person acts according to his time and his class; if he had lived at a different time, or for a shorter time, or on the rough side of life, his reply would invariably be different. But shouldn't we ask whether there are further characteristics in his response? Where is he himself, the living man, who cannot be mistaken for another, who is not quite the same as people similar to him? Obviously, he too must be visible – and will be so if this contradiction is incorporated in his portrayal. The historicizing portrait must keep some lines from sketches showing traces of other movements, other characteristics, within the completed figure. One might imagine a man making a speech in a valley occasionally changing his opinions or making contradictory statements, simply so the echo can confront one sentence with another. (*SzT*, 7, p. 34)

Brecht's Galileo has essentially the (if not *the* essential) features of the historical figure, but includes characteristics which the author considered typical of modern-day scientists, as well as "projections" from the behavior of "ideal" scientists. These are determined by contradictions in society and in the individual: Galileo combines patience and impatience, courage and cowardice, pride and servility, sobriety and enthusiasm, acumen and narrowmindedness, affability and tactlessness, gentle humor and acerbic irony, sensuality and asceticism, commitment and cynicism, democratic ways and kowtowing to the nobles, love of truth and betrayal of truth.

Not all these traits are developed in the same way or to the same degree. Some are contradictory, some are complementary. Some seem negative but have a positive meaning. Impatience is shown by those who are no longer willing to put up with something; tactlessness can be a way of clarifying things; denial of truth can result from a love of truth. The contradictory is not necessarily antagonistic. None of these characteristics have value per se – they derive their significance from the "supreme jurisdiction" of the basic gesture, which comes from that gesture's significance for society. Not all personal qualities can be judged within a specific situation – they must be viewed in terms of the totality and the end. In *Aufbau einer Rolle*, Brecht speaks of a "type of play" that "in its details reasonably depends on a knowledge of the whole" (*SzT*, 7, p. 53). We can get at thc "specific weight" only by adding up every detail that carries weight. As the kaleidescope turns, the various fragments of the stage character finally fall into shape. Our pleasure in this picture would be incomplete if the figure did not have historical and social relevance for past, present, and future; but this enjoyment would still lack something without the idiosyncrasies which make a character the "property" of an audience and of society.

Galileo's behavior reproduces – in counterpoint, as it were – the dialectical growth of the other characters. The enthusiasm of the adult Galileo is repeated in the boy Andrea's passionate adherence to the new cause. Galileo's genius is reflected in the young initiate's intellectual maturation. Andrea's character, however, is an alternative to Galileo's, rather than simply alternating with it. Through following his master, he demonstrates consequences. Although much younger than Galileo, he seems older. Led along, he seems led astray. The result of his devotion: the prototype of a scientist prone to any recantation, denial, refusal, obedience – to whom Galileo's behavior seems natural, rather than dubious, as long as it is a contribution to science. Andrea is not only willing to learn but becomes learnèd as well. Yet while everyone else in *Galileo* should be seen and judged in terms of the end of the play, Andrea is to be judged in terms of his future. So he has at once the rosy bloom of youth and the grayness of old age: intellectual irresponsibility towards mankind. We see corrupt innocence, ruined hope, unfulfilled promise. "Welcome to the gutter, fellow scientist and traitor!" echoes terrifyingly within us. At the end, Andrea adds another line, but we know even this isn't the end of the stanza, whose cynical meaning is clear. "We are actually only at the beginning," he says reassuringly at the close of the play. For better *and* for worse. Galileo sees himself as a dead tree, but Andrea, the "green wood," is not free of rot. We can no more follow Andrea, who has once been led astray, unconditionally than we can follow Galileo: instead, we must find better ways of our own.

Virginia is a further example. This character is based on, but quite different from, a historical model. Her primary function is to demonstrate that the conflict between a new science and an old faith, or – speaking more generally – between social progress and reaction, penetrates the personal and family sphere. Galileo must exist for the whole world, not just for his daughter. He has to ferret out and develop intelligence everywhere; only his daughter's mind is an exception. He accepts the responsibility of being her father and provider but not her intellectual parent. From the beginning, he entrusts her to the Church. Instead of letting her look through the telescope he brushes her aside, saying it is not a toy. His daughter enters the Church to return as a totally different person. Science was her pass into society: Galileo let her circulate as one of his works. She promptly ran into the arms of the Cardinal Inquisitor: the weapon reversed. The unaroused intellect aroused; the misunderstood daughter understood; the girl who was asked nothing asked a great deal. The useless daughter from a good home becomes a useful daughter to the Church.

She still believes that she will marry, and she believes it for eight years, but at the crucial moment she remains for Galileo what she was: a person of secondary importance. Once, she was to be married off as quickly as possible, but now she's left in the lurch. The maiden becomes an old maid. And then she becomes, in effect, a nun. Her only objection to her father's captivity is that she can't be his sole custodian. She is both housekeeper and spiritual advisor to him, supplementing his physical diet with a spiritual one, countering fleshly desires with food for the soul. To the dictates of the two new sciences, she opposes the commands of the old faith, parrying Galileo's logic with theo-logic. She wards off his penitence with the reiteration of charges. She confronts the malice of his ambiguities with the unequivocalness of malicious kindness. She replies to his irony with patience and indulgence. She was once a means to an end for him, and now the situation is reversed. The powerful man is now in her power. The cold that science once brought into their relationship is outdone by the coldness of Christian life.

Never having taught Virginia knowledge, or even tried to teach her, Galileo now cannot be wise. He can only be sly, but his slyness won't save him from damnation and is useless against her condemnation. His hell is terrible not because he has thrown away his own intellectual gift but because he hasn't developed his daughter's – and her own rigidity shows that her life is merely the survival of a destroyed existence.

Ludovico's characterization is also dialectical, although he functions primarily as a type. If he *is* an individual, then it is only despite, not because of, his class. Virginia could have been a different person, but not he. His presence is determined by what he represents, his diction by his class idiocy, his individuality by the rigidity of his caste. Although a man of the world, he is unable to cross the boundaries of his world. He has an expanded horizon – seen from a tower on his estate. When science is accepted by both Court and Church, the scientist's daughter is desirable and eligible for marriage. But the anti-Copernican decree warns him against hasty consequences. It is the father and not the daughter who must endure a period of probation; the daughter need not swear that she is pure, but the future father-in-law must promise to put an end to his impure research. The phases of Venus may have nothing to do with the daughter's behind, but they are intimately connected with the father's appearance. Ludovico may be a scientific layman and a blockhead, but he knows as much as Galileo about the connection between heaven and earth and heaven on earth, and while the Little Monk thinks about the internal agitations of the peasants, Ludovico thinks about the external ones. He has had too much experience with the dynamics of social forces not to realize that the proof of astral motion can be political dynamite. He knows he is right because Galileo grows nasty while Ludovico sticks to the point, remaining discreet and arguing well. When Galileo, losing his temper, goes so far as to threaten to write his works in the Florentine vernacular so that the masses can read them, Ludovico is convinced that this man will always remain a "slave to his passions." Marrying Galileo's daughter could easily jeopardize one's family and social position, so he breaks the engagement.

But although Ludovico in this sense embodies forethought, Galileo incarnates afterthought. And that makes all the difference. Galileo may speculate correctly, but Ludovico calculates correctly. Galileo can act cold but not remain cold. Ludovico, however, can be cool, and turn icy. He is able to remain objective, while Galileo *is* an object lesson, a cause. Ludovico's profile is sharply hewn because it is so impersonal. Galileo carries out functions, but Ludovico is functionalized: a proper manor-lord.

The iron-founder Vanni resembles Ludovico in the way his characterization is placed within a sharply defined social role. Vanni's part in the play is extremely important; without him the Galileo "case" would not be understandable in the way Brecht wished it to be, i.e., as an act of treason against society. But this functionalizes Vanni's role, like Ludovico's. Vanni represents the bourgeoisie of those times. Despite the great respect he, as a layman, has for the scientist, he considers himself on the same level because he is struggling for the same goal: liberation from dependence on feudal power and narrowmindness. He assumes that Galileo can distinguish between friend and foe, and identifies himself as Galileo's friend. He joins the struggle as an economic force that the Grand Duke must take into consideration, for Florence is wedged between the Papal State and the northern Italian city states; she cannot survive without the latter. Galileo's fate hangs in the balance – then he goes over to the Princes and Popes. Vanni has no choice but to leave, regretful but upright, just as he entered. Galileo, who believed he would somehow be able to get out of it as an individual, continues his bootlicking; yet, despite all his writhing and wriggling, he finds no way out.

Of all the characters representing the Church, the Little Monk is the most dialectical: not only a priest but an astronomer. He sees with his own two eyes that Galileo's teachings are right, yet he dare not see this because it is contrary to the Supreme Truth he has been taught. He cannot acknowledge the new knowledge because the consequences will be terrible for the simple people whose misery he is acquainted with and who – in his opinion – so as to endure their misery, need faith in a divine providence underlying the social order. His confusion is great because the contradiction is great. The Little Monk believes that the decree necessarily contains a higher wisdom, but the things he has viewed on heaven and earth, on the moon and in the Campagna, have been so convincing that he cannot take the decree for granted, as do other believers. His passionate craving to unravel the truth from all contradictions is irresistible; it drives him to attempt Galileo's "conversion," and yet forces him to listen to the scientist's arguments, although they not only tear away the scar tissue that religion has spread over the wound in his soul, but enlarge and deepen the injury. The Little Monk confirms Galileo's faith in the gentle power of reason. His actions show that in the long run it will do rulers no good to regimentize thought, influence the minds of their subjects, or enroll as party members the very people they oppress. The chasm between ideology and reality will deepen and widen. Appealed to, called upon, awoken, the "Little Monks" will bring about the victory of reason. Yet at the end of the play he has abandoned research and rests in peace in the church.

Similarly dialectical characterizations can be easily demonstrated for all the figures in the play, and in their language. The dialogue is marked by vivid imagery: the "prosaic," the penetration of new ideology and new "objective" relations on the basis of new conditions of production, is transposed into metaphor. The parabolic diction of the Bible is used verbatim in many ways, because of the very nature of the subject matter; but metaphors create the specific nature of the language, and are used by each character according to his social class and function. As for dialectics, our main concern here, the dialogue is remarkably antithetical, not only in a thesis-and-reply pattern which at times becomes stichomythic, but within individual speeches and lines. Opposing views are transcended and dissolved through gnomic maxims, contradictions resolved by "dictums" in which logic and image form a graspable unity. In this constant creation and transcendence of antitheses, a part is played by the association of images and concepts, and occasionally by the evocative use of alliteration. The syntax throughout, in coordinate and subordinate clauses, is used to develop crucial contrasts.

For example: The curator describes the "slavery under whose whip science sighs in many places." "They've cut their whips out of old leather folios. You don't have to know how the stone falls, you have to know what Aristotle writes about it. Eyes are only for reading. Why bother with new laws of falling bodies, if only the laws of genuflection are important?" The Little Monk explains the agony his parents would suffer if the new concept of the universe turned out to be right: "There will be no meaning in their misery. Hunger will simply mean not having eaten, rather than being a test of strength. Hard work will simply be bending and lugging, and not be a virtue." Galileo's reply to him emphasizes a whole series of contradictions: The Campagna peasants are paying for the war fought in Spain and Germany by the mild Lord Jesus' deputy – and why does the pope place the earth in the center of the universe? "So that Saint Peter's throne may stand at the center of the earth?" He goes on:

> If your parents were prosperous and happy, they might develop the virtues of happiness and prosperity. Today the virtues of exhaustion are caused by the exhausted land. For that my new water pumps could work more wonder than their ridicuous superhuman efforts. Be fruitful and

> multiply: for the fields are barren and war is decimating you! Should I lie to your people?

Finally Galileo sums up: "I can see your people's divine patience, but where is their divine wrath?"

This method of extracting truth from antitheses is also reflected in Galileo's entire approach to research. Thus, before starting to investigate sunspots, he says:

> My intention is not to prove that I was right but to find out *whether* I was right. "Abandon hope all ye who enter – an observation." Before assuming these phenomena are spots, which would suit us, let us first set about proving that they are not – fishtails . . . In fact, we will approach this observing of the sun with the firm determination to prove that the earth stands still, and only if hopelessly defeated in this pious undertaking can we allow ourselves to wonder if we may not have been right all the time: the earth revolves.

"Unhappy is the land that breeds no hero."/"Unhappy is the land that needs a hero." Galileo is trapped in a contradiction of principles from which he cannot extricate himself. At his last meeting with Andrea he says that he has taught knowledge by denying the truth – Brecht drew the truth from contradictions, through the play's murderous analysis. Galileo's "final words" signify initial knowledge: "Scientists cannot remain scientists if they deny themselves to the masses; the powers of nature cannot be fully developed if mankind does not know how to develop its own powers; machines, meant to bring relief to man, may merely bring new hardships; progress may merely progress away from humanity."

The essence of drama is conflict; conflict depends on the existence of antitheses; antitheses are an essential structural element in the dramatic. *Galileo* is antithetical in its parts and its entirety, and these antitheses are in turn transcended through the dialectical nature of its relationships, characters, and language; yet the transcendences themselves are ephemeral. As I pointed out in the beginning, Brecht toward the end of his life came out in favor of a "dialectical theatre," of which *Galileo* – written long before the theory – is a demonstration, not only in its technique but in its aesthetic essence. It is the "merely" narrative and "purely" demonstrative structure, as well as the appropriately "calm" production of this play, that allows us to grasp and enjoy dialectics in the theatre.

NOTE

1. All page references for *Schriften zum Theater* are for the East German Aufbau Verlag edition, Berlin, 1964.

14

THE DISPUTE OVER THE VALLEY: AN ESSAY ON BERTOLT BRECHT'S PLAY, *THE CAUCASIAN CHALK CIRCLE*

Hans-Joachim Bunge

Translated by Bayard Quincy Morgan

Conceptions of Bertolt Brecht's own staging of his play *The Caucasian Chalk Circle* in the "Berliner Ensemble am Schiffbauerdamm" (*première* 7 October 1954) differ from the performance in Frankfort-on-the-Main (directed by Harry Buckwitz *première* 27 April 1955) in this respect, among others, that in Berlin the *Prologue* was performed, whereas in Frankfort it was deleted before rehearsals began.

The *Prologue* is an integral part of *The Caucasian Chalk Circle* and the play has never been published *without it.*[1] In it Brecht shows how two Grusinian Kolchoses settle an argument over the possession of a valley claimed by both villages. The valley is obtained by those who give promise of administering it best, i.e., those who will irrigate it in order to make it produce more fruit.

The goat-raising Kolchos "Galinsk" had been evacuated from the valley by a government order when Hitler's armies were advancing. After the Nazis have been expelled the Kolchos plans to move back, because the peasants are attached to their old homeland and because their goats prefer the grass there.

Members of the neighboring, fruit-growing Kolchos "Rosa Luxemburg" had defended the land as guerillas in the surrounding mountains. In order to stop the enemy they were forced to destroy some of their houses. But between battles they developed a plan for rebuilding the village after the war so it would be larger and more productive. Included in the plan was an irrigation project to develop new vineyards. The project would not pay, however, unless the disputed valley could also be used for this purpose.

In a discussion conducted by experts from the capital, the arguments of common sense prevail over those of love for the homeland, because "one must rather regard a tract of land as a tool with which something useful is produced." The delegates of "Galinsk" are reluctant to give up their former home. But they realize the practicality of the proposals, and furthermore in their new home they well be given state aid to assist them in the breeding of horses.

In their joy over the way such a sound decision had been negotiated, the Kolchos "Rosa Luxemburg" makes plans to produce a play illustrating the discussion: the famous story of the chalk circle. This play is actually a parable showing how in barbaric societies sensible judicial decisions can only be arrived at by chance. One might interpret the story differently (for example, the story could show how the claim to any object is dependent on the labor which is performed for it), but since Brecht conceived of the *Prologue* and the chalk-circle story as a unit, the first interpretation is probably correct. Furthermore, if one is to get the most out of a performance of a Brecht play, it is necessary to understand his technique of confrontation: the confrontation of two legal findings, one from the past, one in the present; or the confrontation of two lands, the one society socialistically organized, the other without such an organization.

After the play's performance in Frankfort, the West German press was unanimously in favor of the omission of the *Prologue*, in which "the political activist had looked very intently over the shoulder of the dramatist" (*Frankfurter Rundschau*): "The *Prologue* with its immense display of comrades true to the communist line, of embattled laughter, and faces beaming with the happiness of fulfilling the Plan, had become the prey of the red pencil" (*Abendpost Frankfurt*). The play, "from which the decayed tooth of the *Prologue* had been pretty thoroughly extracted" (*Westdeutsche Rundschau*), had been "staged without the frame intended for the use of the SED"[2] (*Der Tagesspiegel*, Berlin) and "carefully divested of its bolshevistic wrapping paper" (*Soester Anzeiger*)

In the semi-official organ *Ruhrfestspiele* (*Recklinghausen*), the further observation is made that the deletion was "justified, for it would probably have produced an involuntary comic effect. Besides, it is not meant for us at all, I mean for us here in the West. It is an instruction manual *ad usum Delphini*,[3] a device for protection against criticism in one's own camp. That is really the only way one can take it." "For," writes the *Wiesbadener Kurier*, "the fact that the whole long-winded play had propaganda as its aim should be seen by the merest simpleton. But if one did not or would not see this, the *Prologue* would have knocked it into his head with a sledge hammer."

On the other hand, one can read in *Welt der Arbeit* (Cologne) that the deletion of the *Prologue* was "good, for here no pretext and no alibi is needed, and even the simplest of stories, if only a true poet tells it, has its value and its meaning in itself." Left-wing newspapers said, for example, that the deletion, "in view of the prevailing anti-Soviet psychosis proved to be almost unavoidable" (*Deutsche Volkszeitung*, Düsseldorf). And reviewers from the DDR[4] tried to make out that "such a reaction, which was to be foreseen, had induced the stage manager to make the cut." "Perhaps he even had to do it in order to forestall a complete denial of a permit" (*Neues Deutschland*, Berlin).

In cases where the omission of the *Prologue* was declared to be a defect, it was felt that "the renunciation of the *Prologue* is dishonest, for the weights are shifted, and the public is made to think that a historic fable is all that is meant, that it is nothing more than a colorful stage dream, instead of a presentation of living, present-day conditions. Hence the play comes to us a little like the wolf in sheep's clothing, and points of approximation are feigned where none exist" (*Neue Zeitung*, Recklinghausen). Or: "because without a seductive *Prologue* Brecht (West) appears as the writer of a sentimental play shot through with social criticism, whereas it is only the *Prologue* that displays the most fearful consequences, e.g., the conduct of 'people's judges'" (*Darmstädter Echo*), and "because the idyll in pink, the perfect utopia in its official realism affects us like a fairy tale from which the witch has been cut out" (*Stuttgarter Zeitung*).

Many newspapers had to take the trouble to say the same thing twice: after the *première* in Frankfort and after the guest-performance of the Frankfort theatre in connection with the Ruhr festival in Recklinghausen. Here the stiffly hostile polemic evidently seemed to be especially necessary because the audience consisted for the most part of working people. And since these spectators gave enthusiastic approval to the performance of the (cut) *Caucasian Chalk Circle* and by a subsequent reading of the entire play might perhaps supplement their impressions and form an opinion which deviated from the critiques of the press, one could not simply pass over the deleted *Prologue*, but found it necessary to serve up a "personal opinion" in advance.

The motivation for the uniformity of this "opinion," as to which the more or less perfect verbal agility of the several journalists cannot deceive us, is not hard to see: Brecht located his *Prologue* in the territory of the Soviet Union. The argument, by no means insignificant, over the possession of a valley is conducted in an amusing fashion and leads to an optimistic solution. Since there can be no objection to the procedure as presented, to understand which, and to see that it is good and correct, needs only a slight measure of common sense, one is vexed because the story is set in a socialist land, the only one to be sure where it can at the moment occur at all, but about which reports of a contrary nature are being spread abroad by a high-speed propaganda machine.

It is embarrassing to register this new democratic observance of legality. In some critiques, actually, the "political peril" is quite openly stressed. Hence it seems proper to intimidate a tendentiously trained public in the jargon of political rabble-rousing: "The author has prefixed to his play (1947) a *Prologue* (1954!)" and "is trying in this way to bring it up to date. He wanted to make it palatable to the cultural functionaries of the East by setting his switches in the correct ideological position for the attached play" (*Süddeutsche Zeitung* and *Stuttgarter Zeitung*).

The press in the DDR, one would think, must draw a different conclusion from the *Prologue*. For the arguments of critiques determined by the capitalistic system do not apply here. But this would be a false inference. The difference is almost only the fact that where the *Prologue* was played less is said about it than where it wasn't staged at all.

Neues Deutschland did not mention the performance. In *Theater der Zeit* Fritz Erpenbeck did devote 800 lines to a review of the play and its performance, but all he says about the *Prologue* is that "if one counts it" there are three plots in all. Heinz Hofmann in the *Nationalzeitung* offered Brecht extensive and certainly well-meant suggestions for cuts, but he clearly regards any consideration of the *Prologue* as superfluous. The *Tägliche Rundschau* at any rate writes of the "political significance of a framing action," but to Jürgen Rühle in *Sonntag* "the connection seems to be dragged in by the hair, and in any case the two procedures do not constitute a dramatically necessary unity." A similar attitude is arrived at also by *Neue Zeit* and *Berliner Zeitung*, because the "introductory episode is turned into an indecisive, hardly convincing parallel to the case of the child in the *Chalk Circle* and by-passed the emotional response of the spectator."

The largest amount of space was devoted to it in the *Sächsisches Tageblatt*, and, therefore, the interpretation given there is the most questionable – if one will permit such a superlative. We read there: "What does Brecht want? He wants to instruct, namely, the peasants in a Kolchos who refuse to see that it is correct to turn over one's own land to other people, namely, to such as know how to make that land fruitful (in this case by irrigation). How does Brecht achieve this? For those Kolchos-peasants, who cling to their land and who (in the *Prologue*) only give it up with reluctance, he has a play performed which has the significance of a parable, the play of the 'chalk circle.' Brecht offers an instructive play, with which he would naturally like to instruct the public. It seems to us dubious to make the play parallel to the *Prologue*, when at the close the singer proclaims, 'The children to the motherly . . . the valley to the waterers . . .' The comparison is lame. *This* teaching does not convince. If, nevertheless, the performance came to be a great theatrical event, it was because the plot of the *Chalk Circle* can stand on its own feet without any reference to the *Prologue*."

If critics are right in claiming that the *Prologue* is at least superfluous, then a viewer of both stagings – in Berlin *with* and Frankfort *without* the *Prologue* – should be able to confirm the judgment. For in the final result, in that case, no basic difference would be observable. Differ-ences in the detailed presentation of the several characters by the actors could not have obscured the fact that they were presenting the same story.

However, anyone who has witnessed both performances must dispute this categorically. Although many things in Frankfort, in view of Brecht's detailed and precise instructions for performance, could be presented as they were in Berlin, and although Harry Buckwitz had taken over almost exactly the dramaturgic cuts which Brecht suggested for the Berlin production, in short, although both productions were in general agreement both as to the text and to large areas of the stage procedure, the two performances were very different.

Two different stories were told. In the Frankfort performance, as the critics quite rightly observed, the "tribulations of the maidservant Grusha were presented." The spectator saw how the kitchen maid, after making so many sacrifices, is finally permitted to keep the child. This decision is brought about by Judge Azdak in the fifth act of the play. Undazzled, however, by the brilliant acting of Hanns Ernst Jäger as Azdak, one asked oneself why Brecht had interrupted the Grusha action by inserting an entire act to relate in such detail the history of the judge. For the fact that Azdak is an unusual judge is sufficiently evident in the act in which he adjudicates the child not to the governor's wife but to her maid Grusha. What had led the author to give the plot of his fairy-tale play the substructure of a philosophic contention? The play may need "such a poor people's judge" in order to end as the author wishes, but why does it need the biography of Azdak?

The Frankfort performance would certainly have lost some brilliant acting with elimination of the fourth (Azdak) act, but it would presumably have gained in concentration with respect to its proper objective – the presentation of the Grusha plot – as was marked by Brecht's approval when he saw the full rehearsal. Only he added, characteristically: "If one takes it by itself and detached from the drama as a whole."

In the Berlin performance, which Brecht himself directed, matters were different. The focal point there was not so much the servant Grusha, for all her great role and the famous interpretation of it by Angelika Hurwicz, as the child. For the director in search of the plot of the entire work, the interesting outcome was not: *which mother gets* the child? But: which of the two women is the *best one for the child*?

In Berlin the love scene between Grusha and Simon at the close of the play did not have the same importance as in Frankfort, where it was predominant. After Azdak had determined the right mother for the child, it was good that the child should get a father, and the judge considered the soldier Simon to be suitable. In Frankfort, on the other hand, it looked as if the author were chiefly concerned to reward Grusha for her privations and unselfish labors. So she *did* finally get her *betrothed*, after having almost lost him on account of the child. In Berlin this was *also* the case, as far as the action was concerned, but this happening was of less importance and by no means the "point."

The divergent perspectives for the two performances were, as will be shown, dependent on the inclusion or non-inclusion of the *Prologue*. In contrast to Frankfort, the detailed Azdak episode in Berlin proved itself to be absolutely necessary, because definite expectations of the spectators had been aroused by the linking of the chalk-circle plot with *Prologue* and had now to be satisfied.

In the *Prologue* a peasant woman had said, before the performance of the play about the chalk circle, "it has to do with our problem." The behavior of the peasants in their dispute over the valley invited a comparison with certain modes of behavior which are displayed in the ensuing action. Every procedure can be judged in many different ways, and it always depends on what use one wishes to make of it. In the *Prologue* Brecht indicates definite useful points of view and suggests standards for judging the story of the chalk circle as performed.

"The *Prologue* elucidates the meaning of the play," says Max Schroeder (*Afbau*, 11, 1954). "The play has a fairy-tale character. The victory of the good in the fairy tale is utopian, an expression of the folk's dreams of the future which have no place in the reality of the class society, a victory which may indeed occur in one or the other case but cannot become the truth in a socialist society."

If, as is claimed, the *Prologue* is necessary in order to discover the meaning of the play, the latter cannot be interpreted without the *Prologue*, or may be falsely interpreted. Or, what is the same thing: *The Caucasian Chalk Circle* is not the same play *without* the *Prologue* as *with* it.

Now to be sure Max Schroeder goes on to say, "It is questionable whether the connection between *Prologue* and play is clearly made. In reading I find no cleavage, but in the performance the author's message does not make itself so clear." And he finds support for this view in Käthe Rülicke, who in a critical comparison of the performances in Berlin and Cracow (where the *Prologue* was likewise included) states that evidently it is especially difficult to depict happenings realistically when the actors of a land in which these things cannot as yet occur lack the possibility of direct observation and verification. In her opinion, not only the Polish director but even Brecht himself as director had failed to reproduce the *Prologue* in keeping with the conception of Brecht as author, because the theoretical insights of the director cannot *a priori* make up for the actors' lack of experience.

A failure in stage presentation can be no excuse for theatre critics who have at their disposal the text of the play as well as the performance of it. At least they should be able to see what the playwright intended. For his analysis, Max Schroeder possessed no materials which were not equally accessible to all other critics. And where should the two young critics in the *Forum* (organ of the FDJ[5]) have got their findings if not from the performance? In them – in view of their youth – one can hardly expect the assured gaze of the professional *Litterateur*, but perhaps they have the gift of good and unprejudiced powers of observation. They write, "In our opinion, the *Prologue* serves to vivify a peaceful determination of the right in a socialist society. So much the more striking is the dubiousness, indeed the tragic nature, of adjudication in a predatory society."

If one accuses the author and director Brecht, by whom such plays are extant and to be seen on the stage as *The Mother, Mother Courage and*

Her Children, or *Mr. Puntila and his Servant Matti*, of having written and published something superfluous, and of not having recognized this even when he staged it, surely a more careful analysis is to be advised than one finds the majority of the critics to have printed. Otherwise those writers will all too easily incur the suspicion of having either given expression to a politically hostile critique or of simply tossing off arrogantly flippant judgments. Whereas the former would be explainable from the standpoint of the class conflict, in no case could one excuse mere ignorance.

A famous essay of the Russian literary critic N. A. Dobroliubov was aimed at scholastic critiques when he himself discussed (1859) the plays of A. N. Ostrovsky. His remarks (reproduced here in abridgment) are today once more of importance, and especially in connection with the critiques of the *Prologue* of Brecht's drama.

> We deem it necessary to warn the reader that we do not ascribe any programme to the author, we do not draw up for him any preliminary rules to guide him in planning and executing his works . . . In our opinion, such a method of criticism is extremely offensive to an author whose talent is universally recognized and who has already won the love of the public and a certain share of significance in literature . . . such criticism is unpleasant, because it places the critic in a position of a pedantic schoolteacher setting out to examine a schoolboy . . . Every reader would be quite justified in saying to us, ". . . what we want the critics to do is to explain to us what it is that so often unaccountably thrills us, to explain our own impressions to us and put them in some order. If, after this explanation, our impressions prove to be erroneous and their results harmful, or if it turns out that we are ascribing to the author something that should not be ascribed to him, then let the critics set to work to rectify our errors; but, we insist, they must be rectified on the basis of what the author himself presents to us." We think that such a demand would be quite just, and we, therefore, consider it best to apply to Ostrovsky's productions *realistic* criticism . . . The realistic critic treats the work of an artist in the same way as he treats the phenomena of real life; he studies them in the endeavour to define their norm, to collect their essential, characteristic features, but he does not ask fussily why oats are not rye and coal not diamonds . . . True, there may have been scientists who engaged in experiments to prove that oats become transformed into rye; there have also been critics who tried to prove that if Ostrovsky had altered such and such a scene in such and such a way he would have been a Gogol, and if he had depicted such and such a person in such and such a way he would have been a Shakespeare. . . . We believe, however, that such scientists and critics did not do much to promote science and art. Far more useful were those who brought to the knowledge of the public a few hitherto concealed or not quite clear facts of life, or of the world of art, which is the portrayal of life.[6]

In answer to the assertions of some critics it should be made clear from the beginning that Brecht wrote this play, precisely as we now have it, in 1944 during his expatriation. The *Prologue* was not a later addition. For example, he notes in his diary on September 26, 1944: "Last evening's discussion with Eisler, Helli, and Steff[7] concerning the *Prologue* of the *Chalk Circle*. Steff wants the conflict of the villages to be harsher and more real, on the basis of a genuine disadvantage for the goat-raisers." Brecht made an alteration in 1947 to this extent, that he transferred the negotiations regarding the valley, originally occurring in wartime, to the period after the expulsion of the Nazis. Later changes, which likewise did not affect the main conception and were made during the rehearsals or even after the performance had been in the theatre's repertory for some time, will be reported on hereafter.

In the printed program of the Berlin Ensemble, after a comparison of the plot in the Chinese play and that of Brecht's work we read, "The narrative now shows a new kind of wisdom, a bearing and behavior which rest on a new structure of society. Hence the judgment is different. Hence, too, the play is staged in a land where a new social structure already exists. There the new ideas can be staged. The *Prologue* with its contemporaneous controversy show the applicability of this new wisdom and assigns a historic location to its origination."

It is questionable whether this explanation contributes to the understanding of the play. One can ever surmise that these faulty interpretations, insofar as they are not politically aimed, rest at least in part on the idea that the spectator is from the outset induced to regard the *Prologue* as a kind of booster[8] to thc play proper. In that case it has primarily an explanatory character for the following story, from which a utilitarian effect is to be derived.

But the "new wisdom" cannot have originated solely from the fact that in Brecht's play it is not the biological mother who gets the child – as is the case in the Chinese drama – but "that woman who by assuming the responsibility and by caring for the child has become its mother." Likewise the behavior of Judge Azdak alone, bold and unusual as his verdict is, does not constitute "a *new* kind of truth."

In Brecht's play, Grusha's victory is that of the socially more valuable person, but "in the old Chinese drama, too, the 'motherly one' does not win out solely because she is the biological mother, but because she is also the socially more valuable person," says Max Schroeder in the critique mentioned above. In *both* cases, therefore, the woman gets the child who has proved herself to be the real mother, and it is not unthinkable that that earlier play might have ended as Brecht's does, had the biological mother not proved herself to be motherly. Here as there, a judge acts sensibly, and here as there he does cling to traditional "rights," for in the Chinese drama too it is by no means a question of "normal rights," i.e., those determined by the ruling class and onesidedly interpreted in its favor, and the judge derived his fame from the fact that he did not deliver a formal judgment, or at least that he did not let himself be bribed by the members of the privileged class.

Old as is the yearning of men of all oppressed classes for a just kind of communal society, just as old is the wisdom which invented stories like that of the Chinese circle of chalk. And by the fact that in his play Brecht treats the verdict of Azdak so clearly as a one-time affair, elicited by such astonishing circumstances, absolutely accidental and limited by a brief period of time, he does everything for and nothing against the *old* wisdom. Hence at the close of the play he has the singer say, "Take note of what men of old concluded . . ."

The new wisdom originates from the fact that the Kolchos peasants perform the play in connection with their dispute. And the change which Brecht has made in the old Chinese legend gets productive significance because he conceived the story of the chalk circle along with the *Prologue*. For suddenly, in Brecht's play, what is at stake is no longer a question of motherhood in the sense of the Chinese source.

The question asked in the *Prologue* as to the disposal of the valley, is, who is the most productive user? And more precisely, who gives promise of getting the most out of it? What interests us is not so much who possessed the valley at any time, although the bond with the beloved homeland is by no means denied and the land is not "simply taken away" from its former owner; the important thing is who will administer the land most advantageously *now* – "advantageously" being judged from the viewpoint of the entire society.

As to the story of the chalk circle, "which has to do with our problem," we read in the printed program of the Berlin performance that "the chalk-circle test of the old Chinese novel and drama, as well as its Biblical complement, the judgment of Solomon, are retained as tests of motherhood (by the determination of motherliness)," but that "motherhood is now determined not biologically but socially."

If the selection were made biologically – as in the Chinese example – the mother would be central, but if it is made socially, it is not so much a matter of the mother, and in this case the child is decisive. The mother doesn't need the child but the child needs the mother; and what is decisive for Azdak is not whether he puts a woman in possession of natural or acquired rights, but which decisions is best for the child. The pre-history – how the governor's wife abandoned the child and how Grusha reared it – hardly gets the judge's attention. "I'll . . . not listen to any more lies," he says, and then, "the court has listened to your case, and has come to no decision as to who the real mother of this child is. I, as a judge, am obliged to choose a mother for the child."

The servant Grusha gets the child, not because she took upon herself such great privations on its account and for this reason might perhaps present her merits as a claim to its possession, but because she is willing to keep it "until it knows all words," i.e., because she is useful to the child, which needs the guidance and help of a mother in order to become a useful member of society. The governor's wife, whose biological rights are uncontested, and to whom the judge would perhaps restore the child if this decision were good for the child, does not want the child for its sake but for her own, for the inheritance is bound up with the child.

Poor-folks'-judge Azdak has to be sure a very definite idea of what is good for the child. He asks the maid Grusha, "If he were yours, woman, wouldn't you want him to be rich? You'd only have to say that he is not yours. And immediately he'd have a palace and many horses in his stable and many beggars on his doorstep and many soldiers in his service and many petitioners in his courtyard, wouldn't he? What do you say? Don't you want him to be rich?"

Grusha is silent, but Brecht puts into a song what she is thinking:

> If he went in golden shoes
>   He would cruel be;
> Evil then would be his life.
>   He could laugh at me.
> Too heavy is a heart of stone
>   For human breast to bear!
> Bad and powerful to be
>   Is too great a care.
> Hunger he will have to fear,
>   But no hungry one!
> Darkness he will have to fear,
>   But not the sun![9]

"I think I understand you, woman," says Azdak. He knows which mother he will choose for the child. At this point he already knows it, and the test which he will make shall merely confirm his decision.

It is confidence in the necessary, common-sense decision which likewise determines the action of the experts from the capital in the *Prologue*, after they have examined the documents on the valley project in advance of the general discussion. And just as Judge Azdak by means of the chalk-circle test merely finds out exactly whether he has sufficient grounds for the correctness of his verdict, so the assembly of the two villages in the *Prologue* takes place in order to produce the certainty that no new and more important arguments have been overlooked, or, otherwise, to discuss the existing arguments in common.

But Brecht's play is no parable. The plots of the *Prologue* and the chalk-circle story cannot be regarded simply as parallel, and as if it were indifferent that in one case the decision affects a human being and in the other case a tract of land. No, it is just the difference which must be stressed. In the *Chalk Circle*, the good and the advantage of *one* person is involved; in the *Prologue* not so much the disputed object, i.e., *this* valley, but a valley whose yield benefits many members of society. But the point to which the thinking of the spectator is directed, when he has seen the *Prologue* and the play about the circle of chalk performed for him, is this: that of late men are considering such problems as are exemplified here: "that what there is shall go / to those who are good for it . . ." Thus: "the children to the motherly, that they may prosper / the carts to good drivers, that they are well driven / and the valley to the waterers, that it bring forth fruit."

If the *Prologue* is not to make the story of the chalk circle an actuality, if it is not needed to understand *per se* the plot of the chalk-circle story, but *is* needed to understand Brecht's play and the manner in which nowadays people in a land with a socialist organization judge the concept of ownership, one may ask whether the designation *Prologue* is not misleading. The episode with which Brecht begins his work is of course not written in the manner of Goethe's "Prologue in the Theatre" preceding his *Faust*, for example, or of Hugo von Hofmannsthal's *Prologues*, but rather like *Wallenstein's Camp* in Schiller's trilogy. The dispute of the Kolchos peasants is as much a part of *The Caucasian Chalk Circle* as the life-history of Judge Azdak, which might well be left out if one left out the *Prologue*. Whether or not one calls the controversy which introduces the play a prologue is no longer a formal question at the moment when, by virtue of the formulation, misunderstandings might arise as to its content and its importance – as is the case when one deletes the *Prologue* because one considers it not absolutely part of the work.

Early in August of 1956, when Brecht's attention was called to false conceptions which could be proven by critiques in the press, he changed the title of the episode which plays in the Caucasus simply to *The Dispute Over the Valley* (*Der Streit um das Tal*). Thus he documented unmistakably the necessary inclusion of the present-day controversy in the work as a whole, whose several scenes now have headings of similar form.

Instead of the statement in the printed program of the Berlin Ensemble, "The story now shows a new kind of wisdom . . ." and so on (see supra), it would now perhaps be clearer to say this:

In the story of *The Caucasian Chalk Circle* the origination of an old wisdom is shown, whose novel applicability is to be seen in the present-day dispute over the valley. The productiveness of this wisdom is variable according as its historic place is assigned to it in the two plots. The story of the old Chinese source is legendary. The play with the new verdict in the celebrated test of the chalk circle shows now a new kind of wisdom – a behavior which rests upon a new structure of society. For that reason, too, the play takes place in a land where a new social structure is already in operation. There the new ideas can be staged.

The Caucasian Chalk Circle, therefore, does not "fall apart" into three actions, as some critics assert, but it is composed of them. True, each plot is a self-contained unit – dispute over the valley, story of the chalk circle, and story of the judge – but all three belong strictly together and together make up the whole work, just as within the Azdak-act the single episodes are wholly self-contained – there could be more or fewer of them – but only in their union produce "the story of the judge."

In reality the conception of the work rests upon an alienation of the content of the episode in the Caucasus and that of the chalk-circle story, into which the story of the judge had to be inserted in order to make the alienation effective. It is shown how sensible social decisions, in case of conflicting phenomena of social coexistence, originate or are brought about in two different orders of society. The different length of the two contrasted parts of the play must not mislead us into seeing a difference in weight. On the contrary, it serves to disclose and present the chief contrast as one of historic nature. The two parts, different in content, are also given a different formal treatment. The length of the chalk-circle story is especially emphasized by the brevity of the dispute of the two villages – and vice versa. It is not only that it proved necessary, in connection with the two epochs in which the stories take place, to show more single contradictions in the earlier one, in order to make the happenings recollectible and understandable for those who, living themselves in the present-day parts of the work, perform it on the stage – but the difference in length is a means of documenting the singular value of the historic epoch with its special presuppositions, and thus makes possible the contrast of the two plots.

The contrary nature of the two decisions, in the dispute over the valley and the story of the chalk circle, must find expression, among other things, in the fact that in the latter an exceptional case from legendary tradition is reported, in the former a regular case. For the new manner of not stating the law, but of arriving at sensible decisions determined by the situation, is not restricted to this one example in the socialist organization of society, whereas the determination of the right in the chalk-circle story is absolutely bound up with the existence of Azdak and the time of his service as judge, which again is dependent on the brief duration of the general disorder in the land.

In the chalk-circle story, the one party loses and the other gains. In the decision between the two villages this is only seemingly the case. In reality both gain, because both acknowledge the social order in which they live and which they themselves determine. To be sure, it is simpler to discover the casualness of the judge's decision in the chalk-circle story than the new wisdom in the dispute over the valley. As yet unversed in the use of new methods of thinking and acting, the spectator in the theatre frequently fails as yet to recognize them.

The new social order must be discovered in which the ruling class is no longer the minority whose laws are made in order to preserve its sway, but in which the ruling class consists of the entire working population, whose laws drawn up by all, must be good for all – or they must be changed. Out of sensible considerations a new kind of legality with new legal concepts has been formed.

Brecht added two sentences at the beginning of August 1956, when in preparation for the English visit of the Berlin Ensemble *The Dispute Over the Valley* was rehearsed. When the conflict of the two villages was at its height he had a woman delegate from "Galinsk" say, "By law the valley belongs to us!" Thereupon a member of the Kolchos "Rosa Luxemburg" answered, "Laws must in every case be examined to see if they still are suitable."

These two sentences are of especial importance, because they give the controversial case that majestic perspective which only a Marxist playwright – such as Brecht is – can consciously formulate. If anywhere, the laws of movement and development in human society and in thinking which found their poetic form in this play have been given a pivotal point here.

"The progressiveness of Azdak," we read in the program of the Berlin Ensemble, "resides in the fact that he does not judge by the letter but sees the reality of the law that is made only for the rich. Boldly he turns it about so that it yields something for the poor."

The progressiveness of the villagers in their dispute resides likewise in the fact that they act ultimately against the law of the Soviet Union which actually secures to those citizens who were evacuated during the war on order of the government all rights to the abandoned territory. Whereas, however, Azdak has to prove his progressiveness in defiance of the prevailing social order, in the dispute of the two villages it is the progressive social order which not only justifies this mode of action but promotes it. The progressive thinking of the peasants is shown by the fact that after the presentation of the useful plan of the Kolchos "Rosa Luxemburg" they jointly alter the law, because its observance in the face of the new arguments would be dogmatic – and therewith, in the sense of their social organization, "illegal." By adding those two sentences Brecht did away with that previously possible error: that in the settlement of the dispute an orderly solution might be involved, i.e., a decision which must regularly turn out just so and not otherwise, according to a predetermined and definitive *modus*. As contrasted with the irregular decision of Azdak in his day, the legal finding in the dispute over the valley is to be understood as regular only insofar as the social order in which it can occur guarantees by law a sensible decision, even if for definite unforeseeable reasons it is not a "statutory right."

As a result of this examination of the *Prologue* it must also be surmised that *The Dispute over the Valley* can not only not be a prologue in the sense that it introduces a following play, but that its content is the major objective of the author, and that the story of the chalk circle – as in the play – is performed in order to make the happening clear in its significance. Or, putting it in a different way: in order to make the factual content of the dispute over the valley perceptible and to commend its consideration, it is "estranged" by being contrasted with the chalk-circle story. It is no longer that way, but it is *this* way.

Or is it not noteworthy, and is it not rewarding, to point out that suddenly – and in an undogmatically legal fashion – "right" (in the sense of correct actions) is found such as could not have occurred in other times in Grusinia – or even today in many lands of the world – because the possession of a valley would have been "regulated" by wars?

In not one review has it been pointed out that in the version of the play published in 1949 it is not the Kolchos peasants of the *Prologue* who perform the play, but that a "presentation of the singer Arkadi Tscheidse" is given the hearing of all, of which one peasant woman of "Rosa Luxemburg"[10] says merely, "Arkadi Tscheidse knows all about our discussion. He has promised to recite something that has to do with our problem." Not until the later version in No. 13 of the "Versuche" (1954) was the alteration undertaken at the beginning of rehearsals of the play. In that version the peasant woman says, we "have arranged with the collaboration of the singer Arkadi Tscheidse to produce a play which has a bearing on our problem," and the old man of the Kolchos "Rosa Luxemburg" says, "We have rehearsed the play under his direction," while the singer himself says, "This time it's a play with songs, and nearly the whole Kolchos takes part."

It is only in seeming that this change, after the appearance of the singer has been motivated, serves to explain the presence of the actors, too, who present the story of the chalk circle accompanied by the songs of Arkadi Tscheidse.

The peasants perform the play for themselves. They do so for their own pleasure. But this pleasure is not exhausted in their simply offering some theatrical production or other. They have chosen a play which has to do with their problem. Yet with respect to the present-day case it is not a question of the legal problem *per se*, but of the *manner* in which the decision is made. In the dispute over the valley the decision was revolutionary, but it was given as if it were self-explanatory, in an almost amusing discussion. Anything like a militant dispute is so completely ruled out, although a short while before, i.e., during the Nazi occupation, all the peasants had experienced how people in other regions of the world think about the distribution of land. And in order that they shall not fail to see in what land and under what system they are living, in order that they may recognize in their jointly achieved decision the novelty which they have received in their consciousness, in order that they may comprehend the productiveness and the necessity of further alterations in their socially socialistic thinking, they perform the play: feeling the greatest pleasure in their recognition of the progressiveness of their social order, in which they are placed in a position to alter the world itself.

"The world of today can be reproduced in the theatre, too, but only if it is conceived of as alterable," Brecht replied to a question of Fred Dürrenmatt in connection with the "Darmstadt dialogs" regarding the situation of the current theatre, which took place at the time of the Frankfort *première* of *The Caucasian Chalk Circle*. For "the world of today is only describable to the people of today if it is described as an alterable world."

Many listeners in Darmstadt who are identical with those critics whose critiques of the work were excerpted at the beginning of this essay saw a dogma of party politics in those sentences. They might have been put in the position of seeing in practice, a few miles away from the scene of the dialogs, how Brecht thinks the function of the theatre is actualized – if the Frankfort performance had taken place *with* the so-called *Prologue*.

"The subsequently added *Prologue*" was "a tribute of Brecht's to the red bosses," said the political critique of a West German newspaper. Not the *Prologue* but the entire work is a tribute, and, in fact, a red tribute, i.e., to a social order in which what can only be told as a fairy tale in the story of the circle of chalk is made real.

NOTES

1. This is attested by the special "Bertolt Brecht Number" of the magazine *Sinn und Form* (1949) and No. 13 of the "Versuche," Suhrkamp-Verlag, Berlin and Frankfurt a Main, and Aufbau-Verlag, Berlin, first printing 1954.
2. *Sozialistische Einheitspartei Deutschlands*.
3. Literally, "for the use of the Dauphin," innocuous matter, about equivalent to "pap."
4. *Deutsche Demokratische Republik*, i.e., [Former] East Germany.
5. *Freie Deutsche Jugend*.
6. N. A. Dobroliubov, "Realm of Darkness," in *Selected Philosophic Essays* (Moscow: Foreign Language Publishing House, 1956) 231 ff.
7. Hans Eisler, Helene Weigel, Stefan S. Brecht.
8. *Vorspann* literally means "relay" or "fresh horses." There is no exact English idiomatic equivalent.
9. Translated by Eric and Maja Bentley.
10. In this essay no attention is paid to the fact that in the version of 1949 the names of the two Kolchoses were reversed.

PROLOGUE TO *THE CAUCASIAN CHALK CIRCLE*[1]

Bertolt Brecht

Translated by Eric Bentley

SUMMER OF 1945.

Among the ruins of a war-ravaged Caucasian village the MEMBERS *of two Collective Farms, mostly women and older men, are sitting in a circle, smoking and drinking wine. With them is a* DELEGATE *of the State Reconstruction Commission from Tiflis, the capital.*

PEASANT WOMEN, *left* (*pointing*): That's where we stopped three Nazi tanks. But the apple orchard was already destroyed.

OLD MAN, *right*: Our beautiful dairy farm: a ruin.

GIRL TRACTORIST: I started the fire myself, Comrade. (*Pause.*)

DELEGATE: Comrades! Listen to the report. The Collective Goat Farm Rosa Luxemburg, formerly located right here in this valley, moved East, on orders from the government, at the approach of Hitler's Armies. Now their plan is to return. (*Delegates on right nod.*) But the people of the Collective Fruit Farm Galinsk, their neighbors, propose, instead, that the valley be assigned to them. They would like to plant vineyards and orchards there. Representing the Reconstruction Commission, I request that these two collective farms decide between themselves whether the Rosa Luxemburg should return here or not.

OLD MAN, *right*: First of all, I want to protest against the time limit on discussion. We of The "Rosa Luxemburg" have spent three days and three nights getting here. And now discussion is limited to half a day!

WOUNDED SOLDIER, *left*: Comrade, we haven't as many villages as we used to have. We haven't as many hands. We haven't as much time.

GIRL TRACTORIST: All pleasures have to be rationed. Tobacco is rationed, and wine. Discussion should be rationed.

OLD MAN, *right* (*sighing*): Death to the fascists! All right, I will come to the point and explain just why we want our valley back. Makina Abakidze, unpack the goat cheese. (A PEASANT WOMAN *from the right takes from a basket an enormous cheese wrapped in a cloth. Applause and laughter.*) Help yourselves, Comrades, have some!

OLD MAN, *left* (*suspiciously*): Is this a way of influencing us?

OLD MAN, *right* (*amid laughter*): How could it be a way of influencing you, Surab, you valley-thief? Everyone knows you'll take the cheese and the valley, too. (*Laughter.*) All I expect from you is an honest answer. Do you like the cheese?

OLD MAN, *left*: The answer is: yes.

OLD MAN, *right*: Really. (*Bitterly*) I might have known you knew nothing about cheese.

OLD MAN, *left*: Why? When I tell you I like it?

OLD MAN, *right*: Because you can't like it. Because it's not what it was in the old days. And why not? Because our goats don't like the new grass. The grazing land over there is no good, whatever the young folks say. You can't live there. It doesn't even smell of morning in the morning. (*Several people laugh.*) Please put that in your report.

DELEGATE: Don't mind them: they got your point. After all, why does a man love his country? Because the bread tastes better there, the air smells better, voices sound stronger, the sky is higher, the ground is easier to walk on. Isn't that so?

OLD MAN, *right*: The valley has belonged to us from all eternity.

SOLDIER, *left*: What does that mean – from all eternity? Nothing belongs to anyone from all eternity. When you were young you didn't even belong to yourself. You belonged to the Kazbeki princes.

OLD MAN, *right*: The valley belongs to us by law.

GIRL TRACTORIST: In any case, the laws must be reexamined to see if they're still right.

OLD MAN, *right*: That goes without saying. But doesn't it make a difference what kind of trees stand next to the house you are born in? Or what kind of neighbors you have? We want to come back just to have you as our neighbors, valley-thieves! Now you can all laugh again.

OLD MAN, *left* (*laughing*): Then why don't you listen to what your neighbor, Kato Vachtang, our agriculturist, has to say about the valley?

PEASANT WOMAN, *right*: We've not finished what *we* had to say about this valley. The houses weren't *all* destroyed. As for the dairy farm, at least the foundation's still there.

DELEGATE: If your new grazing land is as bad as all that, you have a good claim to State support.

PEASANT WOMAN, *right*: Comrade Specialist, we're not horse trading. I can't take your cap, hand you another, and say, This one's better. It may be better, but you prefer your own.

GIRL TRACTORIST: A piece of land is not a cap – not in our country, Comrade.

DELEGATE: Don't get angry. It's true a piece of land is a tool to produce something useful, but there's also such a thing as love for a particular piece of land. In any event, what we need to know is exactly what you people would do with the valley if you had it. (*To those on the left.*)

OTHERS: Yes, Let Kato speak.

KATO (*rising; she's in military uniform*): Comrades, last winter, while we were fighting in these hills as Partisans, we discussed how, once the Germans were expelled, we could build up our fruit culture to ten times its original size. I've prepared a plan for an irrigation project. With a dam across our mountain lake we could water seven hundred acres of infertile land. Our farm could not only grow more fruit, it could support vineyards too. The project, however, would only pay if the disputed valley of the Rosa Luxemburg farm were also included. Here are the calculations. (*She hands* DELEGATE *a briefcase.*)

OLD MAN, *right*: Write into the report that our Collective plans to start a new stud farm.

GIRL TRACTORIST: Comrades, the project was conceived during days and nights when we had to run for cover in the mountains. Often, we hadn't even enough ammunition for our half-dozen rifles. We could hardly lay our hands on a pencil. (*Applause from both sides.*)

OLD MAN, *right*: Many thanks to our Comrades of the "Galinsk" and all who have defended our country! (*They shake hands and embrace.*)

GIRL TRACTORIST: As the poet Mayakovsky said: "The home of the Soviet people shall also be the home of Reason!"

(*The* DELEGATES *except for the* OLD MAN *have got up, and with the* DELEGATE SPECIFIED *proceed to study the Agriculturist's drawings. Exclamations such as: "Why is the altitude of fall twenty-two meters?" – "This rock must be blown up" – "Actually, all they need is cement and dynamite" "They force the water to come down here, that's clever!"*)

A VERY YOUNG WORKER, *right* (*to* OLD MAN, *right*): They're going to irrigate all the fields between the hills, look at that, Aleko!

OLD MAN, *right*: I won't look! I knew the project would be good. I refuse to have a pistol pointed at me!

DELEGATE: But they only want to point a pencil at you! (*Laughter*.)

PEASANT WOMAN, *right*: Aleko Bereshwili, you have a weakness for new projects.

DELEGATE: Comrades, may I report that you all agree to give up the valley?

PEASANT WOMAN, *right*: I agree. What about you, Aleko?

OLD MAN, *right* (*bent over drawings*): I move that you let us have copies of the blueprints.

PEASANT WOMAN, *right*: Then we can eat. Once he can talk about blueprints, it's settled. And that goes for the rest of us. (DELEGATES *laughingly embrace again*.)

OLD MAN, *left*: Long live the "Rosa Luxemburg" and much luck to your stud farm!

PEASANT WOMAN, *left*: Comrades, in honor of our guests this evening we are all going to hear the Singer Arkadi Tscheidse. (*Applause*.)

(GIRL TRACTORIST *has gone off to bring the* SINGER.)

PEASANT WOMAN, *right*: Your entertainment had better be good. It's costing us a valley.

PEASANT WOMAN, *left*: Arkadi has promised to sing something that has a bearing on our problem. He knows twenty-one thousand lines of verse by heart.

OLD MAN, *left*: He's hard to get. The Planning Commission should persuade him to come north more often, Comrade.

DELEGATE: We are more interested in economics, I'm afraid.

OLD MAN, *left* (*smiling*): You redistribute vines and tractors, why not songs?

(*Enter the* SINGER *Arkadi Tscheidse, led by* GIRL TRACTORIST. *He is a well-built man of simple manners, accompanied by* FOUR MUSICIANS *with their instruments. The artists are greeted with applause*.)

GIRL TRACTORIST: The Comrade Specialist, Arkadi.

(*The* SINGER *greets them all*.)

DELEGATE: It's an honor to meet you. I heard about your songs when I was still at school. Will it be one of the old legends?

THE SINGER: A very old one. It's called The Chalk Circle and comes from the Chinese. But we'll do it, of course, in a changed version. Comrades, we hope you'll find that old poetry can sound well in the shadow of new tractors. It may be a mistake to mix different wines but old and new wisdom mix admirably. Do we get something to eat before the performance?

VOICES: Of course. Everyone into the Club House!

(*While everyone begins to move,* DELEGATE *turns to* GIRL TRACTORIST.)

DELEGATE: I hope it won't take long. I've got to get back tonight.

GIRL TRACTORIST: How long will it last, Arkadi? The Comrade Specialist must get back to Tiflis tonight.

THE SINGER (*casually*): It's actually two stories. A couple of hours.

DELEGATE (*confidentially*): Couldn't you make it shorter?

THE SINGER: no.

(*And they all go happily to eat.*)

NOTE

1. This version of the Prologue has been used on the American stage since the Lincoln Center production in 1966. It is shorter than the German (and than the English version published by the University of Minnesota Press and Grove Press). It was first printed in the Signet Classic edition, 1983.

Part III:
BRECHT INTERPRETED ABROAD

16

BRECHT AND THE ENGLISH THEATRE

Martin Esslin

That future historians of English drama will describe the period since 1956 as an era of Brechtian influence is quite possible. If so, the phenomenon will be an illustration of the quirks and ironies of cultural diffusion between nations: for that Brechtian era had a great deal of talk and discussion *about* Brecht and what he was *thought* to stand for, but few valid productions of Brecht, little genuine knowledge about Brecht, and hence little evidence of any influence of Brecht's actual work and thought. The "Brechtian" era in England stood under the aegis not of Brecht himself but of various second-hand ideas and concepts *about* Brecht, an image created from misunderstandings and misconceptions. Yet, even though Columbus thought he had landed in Asia, he nevertheless discovered something; even though the idea of Greek tragedy on which the theatre of Racine and Corneille was based may have been wrong, the value of the work of these dramatists is undeniable; and whether the amalgam of ideas and heartsearchings that became known in England as the Brechtian influence was a true reflection of his work or not, in the last resort some interesting innovations results from it – and the British theatre will never be quite the same again.

Moreover (and this is a measure of the English critics' inability to contribute to the artistic progress of the English stage) this undeniable influence of "Brechtian" ideas established itself in the face of stubborn and often vicious attacks on Brecht by the vast majority of daily and weekly theatre reviewers, who not only dismissed a whole series of productions of Brecht's plays in English with contempt (which most of them fully deserved) but consistently denounced Brecht himself as a fraud and the inflated idol of faddists and perverse intellectuals.

The one exception among these critics and the one whose merit – or fault – it was that Brecht's name suddenly achieved the currency of a cultural status symbol to be reckoned with among members of the theatrical profession and some sections of the public, was Kenneth Tynan. Tynan became drama critic of the London *Observer* in 1954, and very soon made the name of Brecht his trademark, his yardstick of values, a symbol that could be thrown into any review of even the most mediocre local offering as a shining contrast, an example of excellence in playwriting, production, ideological commitment, care in rehearsal, dedication to the ideal of theatre as an art rather than as an after-dinner entertainment. Whether consciously and deliberately or by mere instinct, Tynan here repeated the device used by Shaw in the nineties, when he elevated Ibsen into the hero of the theatrical revolution of his time. That Tynan had been stirred by the Brecht productions he had seen is beyond a doubt. Yet as Tynan's knowledge of German was far from profound at the time, he was in no position to appreciate Brecht's first and decisive claim to greatness: his mastery of the German language, his stature as a major poet. Inevitably, this led to a certain deformation of the Brechtian image in English eyes: he came across to the readers of the *Observer* as, above all, a dramatist who was on the side of the angels ideologically, as a great director, and as an example of the potential of a theatre artist working effectively and experimentally within the framework of a wholly state-subsidized institution.

It is here that we touch on one of the most important reasons why discussion about Brecht became so widespread and excited at that particular moment in British theatre history: those were the years which preceded the decision to set up a state-subsidized National Theatre in England. For more than half a century the opponents of such an enterprise had argued very persuasively that state-subsidized theatres – one only had to look at the *Comédie Française*! – inevitably became artistically sterile warrens of potbellied Hamlets and post-climacteric civil-service-status Juliets on pensionable life-contracts, obeying the dictates of officials anxious to use the theatre as a propaganda organ for outworn ideas of the most suspect kind. These arguments could at last be effectively silenced by pointing to the Berliner Ensemble, led by a great artist, consisting of young, vigorous, and anti-establishment actors and actresses, wholly experimental, overflowing with new ideas – and state-subsidized to the hilt. So Brecht became the focal point, the rallying cry of the younger generation of theatrical artists who had realized that the future of the theatre as a serious vehicle for ideas, enlightenment, and beauty, depended on the recognition that the commercial system simply was no longer able to provide the basis for viable drama.

By its very nature, its opposition against the purely commercial aspects of theatre, its insistence on the rightness of public financial support for an art, this movement was one of the left. Brecht's status as a culture hero of Communist East Germany further enhanced his appeal to these circles – and correspondingly diminished his chances of ever pleasing the artistic and political right wing. The year 1956 was the *annus mirabilis* in the development of this left-wing movement. It saw in April the opening of the Royal Court as a nursery of angry young playwrights and in late August and early September the first visit of the Berliner Ensemble to the Palace Theatre on Cambridge Circus. By a tragic coincidence Brecht had died shortly before the date of the Ensemble's opening performance; his note urging the members of the company to play lightly and not too slowly to please an English audience was one of his last public pronouncements.

The critical reactions to the three productions the Ensemble brought to London (*Mother Courage*, *The Caucasian Chalk Circle* and an adaptation of Farquhar's *Recruiting Officer – Pauken und Trompeten*) was on the whole lukewarm; but the impact on the theatrical profession all the more profound. Ironically, however, because hardly anyone in the English theatre knows any German, this impact chiefly manifested itself in those spheres that remained unaffected by the language barrier: in stage design and lighting and in the use of music. Indeed, as far as design is concerned, one can safely say that practically *all* British stage design, outside the area of the most old-fashioned drawing-room comedy, today derives from the work of the main Brechtian designers, Neher, Otto, and von Appen. The principal lessons learned concerned the lightness of construction of Brecht's sets, their flexibility and mobility (Sean Kenny's vastly successful design for *Oliver!*, which was almost solely responsible for the great success of an otherwise thoroughly mediocre musical, is a good example) and above all their marvelous use of the texture of the materials employed. John Bury, at that time with Joan Littlewood, today the main designer for the Royal Shakespeare Company, has assimilated the last lesson with the most telling and exhilarating results.

The imitation of the use of songs and music in Brecht's work was less happy in its results. A rash of "socially-oriented" musicals with somewhat more astringent musical scores remained, on the whole, without lasting impact. John Osborne's *The World of Paul Slickey* (1959) was probably the most notable – and the most disastrous – of these. Joan Littlewood achieved the largest measure of success in this direction (*Make me an Offer*, book by Wolf Mankowitz; *Fings ain't what they used t' be*, book by Frank Norman) and she was also responsible for what must be regarded as the only really notable work which owed a debt to the Brechtian use of music in Britain in the period concerned: Brendan Behan's *The Hostage* (1959) with its many parallels to *The Threepenny Opera*.

To trace the influence of Brechtian theory and practice on directors and actors is far more difficult. How is one to tell which elements in Brecht a director *misunderstood* and then applied in his work? Brecht's theoretical writings were largely unavailable until the publication of John Willett's selection in 1964, and before then those directors who had no German (the large majority) had to rely on second-hand accounts of what Brecht had said. And even though there were a number of detailed works on Brecht's ideas available after 1959 (when Willett's and my own books were published) the opportunities for misunderstanding were legion. And indeed: neither the critical accounts nor the texts themselves could serve any really useful purpose without a detailed knowledge of the German theatre in Brecht's time, *against* which he reacted in his theoretical writings. Brecht's constant insistence on emotional coolness in acting, on inhibiting the psychological process of identification between actor and character, derives from the prevalent German style of acting, which aims at producing the maximum impression of emotional intensity by indulgence in hysterical outbursts and paroxysms of uncontrolled roaring and inarticulate anguish. These orgies of vocal excess and apoplectic breastbeating had not been known in the English theatre since the days of Kean and perhaps Irving. Hence, the English style of acting already being cooler and more Brechtian than Brecht's own company's, most of his polemics against the heavy German style (and that after all is what his insistence on non-identification and alienation is really concerned with) are totally inapplicable to English conditions. Not knowing this, and thinking that Brecht was attacking the style currently prevalent in England as well as in Germany, some directors made desperate attempts to cool their actors down even further. As a result, for example, William Gaskill's production of *Mother Courage* at the National Theatre (1965) achieved an effect tantamount to miniaturization of the play and its characters. These wild and rumbustious figures, who should exude vitality, Rabelaisian appetite, lechery, and meanness, appeared cooled down into whispering dwarfs and bloodless spectres – an effect which became all the more eerie as the outward aspects of the production (design and lighting) were meticulously and almost photographically copied from the Berlin production, so that one seemed to be watching a play performed by zombies, re-enacting scenes from their lives after having been turned into lifeless puppets. On the other hand, William Gaskill also was responsible for what I regard as the most successful Brechtian production of the period: Farquhar's *Recruiting Officer* (and the choice of play was obviously influenced by the fact that the Ensemble had brought Brecht's adaptation of this very play to London in 1956) at the National Theatre in December 1963. Here Robert Stephens, Colin Blakely, and Laurence Oliver did give performances that were larger than life and yet ironically detached, and the sets by René Allio (Planchon's brilliant Brechtian designer, imported from Lyons) were triumphantly light and flexible (and very much reminiscent of von Appen's sets for *Pauken und Trompeten*). But then, in 1963, the translation of Brecht's theoretical writings had not yet appeared and Gaskill had perhaps not yet heard the news about the need to cool down the fervor of his actors! Peter Brook, the most gifted of the younger generation of British directors, has not yet tried his hand at Brecht. Yet he has probably assimilated the lesson of Brecht most consistently, most successfully, and most organically. Brook's great production of *Lear* with Paul Schofield is frequently described as having absorbed the views of Jan Kott, who sees Lear in the light of Beckett. This is perfectly true; yet it concerns the interpretation of the text more than the actual technique of staging, which was most Brechtian both in the decor (a background of burnished copper – as in the Berliner Ensemble *Galileo*) and in the acting: unheroic, relaxed, free of ravings and rantings. Brook's *Marat/Sade*, generally regarded as an embodiment of the ideas of Artaud, also shows the clear and fruitful influence of Brecht (who, of course, also exercised a decisive influence on the playwright, Peter Weiss) in the use of music, nursery rhyme-type verse and delivery, and the multiple alienation effects produced by the convention of having the historical events acted out by the patients in a lunatic asylum.

Joan Littlewood and Peter Brook's work on plays by other authors, must, on the whole, be regarded as the most positive result of Brechtian influence on the art of stage directing in England. Hardly any of Brecht's plays themselves have received wholly satisfactory performances: Joan Littlewood's early attempt at *Mother Courage* (at Barnstaple in June 1955) was a disaster, mainly because the Theatre Workshop company's resources were too feeble even to allow the music to be performed and so the songs (an essential element) had to be cut, and also because Joan Littlewood herself had to play the title role, an impossible feat for the director of so complex a play. *The Threepenny Opera*, directed by Sam Wanamaker in the Blitzstein version (spring 1956) emerged as far too cosy an attempt at turning this astringent work into a sugar-coated musical. George Devine's *Good Woman of Setzuan* (fall 1956) with Peggy Ashcroft in the leading part also failed, largely because it missed a truly Brechtian style and emerged as a somewhat larmoyant melodrama. But the performance had its moments: I remember Esmé Percy as one of the gods, gloriously camp and hence very much in Brecht's spirit (it must have been one of his last roles, he died the next summer) and John Osborne doubling a variety of bit parts. The Royal Shakespeare's production of *The Caucasian Chalk Circle* at the Aldwych (March 1962) came much nearer to success; under William Gaskill's devoted direction, Hugh Griffith gave a magnificent rendering of Azdak, and Patsy Byrne was very touching as Grusha, but the omission of the Dessau music and its substitution by a far sweeter score added a touch of sentimentality totally at variance with Brecht's intentions. Gaskill's production of *Baal* at the Phoenix Theatre (February 1963) provided a telling illustration of the idiocy of the Anglo-Saxon star system. It was Peter O'Toole's idea that the play should be performed because he wanted to play the title role. And so Peter O'Toole it had to be, although a Baal looking like a young god (even though slightly unshaven) made nonsense of the lines which indicate that he is meant to be a monster of ugliness, while Ekart, whom Brecht describes as a youth of angelic appearance had, for contrast's sake, to be played by Harry Andrews, an excellent actor of heavy and ugly roughnecks. Add to this a translation which turned all the poetry (on which the play depends more than any other of Brecht's works) into jarring and incomprehensible prose and you get a measure of the failure of this particular production. An impossible translation also sealed the fate of *Shveyk in the Second World War* at the Mermaid (June 1963) in spite of Frank Dunlop's very spirited direction and an excellent rendering of Eisler's music under Alexander Goehr. As the translator had failed to render the essence of the play – namely the fact that the Czechs speak a very Shveykian language – the actors had to fall back on a variety of local accents which completely confused the issue: Bernard Miles, an excellent comedian, made Shveyk into a West Country yokel, while some of the other Czechs spoke standard English and the SS-men Cockney. There could have been no surer way of misrepresenting Brecht's ideas of the class struggle. An earlier attempt at Brecht by the Mermaid Theatre, *Galileo* with Miles in the title role (June 1960), had been somewhat more successful, although the Mermaid's actors proved themselves largely inadequate to their tasks, and Miles himself, a fine comedian who yearns to play Hamlet, lacked the ultimate tragic stature, although he gave an extremely skillful and gallant reading of the part. Yet, in this case, the play itself triumphantly overcame the handicaps of acting and direction, and emerged as a moving and thought-provoking *story* – i.e., epic theatre in the true sense.

Tony Richardson, the most successful of the new directors produced by the Royal Court, tried his hand with Brecht in the summer of 1964 in a production of *St Joan of the Stockyards*. For sheer failure on the director's part to understand his text this beat all precedents: for Richardson simply did not realize that the heroic blank verse passages in the play are a *parody* of Shakespeare, Schiller, and Goethe. The production, beset as it was by other vicissitudes – Vanessa Redgrave, who had been cast as Joan, fell out at the last moment and was replaced by Siobhan McKenna – convinced most of the London critics (who seem unwilling to read anything about any play they see and therefore have to rely on what gets through to them in performance) that Brecht was after all a fad and a fraud. This led to a "let's get rid of Brecht!" movement among them which was further strengthened by Gaskill's *Mother Courage* at the National Theatre in the spring of 1965 and finally irrupted into howls of triumph on the morning after the opening of Michel St. Denis' *Puntila* at the Aldwych on July 15, 1965. Quite wrongly, for that production, though it had its faults, was on the whole true to Brecht's intentions. Perhaps too much so: for what really angered the critics this time was the propagandist content, the Communist tendency of the play, rather than any shortcomings of the performance. That this should have struck them as something new and unexpected is a measure of their ignorance of Brecht after so many years of intensive preoccupation with him. In any case, it seemed as though the end of Brecht had come at last in England.

But then, with a truly Brechtian touch of ironic paradox, the whole anti-Brecht movement collapsed within a few weeks. On August 9, 1965, the Berliner Ensemble opened its second season in London at the National Theatre with *Arturo Ui* – one of Brecht's most propagandist plays – and the critics began to rave about the precision, passion, acrobatic prowess, and general excellence of it all. Mercifully, as none of them understands German, they could not be put off by the actual content of this play and of those which followed it (Brecht's adaptation of *Coriolanus*, *The Threepenny Opera*, *The Days of the Commune* and in a special private performance for the theatrical profession, the Ensemble's studio production of excerpts from *Mahogonny*, wrongly titled by them the *Little Mahagonny*, which in fact is a quite different work.) And so the verdict and final summing up of Brecht himself in England must be: if he is only seen without his words being heard, he is successful; if his texts are understood, he is a total failure.

Indeed, the only wholly satisfactory and successful production of Brecht in all these years was the performance of *Happy End* (first staged at the Edinburgh Festival of 1964, transferred to the Royal Court in the spring of 1965) which Michael Geliot directed under the auspices of the Traverse Theatre. Here a director familiar with the original who had had a hand in the translation had succeeded in recreating the feel of the late twenties in Berlin, with the added charm that the period itself has now become encrusted with the patina of nostalgia. One must, however, also take into account that this is a play which Brecht never wholly acknowledged, largely because it was a potboiler hurriedly put together to cash in on the success of *The Threepenny Opera* and is surely the most harmless and commercial of all of Brecht's works. Hence even the London critics could warm to its attractiveness.

So much for Brecht's impact on techniques of staging. There remains the question of Brecht's influence on the *writing* of plays. Here too his impact has been broad and superficial rather than deep. The new wave of dramatists had to acknowledge Kenneth Tynan as their prophet and so they were, willy-nilly, saddled with Brecht as a model, in spite of the fact that most of them had achieved their initial success in a strictly naturalistic – and therefore non-Brechtian – mode. As this largely autobiographical style was bound to yield to a law of diminishing returns, both John Osborne and Arnold Wesker were soon attracted by the possibilities of the epic form. Wesker used some vaguely Brechtian devices of story-telling in *Chips with Everything* (1962), more boldly in *Their Very Own and Golden City* (written 1964, first London performance 1966) where a social theme – the building of cities which are to be both beautiful and owned by their workers – is dealt with in a sequence of flash-forwards and flashbacks with compression of the time-sequence and other epic devices. These, after all, amount to little more than the use of a cinematic technique of montage and cutting. Yet I am sure that without the example of Brecht such techniques might not have been so readily used by authors – and accepted by audiences.

Osborne went considerably further in the use of Brechtian devices than Wesker, not only in writing a satirical music play (*Play Slickey*) but above all in turning to historical subjects. Both *Luther* (1961) and *A*

Patriot for Me (1965) aim at being epic drama with a Brechtian scope and Brechtian technique. In *Luther* the superficial impact of *Mother Courage* is particularly painfully obvious in the disastrously ill-written scene (Act III, Scene 2) of the Peasant War, which opens with a long narration by an anonymous Knight against a tableau of "a small hand-cart . . . beside it the bloody bulk of a peasant's corpse." Here Brecht's conception is present, but misunderstood as a kind of lantern lecture illustrated by charades. Yet this failure on Osborne's part is small compared to the much more fundamental mistake he made with *Luther*, namely the idea that one could embark on a great historical play without a deep understanding of the social, cultural, and political background of the period. *Luther* is in fact anything but epic theatre – it is an attempt to clothe personal psychological problems in the superficial garb of historical drama. The same is true of *A Patriot for Me*, which is a better play than *Luther*, but equally inadequate as a serious portrait of the dying Austro-Hungarian Empire or an analysis of dying empires in general (with applications to present-day Britain). Osborne's understanding of the background is so sketchy, his inability to present whatever knowledge he may have acquired so total, that we are left with a Viennese operetta minus the music. And yet, when he is dealing with the real subject-matter of the play, the problem of the homosexual in present-day English society, Osborne rises to considerable heights of eloquence. His mistake was to try to deal with the subject in a "Brechtian" form.

Far more successful as a historical play is Robert Bolt's *A Man for All Seasons* (1960). Here Sir Thomas More's time and problems are presented with insight and a considerable knowledge of their background. But again the technique of "epic drama" which the author quite openly adopted is no more than superficially related to Brechtian theory. There is a narrator, "The Common Man," who goes through the play and appears also in various roles as ordinary people who remain passive in the face of the hero's sufferings. The story is told as a historical paradigm with applications to the present, but in the last resort this is no more – and no less – than the traditional English history play with moral uplift and a patriotic afterglow, John Drinkwater or Clemence Dane brought up to date.

At the other extreme we find the outright imitation of Brecht – ideology, form, technique and all – notably in the case of the gifted poet Christopher Logue (who spent some time with the Berliner Ensemble studying its methods): the musical play *The Lilywhite Boys* (of which he was part author) achieved some success at the Royal Court but suffered from being pastiche of Brecht rather than original work influenced by him.

Much more fruitful examples of inspiration from the epic theatre are provided by two plays which were the direct result of Peter Hall's conviction, when he decided that the Royal Shakespeare Company under his management would have to do more than just Shakespeare, that the future of contemporary drama lay in the field of the large-scale poetic and epic play. Both John Whiting's *The Devils* (1961) and Peter Shaffer's *The Royal Hunt of the Sun* (1964) were written at Peter Hall's suggestion (although Shaffer's play was eventually produced under the auspices of the National Theatre). *The Devils* makes excellent use of a narrative style of presentation and fluid non-realistic decor and deals with historical facts in an illuminating manner. *The Royal Hunt of the Sun* likewise presents a major problem – the contract between totalitarianism and *laisser-faire* societies – as well as making a bitter statement about faith, and does so in a truly epic style. What it lacks, however, is the ultimate consecration of poetry: the language is efficient, but smacks of purple passages in a public speech.

The truest follower of Brecht – or at least of Brecht's essential attitude – is undoubtedly John Arden. Arden has frequently spoken of his admiration for Brecht, but stresses that he is not aware of direct influence. It is more a case of kindred poetical talents following common models in a more distant tradition – Elizabethan drama, folk song, popular theatre of all kinds. Yet whether the Brechtian influence is directly traceable or not, the fact that it was in the air during the period of Arden's first experiments as a playwright surely is not without significance. The linking of scenes by songs in *Live Like Pigs*, the use of folk song in *Serjeant Musgrave's Dance*, the masks in *Happy Haven* (not long after the Berliner Ensemble had used masks most tellingly in their 1956 appearance in *The Caucasian Chalk Circle*), the whole structure and technique of *The Workhouse Donkey* (with a narrator and copious musicial interludes), the parable technique of *Armstrong's Last Goodnight*, all show a deep and genuine affinity with Brechtian concepts. Arden is left-wing in his personal politics, yet in his plays he is strictly neutral, morally as well as politically. In that sense he is at variance with Brecht. Yet, Arden, like Brecht, is a major poet who uses drama as a vehicle for the special poetry of the stage. In this he embodies what is, in my opinion, the overwhelmingly important example provided by Brecht: that drama is a medium for a major poet, that the quality of this particular type of poetric language and imagination transcends all theoretical and practical rules, devices and gimmicks, even commitment and ideology, and that this alone will produce truly great drama.

17

THE DEATH OF MOTHER COURAGE

Henry Glade

There were nine of Brecht's plays in the Moscow repertoires during the 1966–67 season – has any city in the world equalled this? Acceptance of Brecht was long in coming, however. There were some early Brecht productions in Moscow: *The Threeepenny Opera*, directed by Taïrov at the Kamerni Theatre in Janurary 1930; selections from *Fear and Misery of the Third Reich*, staged at the Lenin Komsomol in September 1941. Then nothing, until 1958. Brecht's plays were neither socialistic nor realistic enough for the Stalinist era.

The Berliner Ensemble's visit to Moscow in 1957 opened a tiny chink in the wall of silence, and set off a wide-ranging critical reaction. Local productions of two of Brecht's minor, non-epic plays followed – in 1958 the Vakhtangov Theatre gave *Senora Carrar's Rifles*, and the following year the Ermolova produced *The Visions of Simone Machard*.

The real breakthrough came with Mikhail Straukh's *Mother Courage* at the Mayakovsky in November, 1960, which launched the first phase of Brecht's acceptance in Moscow. *Mother Courage* is still in the Mayakovsky repertoire; but after seven years with the original cast playing the major roles it has become somewhat of a mechanical re-run.

Straukh has the distinction of being the first director to realize the enormous potentialities of a sovietized Brecht, which he created by grafting Eisensteinian revolutionary pathos and Stanislavskian truth-in-feeling to the anti-war thematics then much in vogue (1960 was the year of the film *Ballad of the Soldier*, Shostakovich's "Dresden Quartets," etc.). Mother Courage is played as Niobe; Kattrin is the play's heroine, in the Dostoevsky–Chekhov tradition of the saintly, seemingly-demented person who vainly attempts to do good in an inhumane world. The final scene is altered in keeping with the tenor of this staging. Yudith Glizer as Mother Courage, broken and grief-stricken after the death of Kattrin, harnesses herself to the wagon upon hearing the call of the trumpets. As several critics observed, there is something animal-like about her as she stamps her feet, tries to move the wagon with one pull, fall, *and dies*.

M. Stroeva in her essay "Approaches to Brecht" in *Problems of the Theatre, 1965*, Moscow, 1965 (p. 83), states the case for such a socialist-realist adaptation:

> Mikhail Straukh did not put on a chronicle about the Thirty Years' War nor even a tragical parable about pre-war Germany, but a topical play. It is a play about the people for our people . . . The position of the director is defined by the times. Brecht hurled a bitter and prophetic accusation at the German people on the eve of war. Through the fate of Mother Courage the playwright foretold the future carnage of those who were to go to war for the fascists . . . These were Brecht's thoughts in 1939. In 1961 Mikhail Straukh has a different approach. His staging expresses a greater belief in the coming wrath of the people. Brecht's historical apprehensions, his prognosis, his warnings are not the decisive thing. What is important is the fact that man *can* block the path to war, *can* climb the ladder to the roof and start beating the drums. Because of the historical experiences of the Russian people greater significance is attached to the humanistic and heroic aspects of the play . . .

In April 1963, the Stanislavski Drama Theatre opened its production of *The Threepenny Opera*, which is still drawing huge crowds. Both actors and audience enjoy themselves immensely in this spirited, light-hearted production, which runs counter to all of Brecht's intentions. In short, it is a Stanislavskian operetta.

The second phase of Brecht's reception in Moscow dates from Yury Lyubimov's directing of *The Good Woman of Setzuan* with his graduating class in the Shchukin drama school (affiliated with the Vakhtangov Theatre) in December 1963. Governmental clearance for the play came only grudgingly and conditionally in the summer of 1963. A Sino-Soviet conference was scheduled, and nervous officials were trying to avoid all possible complications in an already tense political situation. Thus some parts were cut, Chinese costuming was dropped, and all references that remotely could be linked to China were deleted. Lyubimov's direction and the students' performances were so well-received that it seemed a shame to break up the group. Therefore, in the spring of the following year, Lyubimov was appointed director of the Taganka Theatre (officially, the Theatre of Drama and Comedy) and *The Good Woman* has been packing them in ever since it opened there in April 1964.

Lyubimov is the most gifted and exciting Brecht interpreter in the Soviet theatre today. He has been greatly influenced by Vakhtangov, who fused Stanislavskian psychologial realism and Meyerholdian theatricality into what he called "fantastic realism;" this "synthetic" approach creates a unique irony. Even before the play begins, one sees Vakhtangovian effects: the bare stage with a grayish-yellow burlap curtain as backdrop, a poster with the inscription "street scene," and a three-times-life-size lighted portrait of a mockingly smirking Brecht. The actors casually come on stage in their black rehearsal clothes and form a line from which three young men step forward. Flanked by a guitarist and an accordionist, one young man, who is later to portray the water seller, expresses Vakhtangov's ideal: he tells the audience that from time to time it becomes necessary for the theatre to go back to its roots – to the market-place and the street – so as not to lose touch with common, everyday life. The speaker removes his cap, bows respectfully in the direction of Brecht's portrait and the other actors follow suit. After a moment of silence the play begins.

In the street, Wong the water seller grimaces, gesticulates, jokes, and jumps around as he tells the audience of the impending visits of the gods, and plaintively reports his inability to find them shelter. All the characters (except the barber and Shen Te) are played in the dual Vakhtangovian style of representational and presentational theatre (Stanislavski and Meyerhold), emphasizing the latter, (The barber Shu-Fu's performance, however, is purposely over-stylized. He is a wind-up doll, bowing obsequiously, fussing and bustling about, his actions reflecting his empty, vain, and greedy existence. It gets a bit irritating to watch and thus, I think, it is not too effective.) After Wong's efforts to find quarters for the gods have failed, feeling that all is lost, he dances out his despair and his sense of shame for the townspeople.

Shen Te sticks a tousled head out of her tiny curtained-off room and makes her entrance. Zinaida Slavina plays the role with great emotional intensity and involvement. A tribute to her acting is given by Gaevsky in *Teatr*, No. 2, 1967, from which I quote in part:

> Slavina plays as it is not pleasant to play, as one should not play. These frenzied shouts, this high-strung pathos, this merciless spending of nervous energy recall the half-legendary times of the romantic actors . . . An actress of such passionate and stormy temperament in the very center of the most Brechtian and most Meyerholdian of our theatres? . . . She has a rather harsh voice and light and swift movements. She could be a dancer. Slavina's acting ranges from the compassionate to the aggressive with no in-between . . . Her intonation is citified . . . The inner rhythm of her roles is that of the city – tense and syncopated.

Shen Te becomes Shui Ta with a bowler hat, dark glasses and an ivory cane. One can sense her anguished reluctance to turn from kindness and generosity to cruelty and hard-headedness.

A play that seemingly treats of man's inhumanity in the capitalistic jungle must be successful in the Soviet Union. Alongside the obvious anti-capitalistic propaganda values, however, there is a deeper, unofficial significance to its success: for decades the theme of the "little man" vis-à-vis the cold bureaucracy of the State has recurred in Soviet writing. There may also be deep empathy for the heroine's split personality; it is not novel to note the delicate balance of kindness and cruelty in the Russian soul.

In March 1964, two Moscow theatres produced *The Caucasian Chalk Circle*. The Gogol Theatre received superior reviews for its Azdak-dominated production, and the Mayakovsky still has the play in its repertoire. Here Grusha is the central figure, and her foster-mother love oozes with saccharine sentimentality. Many meaningless gimmicks have been tacked to the play, and one cannot blame the audience either for its bafflement or its perfunctory applause.

Bernard Reich (Brecht's close friend and author of the first book on Brecht in the Soviet Union) said angrily to me: "The play's tenor is completely missed by relegating Azdak, and with him the question of a new type of justice, to a secondary place. Moreover, Sverdlin, one of the greatest actors in the Soviet Union, plays Azdak like a paragon of virtue when in essence he is *nechisto*." (A wonderfully apt epithet for Azdak. Most literally it means "unclean" but there is an implication of "evil" and "uncanniness" in it.) However, the production, by V. F. Dudin, does make imaginative use of costuming, grotesque masks, and colorfully primitive stage designs. Music and musical arrangements are by M. Meerovich; incidental music is from Stravinsky.

It is not possible within the confines of this aticle to deal with the complex question of the quality of translations – productions are almost always based on the six-volume Russian edition of Brecht's collected works, on which approximately a dozen translators worked. However, Apt's translation of *The Caucasian Chalk Circle* can be taken as a typical example. The translator holds fairly close to the original, but Brecht's earthy, powerful language is formalized (example: "macht seinen letzten Schnaufer" to "pri poslednem izdykhanii"). Brecht's vulgar expressions are cleaned up (*Arschloch* is changed to *idiot*) or a milder Russian equivalent is substituted ("macht die Beine auf" to "spit s muzhem"). Many names are changed, presumably because the originals would sound ridiculous in Russian; thus the goat-raising kolkhoz (which the translator changes to sheep kolkhoz) is called Ashkheti instead of Galinsk, Shalva is renamed Gogi, Jussup – David, Ludovicka – Tamara.

Mention should be made of a failed production. *The Resistable Rise of Arturo Ui* opened in October 1964 at the Students' Theatre of Moscow State University, and the directors chose really to clown it up. For example, after affecting grief at Dullfeet's funeral the murderers then sit on the coffin and have a smoke and a chew. In the text, the Actor coaches Ui in sitting posture and then asks him how long he can hold the correct position; Ui answers, "As long as you wish." In the Moscow production, the Actor pulls the chair out from under Ui, then asks the question, getting the same reply from a dead-pan Ui. This is pure burlesque.

Ui, played by Vladimir Zobin (an engineering student), makes his entrance to the strains of goose-stepping music. From the start, he is supposed to inspire fear. After Schall's Ui as clown and food (Berliner Ensemble), after Lebedev's Ui as Dostoevskian psychopath (Gorki Theatre, Leningrad), we have Ui as dangerous impostor, who successfully camouflages his ruthless ambitions behind a screen of bourgeois respectability. The ending rehashes Jean Vilar, who in his staging and portrayal of Ui at the Théâtre National Populaire tore off his wig, stepped to the footlights and exhorted his audience not to look but to see, not to talk but to act – before it is too late.

Lyubimov's production of *Galileo* opened in December 1965. The staging is simple but imaginative: a backdrop of panels fashioned from egg cartons and equipped with doors and windows is flanked on each side by flats with holes for heads and hands; the right flat has choir boys' costumes painted on it and the left, monks' cowls. As the play progresses, heads pop into the holes. Choir boys and monks provide for each scene a prologue and epilogue made up from Brecht's mottos and specially-composed songs and poems written for this production by David Samoilov. The monks represent the official and ecclesiastical view while the choir boys back Galileo; the boys double as globe-twirling Young Pioneers who give the play's opening lines.

Lev Kopelev, the noted Moscow critic, translated *Galileo* and was special consultant for this production. In a recent letter he wrote:

> The performance is distinguished by verve, inventiveness and élan, but it is not so much a Brechtian conception as "Schillerian" or "Lyubimovian." Visotski as Galileo is athletic, robust, wild, with a raw voice and melancholy goggle eyes; he is not so much enacting Brecht's Galileo as his own, or Lyubimov's: a rebellious, Storm and Stress type of he-man, ever aggressive, boisterous and eager to enlighten his students and the populace.

I might add that Visotski is the very antithesis of Laughton's Galileo. Almost Spartan, he is a man who would rather pursue a new idea than hanker after old wine. In the carnival scene all hell seems to be breaking loose in an unleashing of all forces heretofore held in subjugation. Lyubimov has added Evtuchenko's *Humor* as preface to the Brecht/Eisler ballad which ends with the lines "Obedience will never cure your woe":

Kings,
        Emperors, and Czars,
sovereigns of all the earth,
have commanded many a parade,
but they could not command
                        humor.

They tried
            to commission
                        humor –
but humor cannot be bought!
They tried
            to murder humor,
but humor
            thumbed
                    his nose at them!

It's hard
        to fight humor.

He's eternal.
            Nimble and quick.
He'll pass through anything,
                        through everyone.
So –
            glory be to humor.
He –
            is a brave man.

(translated by George Reavey.
From: *Half-way to the Moon*, edited by
Patricia Blake and Max Hayward. New York, 1965.)

The Brechtian one-line refrain "How nice it is, for a little change, to do just as one pleases!" (Bentley's rendering) is embellished by Samoilov and recited metrically with demonic emphasis on the beat by the entire carnival crowd:

And this I'll tell you,
That whatever may happen,
I want to be the boss myself,
All right, your Worship?

Why does Galileo recant? Lyubimov shows a man who has been crushed by the reactionary forces of church and court, but this is not convincing, for church and court figures are so burlesqued that they are not really effective and believable foils.

The play closes with a weak and sly Galileo senilely sing-songing a self-accusation. Suddenly he breaks off, straightens up, starts in again, speaking in a youthful and powerful voice. He turns to the audience as if to say: It is all up to you to see to it that the liberal forces here and now win out over any attempts of the Stalinists to reassert themselves. As the pin-spot focuses on Galileo, standing alone in the dark, the Young Pioneers again scurry across the stage carrying their globes. From off stage one can hear them reciting Kipling:

If you can trust yourself when all men doubt you . . .
Yours is the Earth and everything that's in it,
And – which is more – you'll be a Man, my son!

In January 1966, *Mr Puntila and his Servant Matti* opened at the Small Auditorium of the Red Army Theatre, directed by the East German Horst Havemann. His heavy-handed, dogmatic approach to the play turned it into an exceedingly dull affair. Havemann follows the text to the letter; he is so much in awe of it that he does not even omit the ticklish tenth scene. The hilarious "Puntila Engages his Daughter . . ." has been converted into a deadly serious event.

Soviet critics gleefully tore apart this tedious production. As one of them put it to me: "You see, this is an East-German import. Matti is played like a Schillerian Marquis Posa; he is the central figure here, fighting the good fight for the classless society." The setting is solid and workable but not very imaginative. Paul Dessau's music based on Slavic folksongs is used, and a preview of each scene is sung by a buxom actress dressed in peasant clothes and accompanied by a guitarist and accordionist. The melody is cloying and the rendition is coy with winks and smirks.

The eighth production was *Man is Man* which I didn't see, but the critics report that it was anti-fascist rather than anti-bourgeois. The ninth and last production of Brecht's works in 1966–7 was *Fear and Misery in the Third Reich*. Directed by Stein and Durov, it opened at the Lenin Komsomol in March after I left. Moscow critics' first reactions have been favorable.

Brecht is "in" now, and the current vogue shows no signs of abating. And it is interesting to note that the freshest and most successful productions are those that have synthesized a new theatre from old traditions – Stanislavski and Vakhtangov – and current concerns, political and intellectual. Brecht himself demanded that the classics be adapted to suit the times; his own works have become classics now. "The universal character of Brecht's art finds expression in the manifold interpretations of each nation" (Andrzej Worth). During the past season in Moscow the interpetations have indeed been manifold.

BRECHT AND CHICANO THEATRE

Barclay Goldsmith

I

Chicano theatre, in existence for well over a decade, is rooted firmly in the popular culture of the barrio and campo. It has also drawn heavily upon many international forms and styles. It is most often compared with Brechtian theatre and the Brechtian theatre movement, since this also has a popular base. If the mid and late 1970s are a time for reflection, as some say, then perhaps now is the time to examine and define the influence of the German writer and theoretician on Chicano theatre.

The question, "Is Chicano theatre Brechtian?", is important for us beyond mere schematic comparison of acting styles, play structures, and themes. The question requires us to analyze the methods by which popular culture is shaped into "high art" forms. It forces us to account for the parallel manner in which two similar theatrical movements emerged in two separate cultures, in two separate historical movements – with apparently very little contact between performers, writers, or other theatre artists.

II

Bertolt Brecht was highly influenced by forms of entertainment known as "popular presentational." Early Chicano theatre falls into this same category. Presentational theatre drops all pretense at achieving "slice of life" naturalism and attempts to eliminate what is called the "fourth wall" dividing actor and audience. It is a theatre often employing masks, asides, large mimetic gesture, and a device known as "breakouts." In this latter technique, the actor drops his or her character and addresses the audience as performer. Presentational theatre is the basis for such high art forms as late Renaissance *commedia dell arte* (Molière), German expressionism, and the Brechtian epic.

There is much confusion about the term "popular presentational" when the "popular" is added. Most simply stated, it refers to a working-class, peasant, or *campesino* audience who can identify with the subject matter presented through song, topicality of humor, and immediately identifiable archetypal characters. The confusion aries because the mass audiences at which presentational theatre aims differ as history changes economic relationships. What might have been lively and popular a decade earlier becomes suddenly irrelevant.[1]

"Popular presentational" theatre has always flourished during times of social upheaval. Morality plays, a late medieval development, were performed in small towns at the same time that secular control was being wrested from the Church. Commedia troups performed in plazas and squares especially in the sixteenth century, when a new merchant class was challenging the authority of the feudal aristocracy. The Germany of the 1920s and early 1930s was ripe for the rise of a popular presentational theatrical form. The crumbling economy and rending of the social fabric had promoted a new political consciousness within the working class.

One of the popular theatrical forms which emerged in Germany at this time was agitprop. The German Workers' Theatre League estimated that over 500 such groups were performing in 1931.[2] The agitprop play is a short theatrical piece which usually has as its aim the education of the audience either to reflect upon or to redress a particular immediate social grievance. The form first developed in the Soviet Union with cultural worker cadres which traveled by train through the country, urging workers and peasants to wrest control of the land. The term "agitprop" was early defined as follows:

> *Agitation*: the putting across of one idea to many people.
>
> *Propaganda*: the putting across of many more complex ideas to relatively fewer people.

Agitation is generally a call to action around a single idea – better wages, for example. Propaganda takes into account the social or cultural ramifications of an idea and usually calls upon the audience for further reflection. Thus, political theatre varies from being immediate and agitational to long-range and propagandistic. (There is strong distaste for the word "propaganda" in our culture because we associate it with a manipulative distortion of truth or because many audiences are not moved by the simplistic characterizations of much agitprop theatre.[3])

The original European agitprop theatre piece is usually highly visual, using one central metaphor to explain a complicated issue. For example, in a contemporary piece developed by England's Red Ladder Theatre, bakers slice large pieces of bread from a giant loaf. The knives are the means of production and the loaf represents raw material. The slices of bread are then brought back by the workers, who must eat, although leftover slices are accumulated up the side of a ladder by the company owner. When this profit becomes "excess accumulation," the workers are put out of work but must borrow money in order to eat the stockpiled pieces of bread. The owner of the factory has interlocking ownership with the bank, etc. The metaphor can be expanded into an enlarged lesson in economics. Though the visual metaphor is highly theatrical, agitprop characterizations are one-dimensional and cartoonlike. Rarely has an agitprop piece survived beyond the immediate moment of some rally or mass meeting for which it was intended.

It was upon this agitprop form that Brecht based his short plays of the 1930s, the years of his newly found political commitment. Known as *Lehrstück*, they differ from agitprop because character development is stronger and the issues turn from the immediate to the general or long-range. For example, in *The Mother*, Pelagea Vlassova, the protagonist, becomes a committed union agitator, and the play takes us through the stages of her changing personality from a scared, self-effacing woman to a strong leader. The play uses archetypal characters but their development is far more complex than in agitprop. Thus the contradictions are much more subtle.

In addition to agitprop, Brecht admired the Berlin cabarets. He was a devotee of many folk comedians, particularly the Bavarian clown Karl Valentin. Brecht's friend, the director Bernard Reich, states that sketches which Valentin wrote and appeared in demonstrated "that a simple and one-dimensional plot can get across an extremely complicated generalization to an audience and that a small scene can stand for a big problem."[4]

Cabaret shows contained large mimetic gestures, grotesque but still archetypal characters, and subtle breakouts. The actor Valentin always seems to be commenting upon the characters he was playing. It is possible that by watching these cabaret shows and Valentin in particular, Brecht learned to distance his audience from the action on stage. This distancing is one of the main attributes of Brechtian acting.

Brecht was interested in a scientific theatre – a theatre which led to reflection on the part of the audience. Reflection, it was hoped, would lead to action, whereas the traditional European theatre, he believed, had always led to emotional catharsis and passive observation on the part of the spectator. The German playwright introduced the concept of *Gestus* in acting in order to distance audiences from the emotional impact of the play. Briefly, this device is a physical or vocal gesture which illuminates social relationships. The *Gestus* is not unlike a series of rapidly evolving still photos.

An example of a *Gestus* occurs in the following line in an acting exercise based on *Romeo and Juliet* and prepared by Brecht for his actors; "But we will be without shelter, Sir," says an old tenant angrily to Romeo who is about to dislodge him.[5] A *Gestus* occurs in the word "Sir." The actor in rehearsal must search for the right body and vocal gesture which will reflect an angry recoiling away from the first part of the line. The use of *Gestus* reinforces our concept of men and women as capable of change. Our conventional physical and vocal gestures are often masks which we shed and change as social relationships change. The concept of *Gestus* allows for masks, freezes, slow motion and other presentational theatrical devices as long as they illuminate social reality.[6]

Brecht moved away from the agitprop-influenced *Lehrstück* form to epic theatre after World War II. In doing this, he moved from a popular presentational form to a high Art form in which the psychology of the characters is more complex and more reality is illuminated than in his earlier shorter plays. In the epic form, the scope of scenes may span several decades, moving back and forth in time. Epic plays are thus non-Aristoletian, since they forsake unity of time and place. A contemporary social problem is often framed in another time period. For example, the distribution of wealth is a contemporary problem explored in *The Caucasian Chalk Circle*, yet the play is set in the twelfth century. Each scene in the epic form poses one single contradiction or illuminates one problem in such a way that it can be lifted from the main body of the work to stand alone with its own statement. Thus, epic scenes echo the simplicity of the early cabaret acts which had influenced Brecht, and they retain the didactic flavor of agitprop.

III

If we begin our analysis with a comparison between conditions for the Chicano in this country in the 1960s and conditions for the average worker in Germany during the 1920s and early 1930s, we discover vast differences. Until recently, a large proportion of the Chicano population has been rural farmworker rather than (as in Germany) urban industrial. Furthermore, the Chicano has had to confront the problems of a colonized minority within a larger dominant culture. Finally, popular Chicano culture itself has its roots in the historic tensions of three cultures – the Pre-Columbian, Spanish Catholic, and Anglo-American. Chicano theatre clearly reflects these realities and differences.

One of the early dramatic forms developed by the Chicano theatre movement was the *acto*. Performed at first to support the United Farmworker Organizing Committee, *actos* were presented at meetings and in picket lines throughout the West by the Teatro Campesino under Luis Valdez's direction. It was the Teatro Campesino which perfected the *acto* form and inspired several dozen other groups to do likewise.

The *acto* is often called agitprop in the press, but though it shows some similarity to that form, its emphasis on character and cultural identity and lack of emphasis on economic metaphor make it decidedly different. However, in one early *acto*, *La quinta temporada*, (*The Fifth Season*),[7] economic relationships between the farmworker, contractor, and boss do in fact receive thematic emphasis. We see a chain functioning whereby the farmworker picks money from a tree and Don Coyote (labor contractor) takes the money from the farmworker's pocket, stuffing some into his own and passing the rest to El Patrón (The Boss). This chain process is repeated over the four seasons until the Boss accumulates a wad of bills. The fifth season is the coming to awareness, the worker's realization that he must break the chain.

The *acto* is rich in theatricality, deriving from the coloring of its characters. Don Coyote is rendered both as animal-like, by way of rural imagery, and as specifically human, through his slyness and his easily recognizable vocal and bodily gestures.

The *acto* form has now flourished for over a decade, reflecting many aspects of Chicano life. It has urged audiences to redress grievances other than the farmworkers' plight, but it has also evoked the richness of Chicano culture for its own sake. Some of the more traditional characters, like La Calavera (Death) and El Diablo (The Devil), derive from medieval morality plays. While they retain their old symbolic force, their modern reference is ironically striking. Other popular cultural traditions which are decidedly Mexican have been incorporated into the *acto*: *el corrido*, a long narrative song, and *la carpa*, the Mexican traveling circus, which also has its own tradition. Many *acto* characters are decidedly contemporary and are both urban and rural. One of the most satirized is the Chicano professional who does not return to serve in the community (*Los vendidos*).

Variety of language (*Gestus*) is emphasized in Brechtian epic. In Chicano theater, variety of language is used primarily to mirror cultural identity. *Actos* are often written and performed in *caló* – a mixture of English and Spanish. An example is "traite los kids" (bring the kids). Sometimes English words are given Spanish pronunciation: "wáchale" (watch out), or "dame un raite" (give me a ride). *Caló* is a language of survival and its use on stage in and of itself has political implications.

Very broadly speaking, the acting styles of early Chicano *actos* and those of Brechtian theatre show affinity. Both are based on popular cultural traditions and are indebted to agitprop, but both have developed characters more fully than the agitprop form, although for different reasons. Both Brechtian theatre and Chicano theatre have characters who are capable of perceiving, growing, and changing. To show this, both use large mimetic gestures, archetypal characters, and masks. Chicano theatre does not show so constant a concern with *Gestus* to denote contradictions within a character. Conversely, early Chicano theatre is more exuberant, requiring a higher energy level from its actors. The most fully developed Chicano theatre piece, Teatro Campesino's *La gran carpa de la familia Rascuachi*, uses the popular traditions of *el corrido* sand *la carpa* in a whirlwind of sound and movement. The nuances of Brechtian acting would have slowed down the forward movement of this piece, altering its effectiveness.

Two *actos* which most precisely reflect the Brechtian acting style are the Teatro Campesino's *Soldado raso* and *Vietnam campesino*. These short pieces portray quieter, conflicting moods and more subtle, restrained character involvement. In the former play, a young Chicano is taken to war by La Muerte (Death) and eventually killed. In the latter, parallels between the lives and struggles of Vietnamese peasants and North American campesinos are explored. Valdez all but states this in an interview with Françoise Kourilsky: "In *Soldado*, I wanted to create a feeling from within the audience, that feeling of two forces, the duality of life that is a reality."[8]

In comparing Brechtian theatre with Chicano theatre, we must realize that Brechtian theatre was developed by one person (with some collaboration from composers and actors), while Chicano theatre springs from a movement which reflects differences of class, cultural makeup, and political orientation within the Chicano community. Recently, many theatres have broken with the *acto* form and taken up new styles and structural forms, some bearing little relationship to either Brechtian epic or the popular presentational form.

One theatre piece which evolved in the early 1970s and is decidedly epic is Teatro Campesino's *La gran carpa de la familia Rascuachi*. The play unfolds a series of episodic events in the life of a family headed by Jesús and María Pelado Rascuachi. Although this short piece, set to music of a *corrido*, uses the cartoonlike characters of popular entertainment, both husband and wife experience the full gamut of contradictory feelings and torn identities. They are Brechtian not simply because they are complex, but because their specific class, regional, and racial backgrounds show them to be representatives as well as individuals. Their gestures and bodily bearing make quick, illuminating statements about their situation as recently arrived Mexican workers, without visas, experiencing American society, working in the fields, raising a family, moving to the city, and finally going on welfare. When Jesús grabs his hat and emits a *grito* (yell) of joy for having successfully crossed the Rio Grande, the shout, the upward thrust of head and stretching of limbs, make for a memorable moment in the theatre. It is his gesture of hope – universally appropriate for a campesino, yet firmly rooted in the psychology of the individual character.

Another example of the epic form can be found in Teatro de la Esperanza's *La víctima*, a portrait of three generations of a Chicano family in the United States painfully achieving, against odds, a degree of upward economic mobility. In this play, collectively written and directed by the group's members, several actors assume multiple roles. This has the same effect as Brechtian acting style, which allows one character to assume many social stances. The sweep of scenes over several generations in a short theatrical time span and the use of such distancing devices as signs make this piece decidedly epic in the Brechtian sense.

A more questionably example is Teatro de la Gentle's *El hombre que se convirtío en perro* (*The Man Who Became a Dog*). This is based on a play of the same name by the Argentine writer Oswaldo Dragún. The protagonist, a factory security guard, turns into a dog because his superiors treat him like one. Though used in expressionistic theatre, most notably in Eugene O'Neill's *The Hairy Ape* and Elmer Rice's *The Adding Machine*, such transformations run counter to one of Brecht's main tenets, which is that the central character be a reasonable person, manipulated perhaps by outside forces but never helpless. At the same time, though decidedly un-Brechtian in this respect, the play employs many popular presentational devices. Power figures are archetypal, gesture is broad, and there are numerous instances when the audience is directly addressed.

IV

To answer the question, "Is Chicano theatre Brechtian?", one has to consider then, what period, what theatrical form, and even what theater company one is referring to. Luis Valdez has stated on several occasions that he is "somewhere between Cantinflas and Brecht." This statement seems correct. His Teatro Campesino has broadly used the popular presentational style, even though there are dissimilarities, and there is of course an affinity with Cantinflas, since the latter's Mexican films represent the great masses, the underemployed, and the cast-offs, searching for identity. The predicaments he explores are similar to those that interest Valdez.

Chicano theatre cannot be Brechtian in any stricter sense than this for several reasons. As has already been stated, Brechtian character development is more realistic and complex. Furthermore, Chicano theatre lacks the dialectical analysis found in Brechtian epic. True, there has been some contact with Brecht's work at Chicano theatre festivals. The San Francisco Mime Troupe's *The Mother* stirred considerable interest at the 1974 Chicano Theatre Festival in Mexico City. The Teatro Experimental de Cali uses the Brechtian epic form to a considerable extent and has performed widely in the United States. Chicano theatre has actually had a considerable influence on Latin American popular theatres, most notably on TEC, which has produced several works of the Teatro Campesino, Los Mascarones in Cuernavaca, Mexico, has evolved a *carpa* style in its traveling productions, probable inspired by *La gran carpa*. But apart from these instances, it is safe to say there has been little direct contact with the Brecht tradition. Félix and Lilly Alvarez – who played Jesús and Maria in the Teatro Campesino's production of *La carpa* for several years – said that an ex-Berliner Ensemble actor told them after a performance that they were "very Brechtian," yet both actors state they never studied Brecht during rehearsals for that play.

Chicano theatre is Brechtian, then, more in spirit than in specifics. Like Brechtian theatre it is based on popular culture and stresses the dialectics of change. But if it aimed to be Brechtian to the letter, it would become a "hothouse plant." German popular culture has grown out of an entirely different set of historical circumstances from that of the Chicano, and the resultant forms must therefore vary.

Brecht wrote, moreover, with a broad Marxist perspective, and very few teatros, if any, are Marxist in concept, at least in the way Brecht intended, with his merciless exposé of contradictions within a bourgeois value system. On this account, some critics dismiss altogether the possibility of comparing Brecht with the teatros. There are, however, two positions here. One is the viewpoint of critical realism, which argues that we are the sum total of all cultural products, and hence all literature which accurately shows the social tensions of a given historical period has value. This is the view taken by Enrique Buenaventura, TEC's director, in defending the Teatro Campesino's Catholic/Pre-Columbian ending of *La carpa* at the 1974 festival. The Teatro Campesino, he argues, understands the religious convictions of the campesino and to deny them is to deny him his right to a cosmology of his own. It is as if the Soviet Union were to deny Tolstoy simply because he chose to write of religious peasant life. The other position is less conciliatory. It argues that only a given style and content are acceptable for socialist theatre (e.g., Brecht and epic or Gorki and socialist realism). Brecht himself said he did not "give a whit" for Tolstoy, and would have paid to have some German classics not published.

The right relationship between popular art and the struggle for cultural identity remains as yet unsettled. What happens to the social fabric upon which Chicano culture is based as more Chicanos move to the cities? Is there now a Chicano urban culture? Does urbanization rob the Chicano of the basis of popular culture? Can popular theatre be urban or only rural? These have become urgent questions now that the last stronghold, the barrios, seem increasingly to be doomed. "From one end of the Southwest to the other," says Ernesto Galarza, writing of Barrio Pascua in Tucson, "they, like the colonias, stand in the path of Anglo progress. I am not speaking here of points of friction but points of attrition, at which the destructive power of the dominant society is at work."[9]

Thus the struggle for cultural identity is related in intricate ways to the survival of popular culture. While it is dangerous to take a narrow view and say that only the popular presentational style should be valued in Chicano theatre, it is equally dangerous to become international and eclectic, searching for styles and forms which have lost their class and cultural roots. During the formative years of their development both Brechtian and Chicano theatre were concerned with agitation. Both drew heavily on their own popular culture and both borrowed from the popular forms of other cultures. In this way both could remain culturally authentic while becoming international.

Because of its popular roots, Chicano theatre is alive and well. If it has evolved a Brechtian flavor, this is because it has based itself on the needs of the people and has served their cause.

NOTES

1. An extensive analysis of popular culture may be found in Stanley Aronowitz's *False Promises: The Shaping of American Working Class Consciousness* (New York: McGraw Hill, 1973).
2. "Nature and Development of Presentational Political Theatre" (unpublished paper by Richard Seyd, former member of Red Ladder Theatre, London, p. 2.) On file with Teatro Libertad, Tucson, Arizona.
3. Ibid., p. 3.
4. Dennis Calandra, "Karl Valentin and Bertolt Brecht," *The Drama Review*, 18, No. 1 (March, 1974), 86.
5. "B.B's Rehearsal Scenes," in *Brecht*, ed. Erika Munk (New York: Bantam Drama Book, 1972), p. 121.
6. An extensive analysis of Brechtian acting can be found in John Willett's *The Theatre of Bertolt Brecht* (London: Methuen, 1960).
7. *La quinta temporada* and other early short theater pieces by the Teatro Campesino can be found in *Actos: El Teatro Campesino* (San Juan Bautista, Calif.: Cucaracha Press, 1971).
8. Quoted in Francoise Kourilsky, "Approaching Quetzalcoatl: the Evolution of El Teatro Campesino," *Performance*, 2 (Fall, 1973), 37–46. This article appeared originally in French in *Travail Théatral*, 7 (April–June, 1972), 59–70.
9. Edward H. Spicer and Raymond H. Thompson, *Plural Society of the Southwest* (Albuquerque: University of New Mexico Press, 1972).

19

BRECHT AND LATIN AMERICA'S "THEATRE OF REVOLUTION"

Diana Taylor

> Copy Brecht? Never, it would be poor and useless. Imitate him? There's no point. Work with him? Yes.
>
> **Fernando Peixoto, "Brecht, Nuestro Compañero."[1]**

The impact of Bertolt Brecht on Latin American theatre is enormous though perhaps difficult to assess in any straightforward way. Every theatre practitioner in the region, I would venture to guess, knows Brecht's theories, yet, few stage his plays. All of Brecht's works are translated into Spanish and Portuguese and are available in most academic bookstores. No other theatre artist, from Latin America or abroad, boasts a similar status or reach. But no one would claim to do "Brechtian" theatre. This essay attempts to address this seeming paradox by looking at both the historical context within which Brecht gets introduced in Latin America, and at the way that theatre practitioners integrate "Brechtian" elements in their own work.

Brecht fever caught on quickly and spread rapidly throughout Latin America around the time of his death in 1956. Coinciding with the waves of Marxist anti-capitalist struggle that swept through Latin America at the end of the 1950s, culminating in the Cuban Revolution of 1959, Brecht's theories of a socially responsible, critical, and historically grounded theatre, directed at the children of the scientific age, resonated throughout the region. The *Festival of the Nations* (Paris, 1954) had introduced Latin American practitioners to the theory, plays, and stagings that were to become the most decisive single influence on them during the next two decades.[2] Translations soon followed. By the mid-1960s Latin America's most renowned groups and directors (such as Santiago Garcia and Enrique Buenaventura, both from Colombia) were putting on their own versions of *Galileo* (1965) and *Seven Deadly Sins* (1969). Playwrights such as Enrique Buenaventura and Griselda Gambaro adapted the fragmented structure of *Fear and Misery of the Third Reich* to describe the political violence in their countries: *Documents from Hell* (Colombia, 1968) and *Information for Foreigners* (Argentina, 1972) respectively. Other major playwrights, such as

Osvaldo Dragún and Ricardo Talesnik (Argentina), Luisa Josefina Hernández and Emilio Carballido (Mexico), started adapting or somehow engaging artistically with a "Brechtian" epic structure.[3] Politically activist theatre groups (such as *Escambray* in Cuba and *Yuyachkani* in Peru) used "Brechtian" methodology to train actors in the alienation techniques that would encourage critical participation from their audiences. Theatre schools and cultural centers hosted discussions on Brecht's dialectical theatre.[4] Terms such as epic, "culinary" theatre, and *Gestus* became commonplace in discussions about art and society. Brecht's reflections on the "'popular' as intelligible to the broad masses"[5] sharpened the focus of popular (or "New") theatre practitioners in the Americas who were dedicated to raising political awareness among disenfranchised populations.

The evidence of Brecht's impact, then, is overwhelming. But this was no mere "borrowing," and nothing as simple as what we normally think of as literary or theatrical "influence." Brecht fever hit at the height of the Cold War for two main reasons. First, his way of infusing the epic form with Marxist ideology offered one more way of framing and making sense of Latin America's revolutionary praxis and aspirations. Participants and spectators could see in the escalating political events a kind of gestic political theatre. Second, Brecht's efforts to combine anticapitalist ideology with aesthetic principles inspired Latin American theatre artists to do the same for themselves, and in their own way. How could artists who lived surrounded by extreme social inequity and brutal political violence justify being artists if that meant an "art for art's sake" mentality or cooptation into state-sponsored programs favoring special interests? Latin American theatre artists, as opposed to the famous Latin American novelists, had few possibilities for working if they separated themselves from the intense struggles affecting their societies.[6] Enrique Buenaventura aptly summed up their predictment in "Theatre and Culture": "Many Latin Americans who belong to the international republic of arts and letters resolve [the] contradiction by making a radical separation between arts and politics [. . .] The best way to do this is to live in Europe and support Cuba."[7] Brecht offered a contemporary model of a theatre practitioner who had successfully brought politics into immediate conversation with aesthetics, challenging every political system from Nazism to the U.S. House on Un-American Activities Committee (HUAC). The theatre artist, Brecht suggested, was at the forefront of political conflict, not sitting somwhere with his back to it.

Let me start with what I see as the first reason why Brecht became so popular in Latin America. Brecht's epic theatre provided one kind of lens for looking at the intense political drama unfolding in the late 1950s. The Cuban revolution, aside from providing the hope of viable political alternatives for Latin America, also produced a riveting theatrical image. Here was a massive, epic drama if there ever was one – one that "aroused the spectator's capacity for action" (Brecht 1964: 37), that proposed that both human beings and social systems were "alterable and able to alter" (ibid.), that begged for a public capable of making decisions and adopting heroic political stances. In other words, though the revolution worked primarily on the "real" order, it had a significant symbolic component. Without reducing the revolution to a spectacle, it is important to notice that its spectacular components served a vital function. They captured worldwide attention; they rallied followers and admirers by ennobling the revolutionaries while delegitimizing their opposition. The compelling figure of Ché, and to a lesser degree the figure of Castro, dominated the imagination of a huge portion of the population of Latin America. The revolution generated images of epic proportions, which coincided with Brechtian terminology: the frozen frame of Ché in his beret; the green fatigue uniforms of the *Castristas*; the Brechtian *Gestus* as the revolutionary attitude of "men" in action; the episodic plot described by Ché in his diary, his continuing struggle to move the revolution to Bolivia and then to other oppressed regions of Latin America; the enthralled popular audience. Ché's heroic quest embodied the continent's hopes for liberation. The entire sequence was highly spectacular: a new world was being created out of conflict, a new beginning, a new hero or "revolutionary man."[8] Events reactivated the "revolutionary myth" envisioned by Latin American liberation thinkers such as José Carlos Mariátegui.[9] And just as scholars argue that theatre provides one means of forging a collective identity, the revolution too created a sense of national and international identity mediated through an image. Instead of twenty-five politically marginal, economically and culturally dependent countries, Latin America could envision itself as a united, coherent entity, a producer (rather than importer) of cultural images.

Notwithstanding its epic proportions, the theatre of revolution, cannot be "read" according to any strict Brechtian terminology. Although it staged the uprising of the oppressed and tried to expose a bourgeois, capitalist, imperialist ideology, it also imposed its own myths. The contradictions underlying many discussions of "new" or "popular" or "revolutionary" Latin American theatre reflect the paradox that lies at the heart of this and perhaps every revolution. If we continue to examine it according to theatrical terminology (discussions of "revolutionary" theatre tend to conflate the two), we detect a significant overlap with Artaud's dramatic theory as expressed in his collection of essays *The Theater and Its Double*. Unlike the Brechtian dialectical theatre, which insists on space for critical distancing – "Spectator and actor ought not to approach one another but to move apart" (Brecht 1964: 26) – the theatricality of the Revolution encouraged an Artaudian identification, even a merging, with those heroic figures "capable of imposing this supreme notion of the theater, men who [would] restore to all of us the natural and magic equivalent of the dogmas in which we no longer believe."[10] Artaud's theory calls for collective fusion in the name of metaphysical transcendence; the individual assumes the image and takes on the "exterior attitudes of the desired condition" (Artaud 1958: 80). Likewise, the revolution encouraged subsuming the personal to the collective ideal. The actor, committed to the process of creating a new real, "makes a total gift of himself," as Jerzy Grotowski advocated, following Artaud's lead, and "sacrifices the innermost part of himself."[11] But not only in theatre do people give themselves up like Artaud's "victims burnt at the stake, signaling through the flames" (Artaud 1958: 13). The mythification of violence as a source of liberation, whether self-directed or other-directed, in Artaudian theories of a total, essential, and heroic theatre – the "theatre of cruelty" – also forms part of revolutionary thinking, a factor as much in its discourse as in its military strategy. Images of self-sacrifice and surrender characterize works on revolution. Fernando Alegria, in *Literatura y revolución*, describes "the bloody operation" of self-examination and recrimination through revolutionary literature, in which authors and their public undergo a painful and glorious striptease: they unmask, "wash, scrub, fumigate themselves, burn their clothing and expose their flesh to merciless scrutiny."[12] Moreover, revolutions themselves are almost synonymous with violence; though people do speak of "nonviolent revolutions," the term seems contradictory. Hannah Arendt argues in *On Revolution* that revolutions "are not even conceivable outside the domains of violence."[13] This is a position the Cuban revolutionaries themselves, maintaining that the struggle for political power was inseparable from armed warfare, would have accepted.

This giving oneself up to the revolution, then, is not a Brechtian critical or dialectical position. A sudden linguistic shift occurs at the point where one would follow the Brechtian terminology to its logical conclusion, to critical awareness and emotional distancing. Here, the surrender to the revolution is described in natural rather than theatrical terminology: one *becomes* a revolutionary and creates a new reality by giving oneself up to the seemingly irresistible force or process. In this sense, "revolution" means the steady motion of heavenly bodies in orbit, which follow laws of physics beyond human control. For one commentator on Latin American popular theatre, "the new socialist hero" will be neither a pessimist nor a conflicted, tortured individual but "a man caught up in the revolutionary whirlwind" (Artiles 1979: 80).

Just as the Cuban revolution was theatrical, much of the so-called revolutionary theatre of this period incorporated and furthered revolutionary ideology, identity, and images. The theatre of revolution, while functioning primarily on the symbolic order, also aimed at real, political change and saw itself as an important instrument in the social struggle. During the 1960s, collective theatres began to reinforce the grassroots movements with their emphasis on leadership, unity, mass mobilization, and combined force. This theatre manifested the widespread preoccupation with war, either reaffirming or decoding military terminology.

Augusto Boal, who acknowledges Piscator and Brecht as important influences, situates theatre firmly in the realm of political and social struggle. For him, during the early 1960s, theatre was a "weapon" in overthrowing systems of oppression. He describes theatrical "raids" staged in 1963 during the Cuban crisis: "A group of actors meet on a corner and begin arguing about politics to the point of threatening physical violence; people gather around them and the group suddenly begins an improvised performance that deals with the most urgent political issues. Only midway through the performance does the crowd realize that it is attending a play."[14] In Cuba, theatrical groups such as the *Conjunto Dramatico de Oriente* (started in 1961) and the *Grupo Teatro Escambray* (1968) gradually moved away from scripted theatre and staged collective acts of group definition and affirmation. Revolutionary theatre was conceived as a pragmatic, educational, useful theatre, a practical exercise in learning about the revolutionary process and encouraging "public participation in [revolutionary] solutions. Theatre is an excellent vehicle to detect and combat problems," wrote the Cuban scholar, Rosa Ileana Boudet.[15] Theatrical performances also became acts of collective affirmation and group definition. This partial, or selective, use of Brechtian principles to think about localized socio-political conditions is noteworthy. Rather than a simple "borrowing," what we see is the process of transculturation, analyzed by Cuban anthroplogist Fernando Ortiz in the 1940s to describe a tripartite process (acculturation, deculturation and transculturation) whereby one cultural system receives and ultimately transforms material from another.[16] Without dismissing the reality of cultural imperialism, transculturation allows for creativity and selection in the process of cultural transmission.

While the Brechtian epic model offered a lens for making sense of riveting political events, Brecht was also profoundly influential in pointing to ways in which Latin American theatre practitioners could combine anti-capitalist ideology with the aesthetic requirements posed by the theatrical form itself. But again, the question of impact is far more difficult to assess than has been acknowledged. Latin American theatre artists experimented enthusiastically with Brechtian theory and methodology. But Latin America was so different from Brecht's Europe in terms of race, language, levels of literacy, performance traditions and expectations, not to mention the socio-economic realities. The adaptation of a "Brechtian" model to this new context was complicated to say the least.

The example of the renowned Peruvian collective theatre group, Yuyachkani, is a case in point. Members of Yuyachkani stress the importance of Brecht's theory, practice and life in their formation and development as a group;[17] when they began working in the early 1970s, they saw themselves as politically "committed" popular theatre practitioners, doing much the same thing that other such groups were doing in the late 1960s and early 1970s. They challenged the hegemonic systems that placed "Theatre" with a capital "T" and "Culture" with a capital "C" in lofty, aesthetic realms, beyond the reach of working-class people and racially marginalized communities. They worked as a collective, rejecting the playwright- and "star"-driven theatrical models that dominated highbrow and commercial theatre. They took the theatre out of elite spaces, staging free performances that had to do with the real life economic and political conditions of working people. They toured their shows to rural communities with little access to theatre, and involved spectators in productions that focused on community issues. Working under the Brechtian influence, which in Latin America was closely linked to strikes and other class/labor struggles, Yuyachkani was a rough, unpolished theatre that came into being because of a strike. Their first play, "Puño de Cobre" (1972), dealt with a miner's strike, and toured Peru's many mining camps to show solidarity with the anti-imperialist, anti-corporate movement.

What Yuyachkani found, however, was that their "method" was totally incongruent with the context in which they found themselves. Because Marxism privileged class, anti-capitalist and anti-imperialist struggles at the expense of racial, ethnic, and gender conflict, popular theatre groups in Latin America ran the risk of reducing deep-seated cultural differences to class difference. In Peru, and other countries with large indigenous and mestizo communities, the "proletariat" in fact consisted of indigenous and mestizo groups who lived on the margins of a capitalist society for various reasons – including linguistic, epistemic, cultural, and religious – not reducible (though bound into) economic disenfranchisement. A call for solidarity organized around anti-capitalism allowed for cultural trespassing on all sorts of other grounds. The less the practitioners knew the communities they were engaging, the more the discrepancies in power and the lack of reciprocity threatened to place them in positions of moral superiority reminiscent of political pamphleteers or religious proselytizers.

Yuyachkani began to understand that the marginalized groups they were addressing in their own country had their own languages, expressive cultures, and performance codes that the group knew nothing about. Miguel Rubio, the artistic director of Yuyachkani, recalls how during that first play which they performed for the miners, the actors dressed in jeans and played a variety of roles and characters. After the performance, one miner commented: "Compañeros, that's a nice play. Too bad you forgot your costumes."[18] "Much later," Rubio continues, "we understood why the miners thought what they did. We had forgotten something much more important than costumes. What they wanted to tell us was that we were forgetting the audience that we were addressing. We were not taking their artistic traditions into consideration. Not only that, we didn't know them!" Thus began the education of Yuyachkani regarding Peru's ethnic and cultural heterogeneity. They added members from these communities to their group; they learned quechua; they trained in indigenous and mestizo performance practices that included singing, playing instruments, dancing, movement and many other forms of popular expression. They expanded the notion of political theatre to include the popular fiesta that emphasized participation, thus blurring the distinction between actor and spectator. Performance, for Yuyachkani as for other popular theatre groups, became less about implementing "Brechtian" practice than about opening up an arena for learning. But in an important reversal, here it was Yuyachkani learning "our first huaylars, pasacalle, and huayno dance steps [;] between beers and warm food, we started to feel and maybe to understand the complexity of the Andean spirit."[19] Only after they made their own the many elements they had learned – from Brecht, from the Andean communities, and from the Eurocentric theatre training they received in Lima – did Yuyachkani finally offer their tribute to Brecht. In *Encuentro de zorros* (1985), a cart much like Mother Courage's comes onstage pushed by the beggars displaced by Peru's war into the sprawling urban centers. And in that same year, Teresa Ralli, one the group's actors, presented a solo performance, "Baladas del Bien-Estar" in which she performs poems and songs by Brecht.

The impact of Brecht on playwrights is just as difficult to assess. Those of us who have access to the written works notice immediate similarities. And even though the influence seems transparent, this apparent transparency may make it more complicated to understand how the "Brechtian" elements are being deployed and what they might mean to local audiences. It is commonplace to isolate certain Latin American playwrights from their context and analyze how they "imitate" or borrow from foreign sources. While examples of this kind of misreading abound, I will focus on how this plays out in the scholarly interpretations of Enrique Buenaventura. Commentators cannot speak highly enough of Buenaventura or emphasize the importance of his dramatic production. They situate him next to Brecht and Piscator in the European tradition of political theatre and interpret his plays in accordance with Brechtian models. They emphasize his preoccupation with history, note his use of historical figures as central characters (Rey Christophe and Bartolomé de Las Casas), and his theatrical technique of "documentation." The words "Brecht," "history," and "popular" appear in tandem in studies on Buenaventura.[20]

Buenaventura's theatre certainly deserves all the praise it receives, and all the usual observations are in some way "true." He repeatedly acknowledges his admiration of and indebtedness to Brecht. From his earliest pieces onward we can discern Brechtian motifs and techniques: *A la diestra de Dios Padre* (*On the Right Hand of God the Father*, 1960) recalls moments of *The Good Woman of Setzuan*; and his cycle of plays *Los papeles del infierno* (*Documents from Hell*, 1968) is based on Brecht's collection of short pieces, *Fears and Miseries of the Third Reich*. Buenaventura's concern with history, too, is evident throughout.

Documents, as he announces explicitly in the prologue, "is a testimony of twenty years of violence and undeclared civil war," the period in Colombian history known simply as *La Violencia*, which began in the mid-1940s. Furthermore, Buenaventura is certainly a "popular" theatre practitioner. He is committed to social change, even revolutionary change. In 1962 he founded Colombia's first professional theatre and repertory company, the TEC (Teatro Escuela de Cali). Buenaventura's activist stance cost him his teaching position at the Escuela Departamental de Teatro del Valle and resulted in the loss of all governmental recognition and support for the TEC. The showdown with the government came after he staged *Seven Deadly Sins* in 1969. If theatre practitioners were going to criticize the government, he and other practitioners were informed, then they shouldn't expect to be supported by the government. The reply was simple – "government" money did not belong to the government but to the people it was supposed to represent, and Buenaventura would not receive funding to shut his mouth and close his eyes.[21] Buenaventura continued to write plays for the newly named Teatro Experimental de Cali (the new TEC) and began experimenting with collaborative playwriting. The texts of collective pieces emerged after a rehearsal process in which he and other TEC members devised, researched, and shaped a topic. In addition to his Marxist political perspective, Buenaventura addresses a "popular" audience, traveling with his shows to rural areas where people have never seen theatre before. Aesthetically, these activities imply radical departures from traditional and hegemonic concepts of "text," "author," and "culture."

All this information is important, as in the case of Yuyachkani, but the standard interpretation of it has resulted, inadvertently, in obscuring rather than illuminating Buenaventura's importance and his position vis-à-vis his country's crisis. A brief look at the assumptions behind the different critical postures will show why they have failed to touch on what is most innovative and radical about Buenaventura's theatrical practice.

The most obvious limitation of the view that Buenaventura is Brechtian, historical, and popular is that those particular terms are themselves problematic and essentialist; they mean different things to different people, and they suggest that there is one Brecht, one Buenaventura. The case for Brechtian "influence," to be meaningful, would require a host of considerations, perhaps principally of periodization (early Brecht? late Brecht? early Buenaventura? late Buenaventura?), which are not addressed in these studies. What do we mean by Brechtian? Are we referring to a political, dialectical theatre? To theatrical techniques such as having women act men's roles and vice versa? To distanciation? To epic narration? Finding answers would involve an examination of transcultural trends, the process by means of which Buenaventura selects and adapts Brechtian themes and strategies to construct "meaning" in relation to his own specific spectactors, many of whom have never heard of Brecht. The Brechtian elements are not popularly known "pretexts" for spontaneous improvisation, as the *commedia dell'arte* plots and characters were for its audience; nor do they constitute a shared belief or tradition, as biblical stories do for some groups and mythological ones for others. What, then, is the point of introducing these elements? How do these adapted features "read" or "play" when Buenaventura's theatre, in turn, is transplanted to another culture? Moreover, to argue simultaneously that Buenaventura is a Brechtian and a "collective" playwright poses the problem of what we mean by *author* and *oeuvre*.[22] Single-author "works" are difficult enough to establish, let alone compare with texts by other authors. The issue becomes even more troublesome with reference either to Brecht or to Buenaventura as "author": the former collaborated with Ruth Berlau, Elisabeth Hauptmann, and Margarete Steffin, for example, not to mention musicians such as Kurt Weill; the latter gradually became a collaborator in a collective creation. Which Brecht or which Buenaventura are we thinking of? Can we even think of Buenaventura's later works as part of his oeuvre in the same way as we do his single-author plays?

Clearly, too, an emphasis on the Brechtian elements clouds the many important Latin American components of his work. His *A la diestra de Dios Padre*, much like Brecht's *Good Woman*, represents multiple "gods": Jesus and St. Peter try to find and help a good person. What are rarely discussed, however, are the other traditions feeding into this drama, from Spanish mystery plays or *autos sacramentales* to the grotesque humor of Ramón del Valle Inclán's (1866–1936) *esperpentos*, to the farcical, masked *festivales* such as the *mojiganga*. Moreover the different representation of the gods bespeaks different world views and hence radically different "solutions" for surviving in the face of formidable odds.

We could argue that Buenaventura's appropriation of foreign cultural material is Brechtian in spirit. After all, Brecht was one of theatre's most avid borrowers. Even here, however, the emphasis on Brecht is misleading; what we should be looking at is the process of transculturation itself. Just as Brecht's specific use of the elements he borrows makes him Brechtian, so does Buenaventura's use of his make him a new original. Buenaventura himself, from *A la diestra de Dios Padre* onward, calls attention to the process of transculturation by means of which marginalized people absorb foreign models and use them for their liberation: Jesus and St. Peter are furious because their designated "good man," Peralta, has misused his powers, but Jesus acknowledges that he has been outsmarted, that in fact Peralta "has done nothing more than use the powers that I gave him."[23] Peralta will not be easily defeated or excluded; in the final scene, using the very wishes Jesus granted him, he jumps into the right hand of God, determined, as William Oliver (1971: 174) puts it, to "plague God's own creativity" for eternity.[24] This, then, is a counterhegemonic strategy that Buenaventura proposes for his audiences; they are directed not to imitate the West but rather to appropriate the weapons of the powerful and use them for their own decolonization. Moreover, he explicitly refers to this strategy in his theoretical papers; he explains that he and his group purposely chose for production foreign plays that illuminated their own specific problems, notably colonization and dependency: "We knew that the colonizer that imposed his culture was also giving us the instruments of liberation. But we can only use those instruments if we apply them to our concrete reality."

In short, to emphasize the Brechtian elements in this way is misleading. Though it is laudable on the part of the commentators to want to stress the quality and importance of Buenaventura's work by situating him next to Brecht, this emphasis leads us away from those characteristics (by and large non-Brechtian) that most contribute to Buenaventura's importance.

Similarly, we contribute to the critical obfuscation of Buenaventura's work by simply stating that he is one of Latin America's foremost "popular" theatre practitioners, since no one quite agrees on what "popular theatre" means. Rather than allowing for differentiation between many kinds of "popular" or "people's" theatre – Chicano theatre, Piscator's "epic" theatre, Boal's theatre of the oppressed, and others – the term "popular" tends to group them all together, despite their important differences. What does the label "popular" tell us about Buenaventura's own production? That it is for the "people"? Yes, if by that we mean rural and semiliterate audiences along with urban and literate (university student) ones. That it is by the "people"? Buenaventura is a self-taught, highly knowledgeable, articulate intellectual, not a man of the semiliterate circles he wants to incorporate in theatrical activity. That this theatre privileges political over aesthetic effects – that is, focuses specifically on a given set of social problems? Buenaventura has adamantly denied that theatre must sacrifice aesthetics to politics, differing radically in this respect both from Piscator and from more dogmatic Latin American popular groups. "'Popular theatre,' or a 'theatre for the masses,' a theatre for a fixed audience and about a specific set of problems," he says, is "just another trick of the system, as elementary as nationalism, folklore, or agitprop. Because the system has cast out the exploited, should you create a product for them that is no more nutritious than the food surpluses it leaves them? Some maintain that the exploited don't want anything else, that they don't have the capacity to participate in the full and complex diversion of a real theatrical production. . . . To accept that we must do lowquality theatre at the outset to 'elevate' the level of the people is to enter wholly into the system" ("Theater and Culture," 154). The issue of "popular theatre," then, is disorienting; it draws attention away from what Buenaventura actually does, away from the artistic and technical strategies he devises to communicate with disparate audiences and to continue producing outstanding theatre in the face of overwhelming difficulties – traveling to rural areas that lack traditional theatre spaces, working with minimum financial and technical resources, dealing with political ostracism and harassment. His is truly a "poor" theatre in the economic sense of the word.

More important, however, is the fact that Buenaventura does not follow the path of consciousness raising normally associated with popular theatre. Rather than propose a vision or communicate a message associated with a specific ideology, he subverts dominant ideology through a process he calls "deconscientization" (deconcienciación) or "demystification." For Buenaventura, this means seeing through the concepts of "tradition," "history," and race, class, and gender "difference" which sustain the power elite. He undermines the boundaries – social, political, economic, cultural, and historical – by means of which the system excludes a substantial portion of its population as grotesque, poor, dirty, infirm others. He does not simply propose overthrowing the oppressors and grabbing their power, however, perpetuating thus the binary system of oppressed and oppressor. He has no intention of substituting one form of violence for another, or "one set of illusions for another" (Reyes 1963: 22). Rather, Buenaventura is far more like Brecht in the way that he questions the entire system, including the role of the oppressed themselves within it. The sociopolitical demystification proposed by Buenaventura strives toward the same political ends as do consciousness-raising theatres, but the difference is an important one that accounts for the subtle, non-didactic nature of Buenaventura's drama. Like Brecht, Buenaventura seeks to expose, rather than impose, ideology.

While the impact of Brecht is profound on Latin American theatre practitioners, it needs to be understood in a less literal fashion. As I have suggested, different groups have tried, in their own ways, to reconcile the aesthetic and political demands of theatre in their own particular contexts. The convergence of concerns, rather than a specific methodology or practice, brings them together. Ironically, scholars who stress Brecht's influence on Latin American and other colonized regions of the world, fail to mention what I consider its single most important feature: Brecht was a common source of inspiration to dramatists from many colonized and marginalized societies, responsible, indirectly, for introducing them to each other. This larger network of activist theatre practitioners from Latin America, India, Africa, and elsewhere who learned of each other through their shared interest in Brecht remains to be explored.

NOTES

1. Fernando Peixoto, "Brecht, Nuestro Compañero," *Conjunto* 69 (July–Sept. 1986), pp. 104–6. All translations from Spanish are mine, unless otherwise noted. This essay is a reworking of an argument I first put forth

in my study, *Theatre of Crisis: Drama and Politics in Latin America* (Lexington: Kentucky University Press, 1990).

2. See Marina Pianca's overview of this period, "De Brecht a Nueva York: Caminos del teatro latinoamericano,' *Conjunto* 69 (July–Sept. 1986), pp. 93–103.
3. The use of a 'Brechtian' epic structure, to my mind, was very idiosyncratic and at times parodic. In Carballido's *I, Too, Speak of the Rose*, Carballido pokes gentle fun at what he sees as the rigidity of Marxist ideology (as it was promoted in Mexico), and he softens the episodic framework associated with Brecht by transforming it into a heart-beat rhythm associated with oral traditions. However, in his book *Brecht en el teatro hispanoamericano* (Ottawa: Girol Books, 1984) Fernando de Toro argues that Latin American theatre practitioners utilized the 'Brechtian system' ("sistema Brecht"), p. 56. His work is an attempt to show how this is so. De Toro emphasizes that these practitioners do not imitate Brecht, but use his epic theatre as a way of bringing political (marxist) ideology into a congruent aesthetic mode that avoids the pitfalls for Aristotelian identification, catharsis and so on.
4. Gilberto Martínez, "Mi experiencia directa con la obra de Bertolt Brecht," *Conjunto* 20 (April–June 1974), pp. 106–26.
5. Bertolt Brecht, "The Popular and the Realistic," *Brecht on Brecht*, translated John Willett (New York: Hill and Wang,1964), p. 108.
6. While theatre people such as Griselda Gambaro, Eduardo Pavlovsky and Diana Raznovich from Argentina (to name a few), Denise Stoklos and Auguesto Boal from Brazil, Ariel Dorfman from Chile, and others left their countries during the periods of extreme periods of military dictatorship, many theatre people in countries like Peru and Colombia that had suffered chronic political violence chose to stay.
7. Enrique Buenavenura, "Theatre & Culture," trans. Joanne Pottlitzer, *TDR* 14/2 (Winter 1970), pp. 151–6.
8. Freddy Artiles, "Teatro popular: Nuevo heroe, nuevo conflicto," in Sonia Gutierrez (ed.), *Teatro popular y cambio social en América Latina* (Costa Rica: EDUCA, 1979), p. 80.
9. José Carlos Mariátegui, *7 ensayos de interpretación de la realidad peruana* (Lima: Amauta, 1975).
10. Antonin Artaud, *The Theatre and Its Double*, trans Mary Caroline Richards (New York: Grove Press, 1958), p. 32.
11. Jerzy Grotowski, *Towards a Poor Theatre* (New York: Simon and Schuster, 1968), p. 35.
12. Fernando Alegria, *Literatura y revolución* (México: Fondo de Cultura Económica, 1976), p. 11.
13. Hannah Arendt, *On Revolution* (Harmondsworth: Penguin, 1963), p. 18.
14. See Augusto Boal, *Theatre of the Oppressed* (New York: TCG, 1985), p. ix, and "A Note on Brazilian Agitprop," *TDR* 14/2 (Winter 1970), p. 96.
15. Rosa Ileana Boudet, *Teatro nuevo: Una respuesta* (Havana: Editorial Letras Cubanas, 1983), p. 12.
16. Fernando Ortiz, *Contrapunteo cubano del tabaco y el azucar* (Caracas: Biblioteca Ayacucho, 1978).
17. The program notes for "Baladas del Bien-Estar" recognize that "Bertold Brecht constitutes a fundamental element that gave rise to Yuyachkani. His plays, his theoretical writings, his 'Short Organum,' his 'five difficulties with telling the truth,' are texts that we come back to in those moments in which we ask ourselves: how do we continue? Or simple, what should we do? But it's not just his work, it's his life too; it's a living testimony of an exemplary attitude and ethics at the time of rising

fascism in Germany. His pilgrimage, persecution, and later exile, were a key motivation in developing his texts. . . ." 1996.

18. Miguel Rubio, "Encuentro con el Hombre Andino," *Grupo Cultural Yuyachkani, Allpa Rayku: Una experencia de teatro popular* (Lima: Edición del 'Grupo Cultural Yuyachkani' y Escuelas Campesinas de la CCP, 2nd edn., 1985), p. 9.
19. Brenda Luz Cotto-Escalera, "Grupo Cultural Yuyachkaui: Group Work and Collective Creation in Contemporary Latin American Theatre." (Unpublished diss., University of Texas, Austin, 1995) p. 8.
20. The major studies on Buenaventura are Beatriz Risk's *El nuevo teatro latinoamericano: Una lectura histórica* (Minneapolis: Prisma Institute, 1987) and Marina Pianca's work (cited above, n. 2). See also de Toro (cited above, n. 3).
21. Martínez (cited above, n. 4) p. 110.
22. See Michel Foucault, *The Archaeology of Knowedge*, trans. A. M. Sheridan Smith (New York: Panther, 1972), p. 24.
23. Enrique Buenaventura, *Teatro* (Bogotá: Ediciones Tercer Mundo, 1963), p. 140.
24. William Oliver (ed.), *Voices of Change in Spanish American Theatre* (Austin: University of Texas Press, 1971), p. 174.

REFERENCES

Artaud, Antonin (1958) *The Theatre and its Double*. Trans. Mary Caroline Richards. New York: Grove Press.

Artiles, Freddy (1979) "Teatro popular: Nuevo heroe, nuevo conflicto." In Sonia Gutierrez (ed.), *Teatro popular y cambio social en América Latina*. Costa Rica: EDUCA.

Brecht, Bertolt (1964) "The Popular and the Realistic." *Brecht on Brecht*, trans. John Willett. New York: Hill and Wang.

Oliver, William (1971) (ed.) *Voices of Change in Spanish American Theatre*. Austin: University of Texas Press.

Reyes, Carlos José (1963) "Introducción: El teatro de Enrique Buenaventura." In *Enrique Buenaventura: Teatro*. Bogotá: Ediciones Tercer Mundo.

POLITICAL DISPLACEMENTS: TOWARD HISTORICIZING BRECHT IN JAPAN, 1932–1998

Uchino Tadashi[1]

PROLOGUE: SEPTEMBER 1998, TOKYO, JAPAN

SCENE: The middle-sized theatre ("The Playhouse") within the New National Theatre Complex, opened in the fall of 1997. The production of *Buddha*, a play with music. Originally published as a *manga* (comic strip) epic by Tezuka Osamu, adapted for stage by Sato Makoto, directed by Kuriyama Tamiya.[2]

CHARACTERS: Playwright and director Sato Makoto (1942–), a founding member of the Black Tent Theatre Company. Sato was theoretically influenced by Brecht in the 1960s and the 1970s. He is now the artistic director of the Setagaya Public Theatre. Tezuka Osamu (1928–89), the most representative and influential *manga* master after World War II, known for establishing *manga* genre as a "serious" art form with such influential works as *Tetsuwan Atom* (*Iron-armed Atom*, 1951–81) and *Jungle Taitei* (*The Emperor of the Jungle*, 1950–4). Kuriyama Tamiya (1953–), a member of the emerging generation of *shingeki* directors, who is known for his technical mastery of stagecraft. And, of course, the New National Theatre Complex. This theatre complex has three theatres within its oppressive modern architecture. It does not have resident opera, dance or theatre companies. Furthermore, the building was built with taxpayers' money, but the operating budget is designed to come from commercial tenants (and ticket sales) who rent the space in the adjoining high-rise building called the Opera City.

SYNOPSIS: The New National Theatre, Sato Makoto, Tezuka Osamu and Kuriyama Tamiya. The production of *Buddha* at the New National Theatre is a curious and even impressive site to begin thinking about Brecht in Japan. There are complex and entangled sets of contexts and issues in the subject of my essay that are almost accidentally present in this single production.

In 1998, Brecht's centennial year, a celebration of his birth is supposed to have taken place all over the world. There is, however, very little "celebration" in Japan, except perhaps within academic circles associated with Brecht or Germany. Japan's theatre culture takes almost no notice of this "historic" year. Yet there are at least two theatre companies which devote themselves to producing Brecht's plays; the Tokyo Engeki (Theatre) Ensemble and Doro Theatre Company, both of which are considered *shingeki* companies, the one professional, the other amateur. They are the only ones "celebrating" Brecht's centennial in any substantial way. Other major theatre venues, commercial or experimental, have taken little notice of Brecht, his works, his theatrical techniques.

In a 9 September 1998 article titled "Brecht's Centennial: Theatre People are Rethinking Brecht's Contemporaneousness" in *The Nihon Keizai Shinbun* (Kono 1998: 40), Kono Takashi, an editor of *The Nihon Keizai Shinbun* attempts to explain Brecht:

> Brecht criticized established theatre practices and proposed new ideas that included a so-called Alienation effect in which allegorization of social contradictions make the audience think there is something wrong. He advocated a dialectical theatre in which characters' good and evil can be seen as social constructions.[3]

After his short but adequate summary, Kono quotes Sato Makoto: "Its almost impossible to find anybody who was not influenced by Brecht," which is followed by another comment by Nishido Kojin, a theatre critic, "[the] little theatre movement has unconsciously embodied Brecht's theatre theories, including the A-effect." Sato is again quoted commenting "Brecht became classic too early for Japan's theatre culture. But if new translations of Brecht's plays became available and a younger director would direct one of them without any preconceptions, we may able to change the fixed image of Brecht in this country."

Although Sato is well-known for his innovative directing of Brecht's plays in the 1970s, he did not do a production of Brecht in 1998. Instead, he directed *Woyzeck* with his Black Tent Theatre Company at his Setagaya Public Theatre in September of that year, in addition to writing the script for *Buddha*. Little theatre practitioners,[4] who have supposedly, according to Nishido, embodied Brecht's theories, seem not to care that 1998 is Brecht's centennial. In short, nobody is thinking seriously about Brecht on his hundredth birthday when it could be commercially and/or critically feasible to "do" Brecht.

Instead, we have this typically apolitical and ahistorical theatrical extravaganza called *Buddha* at Japan's newest national theatre complex, which features Takashima Masanobu, one of the most famous

TV stars of this decade, as Buddha. It is not impossible, however, to hear a far cry (or the dead rattle) of Brecht in Japan, in this apparently un-Brechtian performance. Tezuka's original *manga* consists of seven parts and sixty-nine chapters or episodes. *Buddha* is published in fourteen volumes in Tezuka's *Collected Manga Works*. Tezuka wrote this epic *manga* in the twelve years from 1972 to 1983, in order to retell the biographical story of Buddha, making full use of his capacity to secularize and popularize in the easily accessible *manga* form the sacred and historical texts which depict Buddha's life and his teachings. The story is full of youthful and romantic adventures and, as Tezuka himself asserts in an afterword, it is totally a "fictionalized" version, thus making the work a typical "Tezuka SF" *manga* (Tezuka 1984: 5).

I don't want to argue either "authenticity" or appropriation in Tezuka's understanding of Buddha's life or philosophy. I just want to note that Tezuka's version is a straightforward negotiation between the complete canonical texts of Buddhism in Japan and his own post-war liberal-humanist "popularization." Using many references to contemporary socio-cultural icons, images, and concrete events, Tezuka tells the story of a suffering individual, who later becomes one of the most influential religious figures in the world history. In his usual entertaining and pedagogical manner, Tezuka is successful in doubling two completely separate historical processes: those of ancient India and of post-war Japan. The suffering of people, chaotic power relations and class struggles in ancient India are given narrative life in such a manner that people living in Japan, with memories of devastating World War II, including nuclear holocaust, post-war chaos and eventual revivification from the material and spiritual defeat, can have an easy access to the story being told.

In staging the original, as if to respond to the essentially allegorical nature and structure of this *manga* epic, Sato introduces, or rather appropriates Brecht's characters into his play; three gods from *The Good Person of Szechwan*. They are supposed to function as narrators of the story, leaders of the chorus, and sometimes, to enact some of the characters in the play.

Although Sato uses some Brechtian "songs," *Buddha* is a straight play, in which the action is depicted through dialogue. But two of the main characters who, curiously enough, are both female, are played by actors who are well-known for their roles in recent popular musicals. The chorus is present on stage most of the time, sometimes singing and occasionally dancing. After Brecht, *Buddha* is not called a musical but a play with music. The intention is to refer to the Brecht's influence (especially *The Threepenny Opera*) rather than American musical theatre.

Inclusion of such Brechtian characters and techniques, of course, does not guarantee any Brechtian effect. What is strangely sad about this production is its aesthetic mediocrity. I say strangely sad, because this production was meant to offer an apolitical aesthetic experience to the audience, but it fails to do so quite miserably despite the gigantic budget given to the director, Kuriyama. There is a huge river (real water) visibly running upstage; real fire, smoke machine effects, and an unnecessarily large chorus with many dancers – forty-seven names are listed in the program. It is simply mediocre, bad theatre. The representation of "Indian-ness" is so amateur and "innocent," that even Indians may find it difficult to criticize the production as a "misrepresentation" of "Indian-ness."

The most disturbing thing about *Buddha* is that it lacks a sense of history both in Sato's script and Kuriyama's staging. Brecht is thus radically decontextualized and demeaned in the production. The question we should ask, therefore, is precisely why such a bad production about an interesting person, with techniques drawn from Brecht, has been presented in the New National Theatre, a venue designated for "representative" cultural products. Productions at this theatre are supposed to have something to do with contemporary ways of constructing Japan's national identity. Is this supposed to be some sort of non-commercial "national" and/or "official" "popular" culture? Is this meant to be one of the end products of "democratization" of high culture in this country? In short, why is political and historical consciousness omitted from this particular production, when even aesthetics have no place in it? What does Brecht in Japan mean in this context?

ACT I: MARCH 1932, TOKYO, JAPAN

SCENE: The Production of *The Beggar's Play* by Tokyo Engeki Shudan (Tokyo Theatre Ensemble).

CHARACTERS: Senda Koreya (1904–94), an actor and director, who would later become one of the most influential *shingeki* practitioners, especially during and after the World War II. Senda will also later become a major force in introducing Brecht's work in Japan. When he organized the production of *The Beggar's Play*, he had just returned from spending four years in Germany. Many *shingeki* theatre practitioners at the time were faced with the possibility of being banned by the military government, because of the leftist proletariat theatre movement before the war. Although *shingeki* was understood by the Japanese government to be a leftist movement, there was, in fact, a political split among *shingeki* practitioners. Since its inception at the end of the nineteenth century, the movement's political sympathies kept changing.

SYNOPSIS: Senda Koreya, after participating in the foundation of Tsukiji

Shogekijo (Little Theatre) in 1924, the first "official" *shingeki* company[5] founded by Osanai Kaoru, grew weary of the company's mainstream, apolitical, and elitist attitudes. Senda left Japan for Germany in 1927. At the time, he considered himself to be a radical Marxist theatre practitioner going to Germany to study the workers' theatre movement. According to Ozasa Yoshio, a theatre historian who describes Senda's adventurous stay in Germany in detail, during his first few years in Berlin Senda was more like an observer but eventually became closely connected with people involved with German Workers' Theatre Association (ATBD) (Ozasa 1990: 570–2). Senda later participated in the first meeting of the International Workers' Theatre Association (IATB), held in 1930 in Moscow. As a consequence, Senda became active in agit-prop theatre in Germany. He returned to Japan to establish a far-eastern division of IATB in 1931 (Ozasa 1990: 577).

While in Germany, Senda did see some of Brecht's work (*Man is Man*, *The Threepenny Opera*, and *The Decision*) and, according to Ozasa, was "very impressed by his work" (Ozasa 1990: 570), but never had a chance actually to meet Brecht. Senda later recollected that he considered Brecht "a slightly leftist bourgeois artist" (Senda 1976: 17–18), who had nothing to do with what he and his German friends were doing. *The Threepenny Opera* (1929), however, seems an exception to his general assessment of Brecht at the time. Senda was "mind-blown and very surprised" (1976: 19).

When Senda went back to Japan, the Japan Proletariat Theatre Coalition (PROT) was dominating the leftist *shingeki* scene. Curiously enough, at the time of his return, Senda did not join the association, but established instead the agit-prop theatre group called Tokyo Proletariat Engei Shudan (Tokyo Proletariat Popular Entertainment Ensemble) which was later renamed Mezamashi Tai (Troupe for Uprising). Senda made his directorial debut with a work titled *Blue Uniforms* in February, 1932. The work demonstrated "how an agit-prop theatre company could be collectively organized with small scenes, narration, chants and songs and how professionals, amateurs and audiences could be interconnected, and how political and economical issues could be dealt with" (Senda 1975: 232).

At the same time, Senda was involved in establishing a theatre collective called Tokyo Engeki Shudan (TES: Tokyo Theatre Ensemble). Yet government officials were ever eager to eliminate the leftist movement. When Japan invaded Manchuria in 1931, the start of the endless invasion of Asia that continued until the end of the War in 1945, many leftist *shingeki* practitioners began to have an extremely difficult time.

There were several *shingeki* practitioners like Tsukiji-za (Tsukiji Theatre Company) and Theatre Comedie more interested in transplanting European psychological realism than in leftist theatre. In fact, before the unexpected death of Osanai Kaoru in 1929 when it had to be disbanded, Tsukiji Shogekijo produced 127 productions, out of which only twenty-seven were written by native Japanese. After Tsukiji Shogekijo disbanded, some newly established companies, along with the publication of some theatre magazines like *Gekisaku* (*Playwriting*, 1932–40), were eager to nurture native playwrights, among whom Kishida Kunio (1890–1954) was the major voice. Though difficult to produce plays because of the War, the 1930s is considered to have been the time when "native" playwriting reached its highest point in the pre-war period (Cf. Ibaragi 1973: 82–8).[6]

The 1930s were also a time when diverse kinds of popular entertainment flourished; many genres of popular entertainment had actually been established in the preceding decades during the Taisho era (1912–26), the first phase of democratization of Japan. Takarazuka, the all-female review, was founded in 1914. Other popular forms like Kei Engeki (Light Theatre), reviews and talkies were attracting large audiences and producing popular stars. Still newer forms of popular culture emerged in the early Showa period (1930s)[7] and were characterized as "Ero (erotic), Gro (grotesque), Nonsense." This was Japan's version of decadent culture and degraded aesthetics. This particular image of the 1930s will be taken up later by theatre practitioners, such as Sato Makoto and Inoue Hisashi after the 1960s. Both of whom were heavily influenced by Brecht's theatre practice and writings.

In the meantime, Senda chose to produce *The Threepenny Opera*, for the first production of TES. His intention was to create a site where cultural producers from a wide spectrum of practices, including *shingeki* practitioners could come together. TES was established, according to Ozasa (1990: 597), for four reasons: in order to bring together *shingeki* practitioners, including fragmented members of PROT, who were hostile to each other because of their ideological and/or personal differences; to experiment with new theatrical forms including music, dance, and cinema; to create opportunities for *shingeki* practitioners, who were suffering economically; to appear in radio programs and movies; and to create a space where interaction between *shingeki* practitioners and talented practitioners working in other venues as commercial theatre, Kabuki, musical revues, and cinema could come together to discover a new "popular" theatrical form.

I quoted Ozasa at length, despite the fact that TES did not last even a year, because the reasons for establishing TES later became the *raison d'être* of the *shingeki* practice, even after the war. The search for a new popular theatrical form became a kind of dogma for *shingeki* practitioners, especially after the war. This dogma was used on many occasions. Brecht was tactfully appropriated accordingly, as whenever *shingeki* practitioners performatively and discursively referred to "a new popular theatrical form," Brecht's presence was to be "felt," directly or indirectly. It is interesting to note, therefore, that

Brecht's play was chosen at this particular historical conjuncture as a site for many forms of performance, including popular entertainments; performers in the production were Senda's close associates, some from PROT, Tsukiji-za, Theatre Comedie, and some from Asakusa Kei Engeki.

Brecht in Japan was doomed, however, from the beginning. As Senda recollects, "Kurt Weill's score was easily available, but the script for *The Threepenny Opera* was not published [in Germany], and we didn't have time to acquire the unpublished script used for its production in Germany" (Senda 1975: 237). As a result, Senda had to "reconstruct" the script from his memory and the scenario for Bapst's movie version. He set the play:

> [i]n Tokyo at the early years of Meiji period and tried to incorporate Weill's music as much as possible. Considering we had to create scenes for those participating in the production, we "faked" something like a script. We could not call it Brecht's *The Threepenny Opera*. Because opera was not popular, it could not become the object of parody as in the original. So we decided to call it *The Beggar's Play*, freely adapted by the Dramaturgy Department of TES. (Senda 1975: 238)

The Beggar's Play was performed at the Shin (New) Kabuki-za in Shinjuku, Tokyo, at the end of March, 1932.

It is difficult to know what the production looked like from the reviews of the day. It included some popular stars like Enomoto Kenichi (nicknamed Enoken) from Kei Engeki and Tsukigata Ryunosuke, a movie star. But it was not a great success. More interesting, however, is the fact that the first production of Brecht in Japan was intentionally distorted for external political reasons: Senda, as a young radical artist, was apparently in a hurry to establish TES as a major force in the cultural circles of the day. It is clear that he saw the possibility of "new popular theatrical form" in *The Threepenny Opera*. He even envisioned this production as the beginning of "organizing a united front" for cultural producers against the fascist government (Senda 1985: 409), but he was not able to pursue this goal in any substantial way. In fact after this first Japanese version of Brecht, it took 21 years for Senda to return to Brecht. In 1940 all the *shingeki* companies, except Bungaku-za Theatre Company (Literary Theatre, 1937–), were forced to disband by an official order from the government, and Senda was subsequently imprisoned on several occasions.

ACT II: MAY 1953, TOKYO, JAPAN

SCENE: The Production of *Fear and Misery of the Third Reich* by Haiyu-za's Training School.

CHARACTERS: Senda Koreya and Haiyu-za Theatre Company.

SYNOPSIS: Brecht was rediscovered in Japan quite accidentally after the war in 1953. During the war years, Senda participated in establishing a new *shingeki* company called Haiyu-za (Actor's Theatre) in 1944, although he was prohibited by officials from appearing in public. Along with Bungaku-za, the only theatre company that was not ordered to be disbanded in 1940, Haiyu-za would become a major force in re-establishing a modern theatre tradition during the post-war period.

The seven years from 1945 to 1952 were a decisive period for *shingeki* practitioners. Their new beginning was based upon what they thought they had achieved before the war; and although they wanted liberation from the fascist domination, post-war everyday reality was extremely chaotic. They were, however quick to recover and to start a so-called Shingeki Joint Production which took place in December, 1945. That they chose to perform Chekhov's *The Cherry Orchard*, which had been one of *shingeki*'s favorites in the pre-war period was symbolic in many ways. Their choice indicated the direction, both theoretically and practically, of New Shingeki.

From the beginning of Tsukiji Shogekijo in 1924, Stanislavsky and the Moscow Art Theatre were considered a kind of "master" model. For *shingeki* practice, as I mentioned earlier, there were public and private struggles over which brand of modern European theatre practice *shingeki* should model itself on. There were those who emphasized the coalition with labor and other social movements and those who wanted to pursue a search for the equivalent of a playwright's theatre. In the 1930s, when a modified version of Soviet socialist realism was adapted as the official aesthetic by mainstream *shingeki* practitioners, some representative works in the vein of Japan's version of realistic theatre were produced. These later overshadowed the way *shingeki* practitioners chose to proceed after the war, which manifested itself in the Joint Production of *The Cherry Orchard*.[8]

Senda was at the center of Haiyu-za revitalizing the *shingeki* practice after the War. He survived a complex relationship with the Japan Communist Party and its cultural policies. The Party re-established itself immediately after the War (1945), and was eager to engage leftist *shingeki* practitioners to disseminate Marxist ideology among the masses. Senda successfully negotiated with the General Headquarters of the U.S. occupational forces in Tokyo (GHQ). In fact, it was GHQ, who summoned Senda and *shingeki* practitioners in October, 1945 told them to "fight against the old" and establish a "democratic" theatre tradition (Senda 1980a: 353). By tactfully negotiating with both the Communist Party and GHQ, Senda continued his radical project of establishing a leftist modern theatre tradition in Japan. For Senda this meant developing a European-style theatre production system.[9] Senda wanted the Haiyu-za theatre company to grow into a European-style theatre company, with its own space and training school. It was to be supported by patrons and diverse kinds of audience organizations. Before acquiring a theatre for Haiyu-za at the heart of Tokyo, Senda helped organize its training school in 1951 and for its second graduates, he decided to produce Brecht's *Fear and Misery of the Third Reich*, because he accidentally came across the text in a bookstore in Kyoto. He "chose the text not for its content but for its many scenes and characters which were quite convenient for the kind of production he wanted to do" (Senda 1985: 409). Senda wanted every graduating student to participate in the production and *The Third Reich* was the kind of play that would make that possible.

Senda's ideological ambiguities would later be critically interrogated by many (cf. Kan 1981a: 73–5), because 1950 was the year when the red purge policy of GHQ began to dominate political and cultural life. The fact that most members of Haiyu-za were not purged does not prove much. More importantly, directly political theatre activities usually referred to as *jiritsu engeki* (independent theatre), consisting of amateurs' and activists' theatre practices within actual working environments were systematically banned and erased by GHQ and by the Japanese government through the next decade. This drastic policy change of the occupational forces took place because of the Korean war. Most *shingeki* practitioners had to come to terms with the fact that liberation from the fascist government by the U.S. forces meant another kind of governmental control. Pre-war social and cultural structures and power relations (and actual political figures) were, for the most part, kept "alive." Most symbolic was the continuation of the emperor system by GHQ.[10] This, it was thought, would give stability to Japan as a newly appointed ally of the U.S. It was as if the social structure and agencies did not change at all, but were simply given different names.

Senda's main objective in those years was to "popularize" and to "professionalize" *shingeki* theatre practice (Senda 1980b: 333–6). What Senda meant by "popularize" was that he would solicit the help of providers/creators of professional cultural products for what he calls "mature adult" audiences. He worked hard to organize the "unenlightened" masses into appreciative "adults," as he was intent on providing good non-commercial theatre to the people. Senda was an "old leftist" theatre practitioner and, to that extent, he was political and his political project did have a certain validity and relevance at least in the first decade after the War.

Yet Senda wanted to establish a Western dramatic tradition in Japan in which Western modern drama was produced in what he thought to be authentic and even traditional ways, employing the Stanislavsky style of psychological realism.

In the program note he wrote for his production of *Third Reich* (1953), he notes:

> We decided to work on Brecht's *Fear and Misery of the Third Reich* not because we wanted to show an example of "Epic Theatre," or a "Learning Play." I am now seriously spending most of my time studying what is called "dramatic theatre" and "empathetic" acting techniques, therefore students who will be performing in this production are those who have been educated in that line of theory. (Senda 1976: 141)

According to Senda, Brecht's theory was the antithesis of the dominant Western dramatic tradition. As there was no such tradition in Japan, one had to be established before it could be criticized or overcome. Here we can observe the often-mentioned schizophrenic effect of the modernization of Japan, where Stanislavsky and Brecht were introduced almost simultaneously and as if they were not in contradiction.

Senda was very cautious about introducing Brecht even after this production, because "popularization" and "professionalization" of Haiyu-za, as was already mentioned, was his first concern. Brecht's theatrical ideas were too "unfamiliar" (Senda 1985: 411). Senda did continue to direct Brecht's plays not with the Haiyu-za Theatre Company but at other venues. The first production of Haiyu-za's Brecht had to wait until 1961 when Senda directed *The Good Person of Szechwan*. This was after *shingeki* practitioners actively protested the signing of Japan–U.S. Security Treaty in 1960.

ACT III: OCTOBER 1968, SHINJUKU, TOKYO, JAPAN

SCENE: The Shinjuku Riot by students at Shinjuku Station on International Students' Day.

CHARACTERS: Brecht in Japan, Senda Koreya, Inoue Hisashi (1934–), and Angura Theatre Practitioners, including Sato Makoto and the Black Tent.

SYNOPSIS: After a series of initial programmatic introductions of Brecht's work by Senda, Brecht was more widely disseminated in the 1960s. Senda had been translating Brecht's plays since 1953. These were later collected and published along with Brecht's stagings, as *Collected Plays by Bertolt Brecht* (5 volumes, 1961–2). Brecht's theoretical writings were slower to appear in translation, the first appearing in 1953, translated by Komiya Kozo. But it was not until Senda published *Can the Present-day World Be Reproduced by Means of Theatre: Brecht's Theatre Theories* (1962) that an "authoritative" translation of Brecht's theories appeared in Japan. With this book, Brecht became one of the most widely read authors not only among theatre practitioners, but also by political activists, philosophers, literary figures and other cultural producers.

In this context, it becomes very difficult to follow the whole spectrum of Brecht's influence in Japan. The main threads are: Senda's introduction of Brecht, mainly to *shingeki* practice, and the more subtle and complicated influence of Brecht on Angura theatre practice and its practitioners.

Although Japanese theatrical history of the 1960s is currently remembered for and mostly discussed in terms of the rise of the *angura* theatre movement, *shingeki* was still very active all through the decade. The failure of direct political activism against the Japan–U.S. Security Treaty in 1960 brought about a deep change in Japan's political climate. There was widespread disillusionment with the idealistic notion of socialist revolution. This change in the political climate took the form of a hegemonic struggle between the Old Left and the New Left, especially concerning organizing an effective resistance against renewed imperialistic alliance between Japan and the U.S. While prolific productions of the democratization narrative and of "modernization theory" were carried on by the authorities and the dominant cultural producers in many spheres, including academia and popular media, Japan as a whole was experiencing drastic social and economic changes. People became tamed citizens or "*shomin*," a word which came to mean, at least in some quarters, the newly emerging bourgeois class especially in cities like Tokyo. The 1960s was the time in which Japan's post-colonial and post-war national identity was established mainly through the process of economic growth (the income-doubling project by the ruling Liberal Democratic Party) and manifested in mainstream cultural products, such as commercial films and television dramas, which tended to emphasize Japan's cultural "tradition."

Interestingly enough, *shingeki* never became a mainstream cultural product. Major *shingeki* practitioners were seldom interested in newly discovered and/or invented Japanese "tradition." Most of them were still stuck to the idea of "Japanizing" what they had decided was Western modern theatre tradition. For Senda and his followers, at least, Brecht and Brechtian theory was still something to "study" rather than to "appropriate." This phase lasted almost forever. Senda established a "Brecht Study Group" within the Haiyu-za Theatre Company in 1963, that would be reorganized into his "Brecht's Group" in the next decade, which continued to exist from 1974 to about 1990. Therefore, Brecht's name was gradually becoming almost inseparable from Senda's in the 1960s, and in 1968, as if to prove his status as the major and the only Brechtian in Japan, Senda was invited to represent Japan in "Brecht Dialogue 1968" in East

Berlin. Brecht, therefore, continued to be perversely canonized by Senda and other *shingeki* practitioners. Brecht became classic, as Sato mentions in 1998, but not necessarily in a straightforward fashion. Brecht in Japan, as far as Senda was concerned, has always been displaced from the mainstream *shingeki* practice, as if to say Brecht is what Senda really wanted to do, but had to wait till the audience become more "mature."

Ironically enough, this perverse way of canonizing Brecht by displacing him from mainstream *shingeki* practice, which continued to identify itself against mainstream cultural producers and their products, made it possible for Brecht to be taken up by some newer generations of *shingeki* practitioners. Playwrights of the post-war generation such as Fukuda Yoshiyuki (1931–) and Miyamoto Ken (1926-88) started to write plays *against* the previous generation of *shingeki* practitioners, including Senda, with apparent Brechtian influence, creating overtly political plays especially after 1960, from the New Left ideological perspective. These plays were more subtle and self-reflexive in their notion of the political, using Brechtian epic theatre style and allegorical structure. Brecht in Japan, i.e., Brecht as a displaced political playwright and theatre theorist of the "alienation-effect," began to have a stronger impact on Japan's theatre culture than Senda's faithful introduction of his work. Diverse contemporary theatre practices included the emergence and rise of various kinds of contemporary "popular" theatre within and around *shingeki* and the other new trend that would later be categorized as the *angura* (underground) theatre movement. The former would accumulate in the person and work of Inoue Hisashi (1934–), one of the most popular playwrights in post-war Japan and a professed supporter of the Japan Communist Party, whose most recent work (*Kamiya-cho Sakura Hotel*) was chosen to be produced for the opening of the New National Theatre in 1997.[11] The latter would culminate in the work of Sato Makoto.

One of the formalistic characteristics of Inoue's line of playwriting is the concept of the musical play as a serious but "popular" art form. This is in opposition to other forms of commercial "popular" entertainment, such as imported and appropriated versions of American musical theatre. In fact, it is difficult to tell the difference. Inoue has a concrete image of whom he writes for and with: "*shomin*" of Japan. *Shomin* can be translated as commoners, but it can be more precisely defined as follows:

> It [*shomin*] refers to common masses. The notion of shomin is different from that of citizen or people in that the latter are conscious of their political position and their class under particular historical conditions. It is also different from the notion of unorganized masses in an industrialized society, or "common people," who are identified by anthropology as

> those who retain traditional life styles and indigenous culture. In short, shomin are "people who are unconsciously immersed in the conventional value system" (Hidaka Rokuro). But the notion of shomin emerges, in such expression as "shomin kankaku" (shomin's sensibilities), when intellectual discourses or governmental policies are felt to be so far away from the actual, in order to criticize those from a perspective of "seikatsu-sha" (actually living people). Because they are "shomin," leading their own "small" lives, without any recognizable social, financial, political status, they could have an actual meaning on such occasions. (*World Encyclopedia*, Heibon-sha)

The *shomin* class decisively became the dominant agency for ideology of post-war democracy toward the end of the 1960s. *Shingeki* still stuck to the notion of *taishu* – the unorganized masses in industrialized Japan – as the target audience that they would "educate" and "enlighten." Inoue's innovation was, coming from the *shingeki* tradition, with his experience in working as a writer in mass media, appropriating Brecht to devise his version of "popular theatre" in Japan. Most of his plays, including many of his music theatre works, have allegorical narratives, decisive humor, sentimental "good" scenes and mild political messages. It is not accidental that arguably his most Brechtian play, *Yabuhara Kengyo* (1973) won great critical acclaim. As this play abundantly demonstrates, Inoue was apparently against art theatre, political theatre, and commercial "popular" theatre all at once and wanted to provide *shomin* with what they thought they wanted. He was never avant-garde, politically active, nor commercially popular. He kept to a middle ground, as if to assert that it is the only site where the "true" notion of the popular can be constructed. Being mediocre, being in-between perhaps has been his strength all these years. As the first playwright to be presented at the New National Theatre in 1997, his "triumph" was echoed in the curious mediocrity of the production of *Buddha*, a play with music. The politics of Brecht in Japan has produced some very un-Brechitian results; his notion of the "popular" without any ideological echoes found the easiest and fastest way into Japan's theatre culture.

We are, however, still in 1968, when the *shomin* class is still almost invisible and Brecht in Japan is in the first phase of diverse appropriations by other theatre practitioners, most notably *angura* theatre practitioners, who made themselves quite visible by the end of the 1960s. Brecht, of course, was not their only reference; there was Artaud – *Theatre and Its Double* was already translated in 1965 as were works by Sartre and Beckett. Just as the *tsukiji shogekijo* theatre practitioners were faced with diverse "choices" at the beginning of their existence in 1924 – decontextualized and dehistoricized names, -isms, and writings were simultaneously imported – *angura* theatre practitioners, in an attempt to articulate their cultural and political positions, had to negotiate their theoretical, political, aesthetic, collective and personal concerns with layers and layers of information in the form of translations, journalistic and academic writings and so on. For *angura* theatre practitioners, immediacy of information was most important and the context in which ideas were imported and appropriated did have a serious effect on their understanding and use.

Brecht's name then was conceptualized as a kind of absolute canonical text in Japan's theatre culture by the middle of the 1960s, because, as we have seen, his name was inseparable from Senda's theatre practice. Brecht's political and aesthetic implications were considered authoritative and thus out-of-date when major *angura* theatre practitioners began to make themselves visible. Kara Juro (1940–) formed his Jokyo Gekijo (Situation Theatre) in 1963, and, as the name of his company indicates, his frame of reference was decisively Sartre and existentialist philosophy and aesthetics. Suzuki Tadashi (1939–) started his career directing some of Sartre's plays during his university days in the early 1960s, and participated in the formation of Waseda Shogekijo in 1967 with Betsuyaku Minoru, a playwright writing plays in the Beckettian absurdist tradition. It is more difficult to locate Terayama Shuji's (1935–83) sources of reference, but Brecht was not obviously one of them; in fact, he would later explicate his own theatre theory, as Nakajima Hiroaki brilliantly demonstrates (Nakajima 1997), *against* Brecht or at least, against what Terayama thought Brecht stood for.

Significantly, most initial *angura* practices were not overtly political. Politics were notably outside their performance spaces, especially toward the end of 1960s, for the renewal of the Japan–U.S. Security Treaty was approaching in 1970, with Japan's direct and indirect involvement with the Vietnam War. This time, however, the ontological formation of political activism was completely different from the previous decade, as the notion of orthodox Marxist revolution by underprivileged masses had become archaic; in 1960, the revolt was initiated by labor unions and university student organizations, but the Shinjuku Riot in 1968 was not really an organized riot. It was an accidental and spontaneous eruption of the unorganized energy of university students, and was so full of contradictions that its political content could not be easily articulated. The riot was more a cultural than political event. As Kan Takayuki appropriately describes, the riot made "the political a festive event" (Kan 1981a: 189), by which he meant that the notion of the political was drastically challenged at the end of the 1960s, after tremendous economic growth had been achieved.

It is interesting, therefore, that Kan, a major theorist and practitioner of *angura* theatre, sees the appropriation of Brecht as a major factor in this whole process. While referring to Sartre as the most important figure in the configuration of politics and aesthetics in *angura* theatre practice during the early 1960s, Kan includes Brecht as another important influence:

> Komiya Kozo's translation of Brecht's *Theatre Theories* was such a bad translation that one third of the whole book was almost incomprehensible; nonetheless, we attempted to read from that bad translation, what Brecht's critical theory was and what his alienation theory meant. There was a lot to learn from his alienation theory in terms of a general notion of the critical mind and how we should relate theory to praxis. But this was not enough to teach us a valid methodology for changing the theatrical language and the relationship between language and the body. . . . I must say our understanding of Brecht remained in the sphere of intellectual "recognition." But it was important for us that it reached the sphere of the level of physical expression. (Kan 1981b: 176–7)

Angura theatre practitioners were more interested in Brecht as a theorist than as a playwright. They were not naive enough to believe that they could "transplant" Brechtian theory as it is, whatever its meaning. Brecht was a resource for devising their own theories, from which they would go on to generate their respective theatrical performances. Kan's passage can be read as a confession that they failed to translate Brechtian theory, including its political aspect, into performance.

The notion of "alienation," nevertheless, did become a key concept for *angura* theorists and practitioners, including Kan. The meaning of "alienation" differs from one to the other. Yet none of them seems to have included the most important aspect of the "alienation effect", since it mostly seems to have remained for them within the realm of aesthetics. The "alienation effect" was used for what was understood as its shock value. Many *angura* theatre practitioners sought to revolutionalize theatrical language, especially physical language as the most effective means for the A-effect. At first very political in its aesthetic and historical implications, this newly devised theatrical language later became stabilized and its political implications were lost in the 1970s. In other words, most *angura* practitioners were not able to respond to the symbolic event of the Shinjuku Riot in 1968, in which the old notion of the political was drastically challenged. Both *angura* practitioners and the Shinjuku riot were political only because of their positions within the historical process. Around 1968 with a radical paradigmatic shift in theatre practices, the political began to be gradually displaced from Japan's theatre practices, which was nevertheless part of a political cultural process. During that process, the political Brecht was consensually erased from Japan's cultural memory and we were given Brecht, the great playwright.

EPILOGUE: JUNE 1969, TOKYO, JAPAN

SCENE: Jiyu Gekijo (Theatre of Liberty) and Rokugatsu Gekijo (Theatre of June) decide jointly to form the Engeki Center 68/69, which later became Center 68/71 (1971), and still later, the Black Tent Theatre Company (1990).

CHARACTERS: Sato Makoto and Members of the Black Tent Theatre Company. While most *angura* companies (Suzuki's Waseda Shogekijo, Kara's Red Tent, etc.) were lead by charismatic patriarchal figures, and their collectivity, consciously or not, almost always replicated Japan's typical familial structure, the Black Tent was, and still is, a theatre collective, faithfully reflecting the ideals of post-war democracy. Its structure is quite close to that of the European public theatre system, although they do not have an artistic director and they were not publicly funded until the late 1980s. Sato Makoto is undoubtedly a major figure in the collective, but there are also Saito Haruhiko (actor), Yamamoto Kiyokazu and Kato Tadashi (directors), and Tsuno Kaitaro, Saeki Ryuko, and David Goodman (all dramaturgs). Sato is a graduate from the Haiyu-za Training School, which Senda established, and most other practitioners are also directly from the *shingeki* tradition. Tsuno Kaitaro at the time was a member of Shin Nihon Bungaku (Alternative Japanese Literature), an important cultural site both for the Old Left and the New Left, in which Brecht was often discussed and written about since the beginning of the 1960s. Saeki, now a professor of French Literature at Gakushuin University, is an expert on French theatre. In short, most members are cultural elites who are well-informed about contemporary Euro-American theatre practices and theories and leftist political and cultural theories.

SYNOPSIS: The Black Tent theatre company during the late 1960s and early 1970s kept the many faces of Brecht we have been discussing operative. They were very conscious of their position within Japan's theatre culture, and, as a displaced successor of pre- and post-war *shingeki* practice, they tried to reinvent and reinscribe Brecht in Japan, negotiating Senda's Brecht, Inoue's "popularization" of Brecht, and other *angura* practices, including those inspired by Artaud and the Absurd.

Their slogan was "Theatre for Revolution" and in 1969, they issued a manifesto entitled "Communication Project No. 1," in which they promised to organize their theatre practice as a radical social movement. It included the notion of the Base Theatre, a permanent theatre space, with a repertory system, in Tokyo; the Migrating Theatre, a mobile theatre practice performing and sometimes doing workshops all over Japan; and publication and pedagogy. Accordingly, they started to perform their works all over Japan in their black tent. Their work was meant to be a serious response to what was happening in Europe and the U.S. around 1968. They naturally didn't mean Socialist revolution when they put "Theatre for Revolution" in their slogan. Rather they were concerned with revolutionizing and/or transforming the socio-political status quo through cultural experience, by establishing hybrid sites for resistance against dominant cultural practices. In 1968 Japan, however, was situated at a historical conjuncture that signaled the completion of the post-colonial moment and the process of reconstructing and restructuring national identity. In cultural practices, what H. D. Harootunian calls the "National Poetics," had by then become the dominant ideological device to "eliminate the realm of criticism that once belonged to the space of culture" (Harootunian 1993: 215–16).

In light of the concept of "National Poetics," the Black Tent's political project was destined to fail. Their conscious strategy of decentralization through diasporic journeys, therefore, was understood more often than not as the romantic political gesture of cultural elites. Before their project faded away, it provided the last vital moment for Brecht in Japan's theatre culture. Most notably, Sato's plays are rich examples of this; in his five serial plays with Nezumi Kozo Jirokichi (1969–71) as a protagonist/anti-hero – Jirokichi is a mythic robber in the Edo period, a chivalrous robber who robs the rich for the poor, and a transformation of Mack the Knife in *The Threepenny Opera* – and in his three serial plays entitled *Comedies: The World of Showa Trilogy* (1972–9), Sato and members of the Black Tent explored the possibility of historicizing twentieth century Japan, by appropriating many aspects of Brecht's work.

Abe Sada-Desires of Showa (1973) is the first play in *The World of Showa Trilogy*, and in it Sato uses only Weill's music for *The Threepenny Opera*, itself a very political gesture and perhaps most representative of Sato's reinvention of hybridized Brecht in Japan. Sato attempts to articulate the historical process by which the possibility of revolution has been systematically erased from Japan's public imagination. In devising an overtly allegorical narrative and using the epic theatre format, Sato transforms the actual 1930s' historical figure of Abe Sada, known for having cut off her lover's penis, into the symbolic by portraying the *shomin* class as representative of the status quo, while embodying the possibility of female sexual transgression. The real protagonist in this play, however, is a Showa Emperor, who is drastically demeaned into the timid leader of a small closed community. He is the one suffering from a castration complex/fantasy, the possibility of which is demonstrated by Abe Sada, and fearing that his penis will be cut by the people in the community, he declares martial law. Revolution is impending all through the play, but it never happens and the emperor enjoys a natural death at the end, some fifteen years later.

As I have shown, a political and cultural revolution was forever emerging all through the 1960s, but it never "happened." Sato's *Abe Sada* is an allegory of the 1960s. It is significant that Brecht in Japan revealed himself in such a manner, as he was exceptionally successful in inscribing himself within Sato's text, although he has to be (re)discovered, as I have been attempting to do, from a Harootunian "National Poetics," which urges us to forget and erase; to forget and erase the fact that history is willfully forgotten and cultural memory can be systematically and consensually erased.

The Black Tent returned to Brecht in their "Brecht Renaissance" project in the late 1980s and early 1990s (1989–93). In the intervening years, as if to correspond to Japan's neo-colonial economic invasion of other Asian countries, the Black Tent turned to Asia, via Brecht and Augusto Boal, and via their respective transplantation and appropriation by some Asian theatre practices. Notions of workshop and pedagogy, accordingly, have become more important in the Black Tent's theatre practice as well as the forming of alliances with other Asian theatre practitioners and practices. Their political project, however, has not been visible in Japan's theatre culture, because of its subtlety, its political ambiguities, and its apparent lack of recognition of specific historicity(ies) that each Asian country was then staging.

When the Black Tent came back to Brecht in the late 1980s, he was considered by some a "classic" playwright with the status of Shakespeare. Other theatre practitioners in Japan were more interested in producing Brecht's plays rather than using Brecht to reconfigure their theory and praxis. The younger generation of spectators either had never heard of Brecht or had only a very fixed image of him. Trapped between these radically demarcated positions and statuses within Japan's theatre culture, Brecht had to start "proving himself" after more than fifty years of his existence in Japan. Brecht's theatrical identity was at times fatally associated with those who tried to stage his plays. Ironically, the potential of his political perspective was mostly lost or not even a subject for radical theatre practitioners in Japan. Even after Brecht's centennial year, it is very difficult to feel his presence, ghosted or not, where I come from.

NOTES

1. In this article, when spelling the proper nouns of Japanese names, I will use the order usually used in the Japanese language; the family name first, and the first name last.
2. While I was writing this article, Kuriyama Tamiya was appointed the next artistic director of the New National Theatre, starting in the year 2000.
3. In this article, all the translations are mine, except the quote from H. D. Harootunian's article.
4. *Shingeki* literally means "new theatre," the word coined in the nineteenth

century, as opposed to the traditional forms such as Kabuki and No, identified as *kyugeki* (old theatre). See n. 5 for more detailed discussion of the notion of *shingeki*. As for the use of the terms *angura* (underground theatre) and "little theatre," there still is an ongoing controversy how we define these terms. *Angura* usually refers to a wide variety of radically new theatre practices emerging in the late 1960s. The term "Little Theatre Movement" came to be widely used in the 1980s, as the newer generations of theatre practitioners lost the sense of being "underground" though were still performing in small theatres. The "Little Theatre Movement" as a whole is supposed to include *angura* theatre but some critics do not agree. Newer practitioners and practices, they claim, lost the sense of being a movement, when they were no longer underground.

5. *Shingeki* at best is an ambiguous term. By definition, it is supposed to refer to all theatre practices which have nothing to do with traditional theatrical forms. In a more exclusive usage, it refers to modern theatre practices which were heavily influenced by equivalent Western (mostly European) theatre. Preceding *shingeki* companies such as Bungei Kyokai (Literary Association, 1906–13) and Jiyu Gekijo (Theatre of Liberty, 1909–19) are considered pioneering *shingeki* companies, but in my conception, Tsukiji Shogekijo was the first serious and influential attempt to transplant modern Western theatre practices in Japan, including their production system, acting style, and aesthetic and political concerns.
6. In pre-war *shingeki* practices, there was a conflict between politics and aesthetics. Tsukiji Shogekijo, for instance, was considered more aesthetic than political (that is why Senda left the company for Germany). As we will later see, while both positions were hypothetically integrated into one under the name of Socialist Realism during the 1930s, this radical binary operated in both *shingeki* practice and its theory even in the post-war period. It is usually understood that pioneering *shingeki* practitioners on both sides tried to imitate Western modern theatre practices; they wanted to look "as if" they were "Westerners" by using wigs and false noses. It may sound ridiculous now, but if you are familiar with Japan's traditional theatre culture, *shingeki*'s way of imitating "Westerners" was such a fictional, even fantastic "as if" style that it was not far from the exaggerated make-up and gestures of Kabuki. I therefore suspect that *shingeki*'s acting style might have an "alienation effect," as not so many audiences at the time were familiar with how "Westerners" looked and behaved. It may be more appropriate to understand *shigeki*'s way of "imitating" Western acting style as a hybridizing project of juxtaposing (essentialized) Japanese bodies with (idealized/exoticized) Western looks, gestures and behaviors. The same kind of theoretical inquiry should be made into how the "native" playwrights appropriated what they claimed to be the dramaturgy of Western psychological realism.
7. Japan's system for designating eras by years is called *gengo*. After the Meiji period, it was decided *gengo* would be according to the life of the emperor. When an emperor dies, new *gengo* are designated with the enthronement of the next emperor. Thus in the years covered in this article, Japan has had Meiji (1868–1912), Taisho (1912–26), Showa (1926–89) and Heisei (1989–) with four emperors. It is now customary to call emperors with *gengo* such as Meiji Emperor or Showa Emperor.
8. This joint production was possible by referring to the "origin" of *shingeki*. By referring to the pre-revolution rather than post-revolution Moscow Art Theatre (Chekhov and Stanislavsky) as their "origin" and theoretical model, the post-war *shingeki* practitioners, consciously or not, confessed

their ideological ambiguities. *The Cherry Orchard* was chosen as an obviously apolitical piece of work which different *shingeki* practitioners with different ideological backgrouds could agree on producing.

9. You may detect a certain degree of politically charged rhetoric in Senda's way of positioning himself within Japan's theatre culture. In his case, especially after the war, his politics were not so much about Marxist revolution, but a gradual democratization of the country. He did not want to mingle with the Communist Party or with GHQ. GHQ, accordingly, did not consider him to be "dangerous" to their policy in the post-war Japan, but rather to be a potential cultural agency for democratizing Japan.
10. The Emperor denied his divine lineage on 1 January 1946. It was to save him from being accused of his wartime responsibility. In the subsequent restructuring process of Japan's social and political system, the "definition" that the Emperor is just a "regular" human being was appropriated, as is cleared stated in the Japanese constitution, to reintroduce many pre-war "elements" (social institutions, personnel, and so on).
11. It may sound confusing. How is it possible that a play written by a professed supporter of the Japan Communist Party is chosen to be performed for the opening of the New National Theatre? First of all, the Japan Communist Party is a legitimate political organization, and anyone has a constitutional right to support it. Second and more importantly, Inoue has long been thought to be an anti-emperor system writer, but this new play, according to theatre critic Nishido Kojin was apparently written to "cunningly evade the issue of Showa Emperor's war responsibility" (Nishido 1998: 27) though it pretends to take up that very issue. The New National Theatre is the place, as Nishido also points out, where the emperor family are supposed to have all the rights to visit, and Inoue was given a chance to raise the issue of war responsibility, but he was not able to face the challenge.

REFERENCES

Brecht, Bertolt (1961–2) *Collected Plays by Bertolt Brecht* (5 vols), ed. Senda Koreya, translated into Japanese by Senda Koreyo, Kato Ei, Komiya Kozo, Uchigaki Keiichi, Iwabuchi Tatsuji, Tokyo: Hakusui-sha.

Harootunian, H. D. (1993) "America's Japan / Japan's Japan." In *Japan in the World*, ed. Masao Miyoshi and H. D. Harootunian, Durham: Duke University Press, 196–221.

Ibaragi, Ken (1973) *Shingeki Sho-shi* (*A Short History of Shingeki*), Tokyo: Mirai-Sha.

Kono Takashi (1998) "Brecht Seitan Hyaku-shunen – Gendaisei Mi naosu Engekijin" ("Brecht's Centennial – Theatre People are Rethinking Brecht's Contemporaneity"), *Nihon Keizai Shinbun* (*The Japan Economy Newspaper*) (9 Sept.), 40. Tokyo: The Nihon Keizai Shinbun-sha.

Kan Takayuki (1981a) *Sengo Engeki* (*Post-war Theatre*), Tokyo: Asahi Shinbun-Sha.

——— (1981b) *Zoku Kaitaisuru Engeki* (*Decomposing Theatre 2*), Tokyo: Renga-shobo Shin-sha.

Nakajima Hiroaki (1997) "Brecht to Terayama Shuji (Brecht and Terayama Shuji)," *Doitsu Engeki – Bungaku no Mangekyo* (*German Theatre – Kaleidoscope of*

Literature), Tokyo: Dogaku-sha, 191–208.

Nisido, Kojin (1998) "Mondai to Shiteno 90 Nendai Engeki (Theatre Culture in the 1990s as a 'Problem')," *Teatro* (Aug. 1998), 25–9. Tokyo: Teatro-sha.

Ozasa, Yoshio (1990) *Nihon Gendai Engeki-shi* (*The History of Japanese Contemporary Theatre*), vol. 3, Tokyo: Hakusui-sha.

Senda, Koreya (1975) *Mo Hitotsu no Shingeki-shi: Senda Koreya Jiden* (*An Alternative History of Shingeki – An Autobiography*), Tokyo: Chikuma-shobo.

——— (1976) *Nijju-seiki Engeki: Brecht to Watashi* (*The Twentieth Century Theatre – Brecht and I*), Tokyo: Yomiuri Sinbun-sha.

——— (1980a) "Kaisetsu-teki Zuiso 1945–49 (An Explanatory Essay: 1945–49)," *Senda Koreya Engeki Ronshu* (*Collected Theatre Writings of Senda Koreya*), vol. 1, Tokyo: Mirai-sha, 343–92.

——— (1980b) "Kaisetsu-teki Zuiso 1950–54 (An Explanatory Essay: 1950–54)," *Senda Koreya Engeki Ronshu* (*Collected Theatre Writings of Senda Koreya*), vol. 2, Tokyo: Mirai-sha, 329–84.

——— (1985) "Kaisetsu-teki Zuiso 1955–59 (An Explanatory Essay: 1955–59)," *Senda Koreya engeki Ronshu* (*Collected Theatre Writings of Senda Koreya*), vol. 3, Tokyo: Mirai-sha, 335–445.

Tezuka Osamu (1984) "In Completing the Work," *Buddha*, vol. 14, Tokyo: Kodansha.

21

THE ACTOR'S INVOLVEMENT: NOTES ON BRECHT – AN INTERVIEW WITH JOSEPH CHAIKIN

Erika Munk

CHAIKIN: I'd like to start with a quotation from Brecht –

> The problem holds for all art, and it is a vast one . . . which can be expressed so: How can the theatre be both instructive and entertaining? How can it be divorced from spiritual dope traffic and turned from a home of illusions to a home of experience? How can the unfree, ignorant man of our century, with his thirst for freedom and his hunger for knowledge, how can the tortured and heroic, abused and ingenious, changeable and world-changing man of this great and ghastly century obtain his own theatre, which will help him to master the world and himself?

This fairly well sums up the kind of questions Brecht forces the actor to face – the most important and most difficult ones.

MUNK: To start with such questions is somewhat overwhelming; let me narrow them down. Can Brecht's theatre instruct and entertain an American audience? And how should American actors approach Brecht's theatre so that it becomes effective?

CHAIKIN: Brecht is a great teacher and dramatist. He wrote things which we now must find ways of performing, and he wanted to talk to, or create, revolutionaries. But today's revolutionaries, in this country at least, are not interested in formal expression, least of all words. People are becoming adults in an absurd time when the extinction of the human race is table talk. People are rejecting the savings-account-of-experience and living now – there is nothing outside the moment. But Brecht's plays and his own directing are severely formal, meticulously worked out and pared down. The need is to find a stage behavior that could engage us and be true to Brecht. Otherwise we will all, young and older, fall into deeper silence. Brecht engages man ethically by making him think, but the whole mind-blasting thing represents no thinking. Let alone theatre-going.

MUNK: What about by-passing the theatres and taking Brecht to the audience, in the streets or parks?

CHAIKIN: Though he didn't intend it, Brecht's plays are too sophisticated for such a theatre, where all points have to be made very loudly and broadly.

MUNK: Even the *Lehrstücke*?

CHAIKIN: I wasn't thinking of them, because I don't believe he wrote the purely didactic works to mean anything beyond his own time. They wouldn't be either entertaining or meaningful now. They're political in a very precise way – but hippies, for example, think that no matter what side you're on, once you're in the argument you're in the ring, and you ought to keep out of it. Meanwhile the new left people would find the political terms of the *Lehrstücke* irrelevant, and the militant don't want to listen to anyone but themselves.

MUNK: You may be doing a Brecht production in the next few months; do you think about where it will be done and what kind of people you'd like to have come to it?

CHAIKIN: No, Peter Brook was advising me about that, and he said that in the theatre we are deprived of the satisfaction of an immediate sense of an effect from our work. Even if you do a political piece you can't see a pebble fall here and a ripple appear there. Perhaps in the theatre of parks and demonstrations, but not in one which is open just to a given paying public, which unfortunately is the only thing now feasible for a major Brecht play – say, *Mother Courage*.

MUNK: In this context, how do you want to see Brecht performed?

CHAIKIN: You have to start with why he's important, beyond the fact that he wrote good plays. Then you must depart from the theories and from the museum aura around him, and build a way of subverting, infiltrating, hopefully altering, the consciousness of the audience. Just communicating messages is almost as boring as pure self-expression. Brecht's theatre is largely a propaganda theatre, and if the means that he used aren't useful now, the way they may have been, then others have to be used. If you think these pieces are worth it, as I do.

MUNK: Why do you?

CHAIKIN: Below the messages, he is full of inquiries, of irony, continually saying, "Look at this action, it's not as it appears!" Brecht would have been the perfect member of the Living Theatre, one who wants to understand how to live, how man should be to man. There are questions of man to dream, as in Pirandello, and man to thought, as in Shaw, but Brecht is concerned with man to man. Though he probably didn't succeed in living well with other people any better than most of us do.

MUNK: You were acting with the Living Theatre when they did their Brecht productions in New York, before they went to Europe. How did they, and you, approach him?

CHAIKIN: Well, we did two major Brecht productions. The first, *Jungle of Cities*, doesn't really ask of the actor what the later works do. You go about it with a tension similar to that with which you go about, oh, something between a naturalistic writer and Ionesco. *Man is Man* is a different story. We decided on the Nellhaus adaptation, and then wrote to East Berlin and got a complete run-down on how the actors should work, what the values should be, and so on. Julian Beck read these aloud, we talked about it at length, tried it as best we could, and found that it remained theory, unable to become an active working process – though we made great efforts.

MUNK: Looking back, was the problem in the theory or in the company?

CHAIKIN: We had just so many weeks for rehearsal, and not enough laboratory time. After the show opened and had run for a while, however, we came to discover some of the values we hadn't understood through the theory alone.

MUNK: Did the production change then?

CHAIKIN: Yes, mainly in that we developed a real confrontation with the audience.

MUNK: Did this affect the way you played Galy Gay?

CHAIKIN: I went through a personal transformation. I had been at the Living Theatre for a while and had done many things – *The Connection* and so on – and I was interested in a very fancy career for myself as an actor. I thought the opportunity to play this terrific role would give me all the chance in the world to further this career, and I had an agent and a personal manager and a lot of projects waiting. But in doing the role every night, saying the lines, finding my own involvement with the play, I changed little by little. Like Galy Gay. And I couldn't go back to those aspirations. But one thing I know is that Brecht has a terrific suspicion of principles and ideas. It's the real person, who takes up a volume of space, that he is concerned about. And a lot of idealists won't bring you a band-aid when you're bleeding.

MUNK: Was your approach to acting changed, as well as your idea of your career?

CHAIKIN: All of it. I started to think about some of those theories, even when I was on stage. I've read Marowitz and Esslin, and the others who say that the theories aren't true, that people are moved to the end of *Mother Courage* and so there isn't really any alienation and the actors are just actors. I don't think that's so.

MUNK: Was this particularly obvious when you compared Brecht to the Stanislavsky-ish training you and most American actors have had?

CHAIKIN: Stanislavsky was a director who directed other people's plays. Brecht mainly directed his own plays, and always kept foremost the idea of the entire play. When the actor scores his role in most plays, he is constantly concerned with the stakes of his character. He supports his actions by the character's motivations, and is hardly involved with the whole. The moment-to-moment reality is a circle of concentration that includes only the other characters, and he is unselfconscious in relation to the audience. What is radical in Brecht is the requirement that the actor as a private person be deeply concerned with the subject matter of the play. He is on stage within the given circumstances, but also sharing with the audience a response to the character's predicament.

MUNK: If in the Stanislavsky system the actor's attention is always on the character's needs, where should it be in Brecht?

CHAIKIN: If I am playing Galy Gay, which self is inside the disguise of the character? It is an actor, involved with the stakes of the play, not with total identification of himself and the character. The actor's attention, which might otherwise be on the character, is here connected to the spectator. Moment to moment the play is between actor and audience, as the actor's attitude changes about the character and his circumstances. The audience is the actor's partner as he plays the role of the character for the other characters. Yet the actor should not – and does not have to – wink, woo, or pander to the audience: there is a tacit understanding. The actor, as his character, is sincere in relation to the other actors but performing in relation to the audience.

MUNK: A specific example?

CHAIKIN: Brecht was not concerned with the presentation of the inner life, but with the deed. Three soldiers bribe Galy Gay with a box of cigars. He resists the offer, then he capitulates. The audience should clearly see, first, the ploys of the soldiers and Galy Gay's dilemma, and, second, the point at which this innocent can't say no. The four actors share the action. Each actor's focus is the "bribe." The particular choices each makes come out of exploring the forces which move the action toward Galy Gay's capitulation. There is no interest in playing details of the character which are irrelevant to the "bribe."

MUNK: How are the actor's choices made?

CHAIKIN: First, accept Brecht's assumption that what takes place in the world takes place within yourself and that a person is connected to whatever takes place in the world. Then appreciate how Brecht's theories came about, and depart from them. For having understood the first premise, you will be faithful to Brecht's intentions.

MUNK: How does that premise function when you're actually working?

CHAIKIN: It takes the shape of moral things that I can't stop thinking about. Like the sense of what I'm doing when I think something's perfectly innocent, but it's really exploiting people, because that's the social set-up. In what way am I perpetuating this set-up, and how is it possible not to perpetuate it? And then, a sense of anger and frustration that even "hatred against injustice make the brow grow stern."

MUNK: How do alienation effects fit into this?

CHAIKIN: The whole notion of the V-effect is distorted in America because actors think "distance" means "not caring." Quite the contrary. Whether or not Mother Courage bargains too long over Swiss Cheese's ransom, whether Grusha will take the infant aristocrat – these are actions with consequences of which the actor, like the audience, is aware. The V-affect is a means of presenting these events so that the audience can have an unsentimental view of them. It is anything but indifference. The difficulty is that our actors truly care about so little, and frequently are so uninterested in social questions.

Yet Brecht's techniques of allegory, song, impersonation, humor on 10 levels, viable theatrical invention, are all there to illuminate the seriousness of the choices facing men. If the actor is involved with the moral arguments of the play, acting at a distance has the power of spotlighting the forces at work, though it *should* be difficult for the actor to distance himself from something in which he is passionately involved – if two people nearly burn to death in a fire, their retelling in no matter how detached a way, is different from that of two people who are trying to arouse in themselves the fantasized dread and peril of being in a burning house. Yet even at moments of greatest crisis, the actor must be relaxed muscularly – no display of strain must deflect the audience's attention from the problems at hand.

MUNK: I've been told that the actors at the Berlin Ensemble achieve this . . .

CHAIKIN: I long to see one of their productions. I've been there, met the people, seen rehearsals, but I've always been playing in West Germany at night. Judging from rehearsals, the particular choices in their productions are arrived at through so much inquiry that they seem the definite choices. Yet the gestures remain volatile and expressive.

MUNK: This contradicts all those criticisms that the Ensemble treats Brecht's work like the Soviets treat Lenin's body – rigor mortified.

CHAIKIN: Well, there is a problem, but it's not quite like that. I was talking to some people who had seen a couple of productions and said to me that it was staggering, it made everything else seem so amateur. But then they began to describe the productions to me. Brecht would have hated what they said. They said, oh! the way this man came out with his hair painted silver and he never left the stage but as the play progressed it changed into something else, just like a magic trick!

MUNK: That was in *Coriolan*?

CHAIKIN: Yes. All the points they brought home were points that Brecht would have hated people carrying away from the theatre.

MUNK: Can we learn anything from the Ensemble?

CHAIKIN: There is only an analytical interest in doing Brecht as they do it, except for their own company. Like, when I was talking to an actor there, I asked him, what do you think about to start? And he said, the thing we think about first is, what socio-economic class the character is involved in. If any actor in America asked himself that as his first question, he'd go completely dry, but it galvanizes the Ensemble actor into a kind of excitement and vigor. The stakes are entirely different here, no matter whether you're in the Open Theatre or the Actors Studio.

MUNK: Do you use *any* Brechtian approaches in the Open Theatre's exercises and training?

CHAIKIN: Not directly. But there's some kind of relationship, because I am imprinted with Brecht in my own mind. There is no precise technical influence.

Maybe we should go back to the subject of producing Brecht's plays in this country, something which you can't discuss without talking about the theatre scene here. It's like you can't plant rhubarb in certain kinds of soil. The people who put Brecht on may start with something else in mind, but suddenly they're just putting on another play. Rehearsal time is limited, and no room is left for real inquiry, real exploration of the choices. The audience is the same people paying the same prices as always. And the critics are frozen into their set of responses. I have never known a case where a critic's response to actors, directors, or writers has expanded or encouraged their talent – I *have* known cases where, by panning or praising, the critic had crushed or discouraged creative inspiration. That's why I feel about critics the way I feel about the Administration. The producers cater to them, and perpetuate the problem. It's like nobody has any choice.

MUNK: Can we get out this bind?

CHAIKIN: If investors take a different relation to the things they invest in, which means if people have a different relationship to money.

MUNK: Then we have to revolutionize society before we can perform Brecht's radical plays?

CHAIKIN: That's one hang-up with direct political theatre, where the issues are addressed. (And why, incidentally, I think that political films are usually more effective.) Maybe things can be put in perspective if we think about a political theatre where subjects instead of issues are addressed – like the Living Theatre.

The similarity in the acting values of Brecht and Stanislavsky is obvious when they are compared with the radical exploration of voice, movement, and behavior now being made in theatre laboratories in London, New York, Minneapolis, San Francisco, Berlin, Paris, Milan, Poland. These groups work in sessions that are not classes (where what is taught is already known by the teacher) or rehearsals (which are preparations for a planned production). They've gone on to oriental theatre, yoga, Artaud; and the discipline has shifted from reality to subjectivity. Actors play images as in a dream, men as primal creatures. There are disembodied voices, zombies, cartoons, gods, machines. There is a sense of alarm, a rediscovery of joy. The premise is that we represent ourselves falsely even when we are most sincere, and thus that to play characters as we play ourselves limits the imagination. They all agree that we are stunned creatures living in an untenable world.

MUNK: Wouldn't Brecht agree?

CHAIKIN: He had the sense of alarm, but there's not much joy in Brecht, not even in the songs – which is one reason he's hard for the young audience to approach. Brecht was writing in a joyless world.

MUNK: Aren't we?

CHAIKIN: He felt it directly, he fled it, while we feel it like a cancer growing and growing, which we can't leave behind. Yet perhaps this makes Brecht's work all the more necessary, *if* we can find techniques for bringing it to the young. Our circumstances are very different from Brecht's time, but the bullshit is largely the same, and while liberal and reactionary have wildly opposing views, they lead identical lives. A person is who he pretends to be. All the while I put off taking any action for or against what I see, my life recedes before me.

It passes. It passes. It passed. Brecht's works are intended to be a call to action – action as a form of choice, choice based on what I see. As Laing said in *The Politics of Experience*:

> If we are stripped of experience, we are stripped of our deeds; and if our deeds are, so to speak, taken out of our hands like toys from the hands of children, we are bereft of humanity. We cannot be deceived. Men can and

do destroy the humanity of other men, and the condition of this possibility is that we are interdependent. We are not self-contained monads producing no effects on each other except our reflections. We are acted upon, changed for good or ill, by other men; and we are agents who act upon others to affect them in different ways. Each of us is the other to the others.

22

BRECHTIAN THEORY AND AMERICAN FEMINIST THEATRE

Karen Laughlin

In tracing the roots of American feminist theatre, critics have emphasized the importance of the Off-Off-Broadway theatre movement of the 1950s and 1960s, in which many of today's feminist theatre practitioners took an active part. In the work of groups like the Open Theatre, women found political interests and experimental techniques compatible with their own.[1] Perhaps because of the obvious historical links between these groups and the feminist theatre of the 1970s, little attention has so far been paid to the role of Brecht's plays or theories as models and inspiration for women playwrights.[2] Yet Brecht's work has also played a significant part in shaping the emergent feminist theatre in the United States. Individual playwrights, feminist theatre groups, and other women who have assumed leadership roles in the contemporary theatre have linked their work with Brecht's in a variety of ways.

Beyond showing an obvious appreciation for Brecht's plays, American women have found three principal aspects of Brecht's evolving theatre aesthetic particularly useful in the development of a theatre which "privileges the experiences of women, illustrates their oppression or shows opportunities for liberation."[3] Brecht's comments on acting and the actor–audience relationship have been incorporated in the search for a feminist acting style and related efforts to highlight the oppressive nature of gender distinctions. The argument for the 'historicizing' of dramatic events has aided women eager to reclaim and re-examine history from a woman's perspective while at the same time revealing the social and political forces at work in shaping women's destinies. And, finally, the structuring devices and narrative methods of "epic theatre," as developed by both Brecht and Erwin Piscator, have been useful to feminists seeking to move away from realism towards a presentational style more relevant to women's experiences. In borrowing from Brecht, however, feminist theatre practitioners have often adapted his theories to suit the unique perspective and demands of feminist dramaturgy.

In her diary for 28 December 1949, Judith Malina wrote, ". . . read Brecht's *Good Person of Setzuan*. A good play, but it's difficult to do parable propaganda theatre."[4] Though she may have found it difficult, Malina went on to stage powerful productions of Brecht's *He Who Says Yes and He Who Says No* in 1951 and his *Antigone* in 1967. While Malina was bringing Brecht to the attention of New York theatre audiences (and of those women coming under the influence of "new theatre" groups like Malina and Julian Beck's Living Theatre), women, who were finally beginning to assume directorial roles in American regional theatre, were putting Brecht's plays on the stage, Nina Vance, for example, opened her new Alley Theatre playhouse in Houston with Brecht's *Galileo* in 1962, while in the previous year Zelda Fichandler, a key figure in the regional theatre revolution, opened a new theatre in Washington, DC with the first American professional production of *The Caucasian Chalk Circle*.[5]

Other theatre groups have not only staged but have also adapted Brecht's plays. In 1973 the American Alive and Trucking Theatre Company adapted *The Exception and the Rule*, staging it along with their own piece, *Ally, Ally, All Come Free*. In the same year, on the other side of the Atlantic, London theatre audiences saw an adaptation of Brecht's *The Mother* by feminist playwright Pam Gems. Three years later another American group, At the Foot of the Mountain, produced *Raped: A Woman's Look at Brecht's "The Exception and the Rule*." The title of this piece suggests less an adaptation than a critique of Brecht's play. Yet even this example indicates the extent to which contemporary feminist playwrights and theatre groups have been not only aware of but also influenced by Brecht's work. In the words of playwright and director Roberta Sklar, who herself directed *The Good Person of Szechwan* while in graduate school, "Like anyone I have ever known who became seriously involved with a Brecht play, I was changed by it."[6]

Not all of the women and groups who have worked with Brecht's plays have commented so explicitly about the influence of his work on theirs. Yet both the dramatic works and the theoretical statements of several feminist theatre practitioners suggest that these groups have both adopted and adapted a Brechtian acting style. Like Brecht, they have sought a style of acting designed to reveal the workings "as well as the machinery of society which surround the modern playgoer in his daily life, so that the playgoer will *notice* . . . and criticize and change them not simply accept them as inevitable."[7]

American feminist theatre's debt to this aspect of Brechtian theory can be seen in Karen Malpede's comments on the work of three feminist theatre groups based in New York: Emmatroupe, established by Eleanor Johnson and Judith Kataloni in 1975; The Women's Experimental Theatre, which was founded by Clare Coss, Sondra Segal, and Roberta Sklar in 1977; and the New Cycle Theatre, founded by Karen Malpede and Burl Hash in 1977. According to Malpede, "Each of these theatres . . . seeks a way of speaking that is also a way of hearing. The audience for each is meant to see the actor understanding . . . the new truths she or he has uttered. The shock of recognition unites audience and actors, and each group is simultaneously moved toward an emotional understanding of the next world action."[8] In Malpede's view, then, these groups develop something very much akin to the empathy between *actor* and spectator Brecht praises in his essay on "Alienation Effects in Chinese Acting," a relationship in which the "performer's self-observation . . . stopped the spectator from losing himself in the character completely . . . Yet the spectator's empathy was not entirely rejected. The audience identifies itself with the actor as being an observer, and accordingly develops his attitude of observing or looking on."[9] Malpede's comment on the participants' "understanding of the next world action" likewise echoes Brecht's insistence that this style of acting should lead the audience to see the possibility for action in the world outside the theatre.

It is difficult to document the actual practice of such an acting style by other feminist theatre groups given the ephemeral nature of theatrical performances. Interestingly, though, a number of feminist playwrights have attempted to write the double role of the Brechtian actor – as the character and as the actor observing and judging the character's actions – into their scripts. Most frequently this involves the use of either role reversals or cross-gender casting.

Myrna Lamb's 1969 parable play, *But What Have You Done For Me Lately?*, provides an instructive early example of this technique. In this play, a pregnant man begs a female doctor to abort a fetus that has been implanted in him against his will. The double role, of course, arises from putting the man in "*the* position usually assumed to be female" and associating his response with that of the many actual "women faced with the prospect of an unwanted child."[10] In so doing, Lamb lays bare the social forces underlying the anti-abortion argument. The man's medically engineering pregnancy strips away the idea of motherhood as "natural" and inevitable while his confusion and terror bring into sharp focus the hardships brought upon women by what Lamb describes as "a society dominated by righteous male chauvinists of both sexes who identified with the little clumps of cells and gave them precedence over the former owners of the host bodies."[11]

In *Babes in the Bighouse*, a docudrama about life inside a women's prison, Megan Terry and Jo Ann Schmidman took the Brechtian acting style a step further. In their own 1974 production of the play at the Omaha Magic Theatre, the authors cast both men and women in the roles of the female prisoners and prison matrons, an act which "led the entire company to a more rigorous study of 'women's speech patterns, their physical and emotional behaviours and just how it is to be a women'."[12] This technique, like Lamb's role reversal, underlines a key discovery of contemporary women playwrights; the inability of male spectators to hear and truly understand what female characters are saying and doing. As Terry and her company observed, "men are socialized to respond to a male body and a male voice; from an early age they seem to be trained to discount what women say". Hence the value of "alienating" actor and character through cross-gender casting: "by putting a man in a dress, in the same constraints as the women characters in the play, it became clear to the men in the audience what women were up against."[13]

But in addition to simply gaining the empathy of male spectators, this technique underlines the socially constructed nature of gender distinctions, leading the audience to "accept from the all-female context of the women's prison that our perceptions of gender are based on social roles, gestures and styles."[14] Terry and Schmidman enhanced this revelation through the use of Brechtian *Gestus*, in a scene involving a giant hypodermic needle used to subdue a particularly rebellious prisoner. As she brandishes the needle, threatening the prisoner, Teresa, with the painful injection, the doctor urges her "to become a lady so that we can help you."[15] With this *Gestus* the playwrights show – in the Brechtian sense – the process of female socialization and its painful impact on the women subjected to it.

In its use of masks to highlight the distance between the actor-character and his or her social roles, Martha Boesing's *River Journal* recalls Brecht's *Good Person of Szechwan.* Boesing's play was first produced by the feminist theatre collective, At the Foot of the Mountain, which she helped found in 1974, and which also produced the adaptation of Brecht's *The Exception and the Rule* discussed above. In *River Journal*, Boesing explores the two principal roles she sees as available to women within patriarchal marriage. The play opens with a wedding ceremony, in which the protagonist, Ann, is given in marriage to a mild and loving man named Myles. Ann's sisters, Vera and Carla, give her exaggerated masks of themselves as a wedding gift. Unlike Ann, who feels trapped and unhappy in her marriage, the two sisters have little trouble relating to Myles; Carla (the nurturing "earth mother") cooks for him and helps him keep track of his belongings while Vera (the coquette or vamp) flatters and eventually seduces him. As her situation becomes desperate, Ann finally dons the masks and takes on each sister's persona, promising, "I'm gonna to be a good wife to you, Myles. I'm gonna do it right."[16] But a horrifying fantasy in which she kills and dismembers her sisters finally leads Ann to discover that the roles symbolized by her sisters' masks are pure invention. As a figure who combines Ann's mother and an avenging Snake Goddess assures her:

> SNAKE/MOM: They're not real, Annie. You made them up. Just like I did before you and just like all the women did and still do who live in a world ruled by men. (*Pause*..) 'Cause it's the only way we know how to survive.[17]

In terms of Brechtian "alienation", the mask device in Boesing's play functions much as it does in *The Good Person of Szechwan.* In both instances, the mask distances the actor-character from the role he or she adopts in order to survive in the given society. The audience, then, is invited not only to recognize these roles as pure inventions (though of undeniable power) but also to examine the social conditions which have caused the characters to take on these alternative identities. For both Brecht's Shen Teh and Boesing's Ann, the masks are necessary for survival within the dominant social systems (of either capitalism or patriarchal marriage) presented in each play. But whereas Shen Teh drops the mask of Shui Ta only when compelled to do so in the trial scene, near the end of *River Journal* Ann purposefully burns the masks which cripple her in an elaborate ritual overseen by Snake. While Ann's alternatives are left unspecified (as are Shen Teh's), Boesing shows her heroine discarding the roles patriarchy has imposed on her as she moves away from her husband and towards the strongly feminine river of her play's title. Audience members, however, are still reminded of the need to duplicate Ann's act of liberation in their own lives as Boesing ends her play with a typically Brechtian call to action:

> ALL (*sing*): The die is cast,
> The dead no longer singing.
> What's done is done.
> The pendulum is swinging.
>
> The question is laid out
> For each of us to ask:
> Whether to hold on
> Or to drop the mask.[18]

Brechtian acting is, of course, closely bound up with Brecht's notion of historicization as a related means of distancing the dramatic events and helping the audience to see the specific and changeable conditions shaping a character's situation. In his "Short Description of a New Technique of Acting" Brecht writes,

> The actor must play the incidents as historical ones. Historical incidents are unique, transitory incidents associated with particular periods. The conduct of the persons involved in them is not fixed and "universally human"; it includes elements that have been or may be overtaken by the course of history, and is subject to criticism from the immediately following period's point of view.[19]

Joan Schenkar's 1979 play, *Signs of Life*, incorporates such historicization in its exploration of the power relations between men and women in nineteenth-century America. Developed and performed under the auspices of the Women's Project at the American Place Theatre, this play interweaves historical "fact" and literary fantasy. P.T. Barnum, Henry James, James's sister, Alice, and Alice's real-life companion, Katherine Loring, are placed alongside two quasi-historical figures: an "Elephant

Woman" named Jane Merritt, modelled on the actual "Elephant Man," and Dr Simon Sloper, who bears the name of one of James's literary creations but wields the "Uterine Guillotine . . . invented and named by the founder of American gynecology."[20]

The principal action of Schenkar's drama takes place on centre stage, in a room occupied alternately by Alice James and Jane Merritt. Here we see parallel scenes demonstrating the oppressive and invasive manipulation of both women by the play's male characters. Jane is put on display as a freak by Barnum and is used by Sloper for a series of medical experiments. Alice's nervous disorder, as well as the breast cancer that eventually kills her, also brings her under Dr Sloper's questionable care, though she is able to fend off his offer to "strike at the root of the evil" in her body by removing all of her female organs with his Uterine Guillotine.[21] She is less successful in resisting the attacks of her brother, portrayed as a kind of artistic vampire, who first plagiarizes and then burns Alice's treasured journal.[22] The parallels between Jane and Alice, both in some sense frail and dependent on the men who abuse while pretending to care for them, indicate a pattern of exploitation that is woven throughout the fabric of Victorian society.

Schenkar enhances the audience's awareness of this pattern by framing these scenes with an elaborate tea ceremony taking place on the stage apron. Here Mr James, Dr Sloper, and occasionally P.T. Barnum intersperse the banal conversation accompanying afternoon tea with more passionate discussions of facts and feelings surrounding the play's female protagonists. The tea ceremony itself provides "historical" distance from the events unfolding on centre stage in that the tea time discussions are all set in a period after the unfortunate deaths of Alice and Jane. As they narrate many of the events in the women's lives, the three men also reveal the attitudes shaping Victorian America's "perverse fascination and horror toward women."[23] With its surface restraint and gentility and its underlying intensity of negative emotion toward women, the tea-time ritual performs a key function of Brecht's "historicizing theatre." As it "concentrates entirely on whatever in this perfectly everyday event is remarkable, particular, and demanding inquiry," this scene "demonstrate[s] a custom which leads to conclusions about the entire structure of a society at a particular (transient) time."[24]

But in addition to pointing out historically significant forces and relationships at work in the past, Brechtian historicization is of course intended to suggest the continued impact of the dramatized conditions in other historical periods. In *Signs of Life*, Schenkar seems to be aiming at just such an effect when she speaks of her desire to instil in the audience "a constant and nervous recollection of familiarity, a shudder of recognition" at the shared "prejudices and inclinations" of her nineteenth-century characters.[25]

This confrontation of past and present is even more forcefully conveyed in the Women's Experimental Theatre's *Electra Speaks*, which draws on Western literary history in exploring the roots of patriarchy's silencing of women. *Electra Speaks* is the third part of the Women's Experimental Theatre's *Daughters Cycle*, a trilogy of plays focused on women within the family. But, whereas the trilogy's first two parts situate their daughters, sisters, and mothers in the present day, *Electra Speaks* turns to the ancient world and picks up the figures of Electra, Clytemnestra, Iphigenia, Cassandra, and Athena from ancient Greek literature and myth.

The play opens with a recitation of "the old story", the story of the House of Atreus as dramatized in Aeschylus' trilogy, the *Oresteia*, Electra's recorded voice, which narrates the familiar account of the sacrifice of Iphigenia by her father, Agamemnon, and the series of murders subsequently committed to avenge previous slayings, is accompanied by "a series of transforming physical and vocal images" that first illustrate and then question what happened to the women in the classical myth.[26] Later scenes employ a variety of additional techniques to dramatize the contradictions between the roles laid out for these women and their underlying, patriarchal assumptions. The tag "They say," for example, indicates the patriarchal voice's canonical version of each women's experience: "They say she did it for the glory of Greece," says Iphigenia. But, she continues, "they don't say she was a young women murdered by her father./They don't say anything about her relationship with her mother./ . . . Everything is what they say./We don't know the ways in which she resisted."[27]

Brecht's suggestion that the actor historicize his actions and remarks by speaking in the third person is given an ingenious twist here, as it is even more forcefully in the scene entitled "Electra tries to speak." Stuttering and gagging as she adopts the roles of "Everybody But Herself," Electra uses the third person to narrate her painful struggle to give voice to her own experience. What Electra speaks, then, is that very struggle, and the problems faced by women in general as they confront the absence of their experience in the documents of patriarchal culture. Her concluding line, "there's probably more she could say," spoken "directly and clearly" to the audience, insists on the link between Electra's situation and that of the present-day spectators.[28]

But it is Athena's monologue in the play's first act which most pointedly links past and present. Just as she defended Orestes in Aeschylus' version of the story, so the Athena of *Electra Speaks* emphatically argues against the women of the House of Atreus, enumerating Clytemnestra's misdeeds and even suggesting that Orestes was pushed into murder by his sister. But Coss, Segal, and Sklar have transposed Athena into a modern lawyer who has little sympathy for women who have not played the role of "Daddy's Girl" as she has. Her view of Clytemnestra as "a slut," her insistence that "no woman is raped unless she wants to be," and her parting threat, "I tell you if that woman were alive today I'd haul her into family court," offer a powerful feminist critique of contemporary justice even while recalling the classical origins of the negative attitudes toward women implicit in it.[29]

But the historical perspective of *Electra Speaks* has an additional motive as well, one that illustrates a significant modification of Brechtian historicization to suit the aims of feminist theatre. In describing their goals for the entire *Daughters Cycle*, Coss, Segal, and Sklar speak of their desire to retrieve "the culture that emanates from [women's] half of the human race" and "to dismantle the past and reconstruct it with [their] own women's consciousness."[30] Thus, even as it reveals the historical conditions shaping women's lives, *Electra Speaks* also represents an attempt to rewrite history by making the attitudes and experiences of the women it features a part of the historical landscape. Like other feminists in the United States and abroad, the Women's Experimental Theatre turned to history not only to reveal the workings of oppressive, patriarchal structures by examining them through "an historian's eye," as Brecht would say, but also to reclaim and reinterpret the past from a feminist perspective.

Denise Hamilton's *Parallax*, developed, like *Signs of Life*, for the Women's Project at the American Place Theatre, embodies this reinterpretation process in its very structure. In a series of vignettes, this brief, one-woman show dramatizes Daisy Bates's leadership of the bitter fight to integrate the schools of Little Rock, Arkansas. The parallax of the play's title becomes apparent through the use of projected slides and televised commentary. These juxtapose the on-stage actions of the generally forgotten Bates with media tributes to Rose Fitzgerald Kennedy, who is lovingly described as "the matriarch of America's greatest political family."[31] Coupled with this display of media power to create a female hero is the revelation that Bates and her husband eventually lost their beloved newspaper owing to the cancellation of advertising contracts. In the process of reminding audiences of Bates's contribution to the cause of integration, then, Hamilton invites them to recognize the role of the media and advertising in the construction of history. In addition, the contrast of Bates and Kennedy underlies patriarchal culture's power to suppress – if not castigate – women who do not fit the traditional mold of supportive, suffering mother.

As a tribute to one of history's forgotten women, however, Hamilton's play also invites us to see Daisy Bates as a role model, to admire her strength and courage even as we are angered by our recognition of the social forces at work against her. In this sense, *Parallax* illustrates a more general trend among American women playwrights, whose reworking of history often features actual women from the near or distant past. Spectators may be incited to see the historical conditions shaping these women's lives and judge the characters and their actions. But often this judgement may not be the focal point of the dramatist's work.

In *Approaching Simone*, for example, Megan Terry displays the heroic spirit and powerful will of Simone Weil in an effort to provide an alternative to masculine models of behaviour. In explaining her rationale for writing *Simone*, Terry speaks of her desire "to come out and be as strong as I can for *other women*. They need models, they need to know that a woman can make it and think clearly in a womanly way. All the heroes are dead or killed or compromised, and women *need* heroes."[32] Julia Miles, director of the Women's Project, appears to share Terry's view. In the preface to *Women Heroes*, a collection of plays she edited and produced, Miles speaks of the need for positive public images of women and describes her project as an attempt to "provide an examination and celebration of the lives of notable, exceptional women."[33] Using a variety of styles and techniques, the six plays in this volume (which includes *Parallax*) explore and often celebrate the lives of real and fictional women, including Colette, Emma Goldman, and athlete Babe Didrickson. While the title character in Brecht's *Galileo* argues "Unhappy the land that is in need of heroes," these feminist playwrights seem to share the view of Galileo's pupil, Andrea, that heroes, or positive role models, are indeed necessary.[34] Unlike many of their European counterparts, these feminist playwrights are not afraid to "romanticize female identity" by building strong female characters embodying women's historical accomplishments and ideals.[35]

While some American feminists have turned to history without incorporating Brechtian historicization, others have applied Brecht's experiments with a historicizing dramatic form to the presentation of more immediate or personal subject matter than the "epic" or "history" play traditionally allows. Noting the existence of a similar phenomenon among British feminist theatre groups, Michelene Wandor argues that, while placing "the individual in his/her social and political context" is a useful and necessary reaction to much realistic theatre, "the epic case can be overstated, if it results in excluding individual and emotional life from a definition of 'politics'".[36] Although this remark may imply an unfair characterization of Brecht's own plays (one thinks again of *The Good Person of Szechwan* and its clear focus on the emotional life of Shen Teh), it highlights a third significant point of exchange between Brechtian and American feminist dramaturgy. For many American women, the structuring techniques and devices of Brecht's "non-Aristotelian" dramaturgy have played a key role in the development of a dramatic form suited to the nature and diversity of women's experiences.

Once again, the comments of Roberta Sklar are instructive. Speaking of her own elimination of linear development in the Women's Experimental Theatre's *Electra Speaks*, Sklar identifies Brecht's use of episodic structure as a source of inspiration for this work. But her application of non-linear form seems quite distant from Brecht's. Observing that "linear sequence is almost irrelevant in *Electra Speaks*," Sklar explains, "What interests me about episodic structure has to do with expressing the inner life . . . At any given moment things are happening sequentially as well as simultaneously . . . feelings don't happen in logical sequence

. . . Episodic structure fits that understanding of reality: that, as every woman knows, life is a constant three-ring circus rather than some linear tale of adventure."[37]

In keeping with Brecht's description of the "epic" (as opposed to the "dramatic") theatre, the short scenes of *Electra Speaks* break up the play's action and help bring the spectator face to face with the patriarchal assumptions underlying women's traditional role. For Sklar, however, episodic structure has an added significance, providing a means of capturing the inner life and a dimension of experience to which she feels women are particularly sensitive.

Other feminist playwrights have also adapted characteristic devices of epic dramaturgy for the presentation of an inner or extremely personal reality. Boesing's *River Journal*, for example, makes frequent use of songs, announced scene titles, and readings from Ann's journal, all of which comment on the action and move the play away from the narcotic effect of the more realistic dramaturgy to which both Brecht and many American feminists object. But the journal readings in particular, with their surreal, often violent imagery, also take us inside the dreams and fantasy life of the play's troubled protagonist. Rather than evoking a broader, historical or political context for Ann's distress (as in Brecht's description of the use of projections in *The Mother*, "to show the great movement of ideas in which the events were taking place"[38]), these readings instead recall Adrienne Rich's belief that "only the willingness to share private and sometimes painful experience can enable women to create a collective description of the world which will be truly ours."[39]

Similarly, both Myrna Lamb's "Space-Age Musical Soap Opera," *The Mod Donna*, and Megan Terry's musical *American King's English for Queens* employ episodic structure, scene titles, and "reflective and moralizing" music which become "an active collaborator in the stripping bare of the middle class corpus of ideas."[40] In both structure and content, these plays stand in sharp contrast to the "culinary opera" criticized by Brecht and represent significant attempts to politicize the musical form that has become a hallmark of American theatre. Yet both plays use a blatantly domestic setting and focus on the American family rather than on more traditionally "political" material.

The Mod Donna explores "mod wife-swapping" which has "turned a bit dissonant, a bit macabre" by interspersing "Soap Opera scenes" of an absurd and exploitative *ménage à trois* with short "commercial breaks" illustrating the dissatisfaction resulting from contemporary consumerism.[41] Central to the play is a musical number entitled the "Liberation Song," which repeatedly asks women whether they have the courage to reject the sexist attitudes and obsessions which make whores of women in bourgeois society. No one in the play appears capable of doing so, least of all the heroine, Donna, who is ultimately rejected by the "boss couple" who have used her to boost the level of sexual satisfaction in their marriage. But when Donna's outraged husband symbolically executes her in the final scene, the Chorus appeals to the audience; a reprise of the theme song culminates in a rousing call for "LIBERATION LIBERATION LIBERATION" from the oppression and degradation of women implicit in modern marriage.[42]

In *American King's English*, Terry reveals the sexism inherent in American English by exploring its use in a "typical" American family. Set in a family home, the play's short scenes dramatize the impact of phenomena such as body language or the language of business, and the confusion created for young women by the generic use of the masculine pronoun. As in *The Mod Donna*, songs reinforce the play's central question, "Do you think like you talk, or talk like you think?"[43] Mom's medley of popular love songs, for example, shows the shallow view of marriage she has adopted from the language of romance, while Dad's subsequent rendition of "HOME, home on the Kitchen-Queen range," effectively demonstrates how the rhetoric of advertising has correspondingly shaped his view of his wife.[44] Both songs, and others in the play, sum up Terry's awareness of the power of language to shape even our most intimate experiences.

In various ways, each of these plays embodies feminism's basic contention that "the personal is political" and thus reorients the content of "political theatre" as Brecht and other male political playwrights have defined it. The plays' intimate, often domestic scenes and settings tend to reflect the tight links between women's public and private lives, the intensely personal terms in which they may see what Brecht calls "social relationships." And whereas Brechtian theory tends to play down the inner life in favour of an "idea of man as a function of man,"[45] feminist playwrights have emphasized the links between inner and social realities. As Sklar observes, "For woman, the internal reality is filled with the social suppression of womanhood."[46] Moreover, even those feminist playwrights whose work is not necessarily focused on the "inner" world, frequently draw attention to the family, marriage, and the traditional work of women as a "basic part of any political structure,"[47] thus redefining or expanding the parameters of the environment that should be of interest to the political playwright.

Perhaps, though, these adaptations of Brechtian theory are in keeping with that theory itself, a response to changes in the "given conditions of men's [and women's] life together" of which Brecht himself speaks in *A Short Organum*.[48] In the earlier essay entitled "The Modern Theatre is the Epic Theatre," Brecht argued,

> True progress consists not in being progressive but in progressing. True progress is what enables or compels us to progress. And on a broad front, at that, so that neighbouring spheres are set in motion too. True progress has its cause in the impossibility of an actual situation, and its result is that situation's change.[49]

The evolving feminist theatre may well be progressing in a direction Brecht never foresaw and might never even have supported. But the state and understanding of political struggles outside the theatre have changed in the thirty years since Brecht's death. And, given these changes, it seems entirely appropriate that the "neighbouring space" of sexual politics should be "set in motion" by techniques borrowed from Brecht and adapted to the needs and aims of today's theatre women. Both Brechtian theory and American feminist theatre appear to have been enriched by this confrontation.

NOTES

1. Both Roberta Sklar and Megan Terry, for example, were associated with the Open Theatre in the 1960s and acknowledge the impact of the outlook and techniques developed with this group on their subsequent work. See Megan Terry, interview, *Interviews with Contemporary Women Playwrights*, with Kathleen Betsko and Rachel Koenig (New York: Beech Tree Books, 1987) 380, and Roberta Sklar, "Roberta Sklar: Toward Creating a Women's Theatre," interview with Cornelia Brunner, *The Drama Review* 24.2 (1980): 30–1.
2. Helene Keyssar's *Feminist Theatre* (Houndmills, England: Macmillan, 1984), for example, notes that the current wave of "feminist drama had its most immediate roots in the political and aesthetic disruptions of the 1960s" (p. 1). Though she goes on to cite Stanislavsky, Gertrude Stein, and others as influential figures, Brecht's name never appears in her discussion of the "Roots and Contexts" of feminist theatre. Elizabeth J. Natalle's *Feminist Theatre: A Study in Persuasion* (Metuchen, NJ: Scarecrow, 1985) is only slightly more helpful since she merely lists Brecht and Piscator alongside Aristophanes, Ibsen, and Shaw as playwrights who, like the feminist theatre groups she studies, have used the stage "to advocate a point of view" (p. 1).
3. This is Sue-Ellen Case's definition of the feminist approach to theatre as cited in Linda Walsh Jenkins and Susan Ogden-Malouf, "The (Female) Actor Prepares," *Theater* 17.1 (1985): 66. There are nearly as many definitions of feminist theatre as there are feminist theatre practitioners. Case's phrasing, however, sums up the salient features of many of these. See the introduction to Dinah Luise Leavitt, *Feminist Theatre Groups* (Jefferson, NC: McFarland, 1980) for a fuller discussion of the problems of defining this phenomenon.
4. Judith Malina, *The Diaries of Judith Malina: 1947–1957* (New York: Grove Press, 1984) 94.
5. Dorothy B. Magnus, "Matriarchs of the Regional Theatre," *Women in American Theatre: Careers, Images, Movements*, ed. Helen Krich Chinoy and Linda Walsh Jenkins (New York: Crown, 1981) 221, 223.
6. "Roberta Sklar: Toward Creating a Women's Theatre," 28.
7. Timothy J. Wiles, *The Theater Event: Modern Theories of Performance* (Chicago: University of Chicago Press, 1980) 71.
8. Karen Malpede, "Feminist Plays and Performance: Ending the Violence We Have Known," *Women in Theatre: Compassion and Hope*, ed. Karen Malpede (New York: Drama Books, 1983) 233.

9. Bertolt Brecht, *Brecht on Theatre: The Development of an Aesthetic*, ed. and trans. John Willett (London: Methuen, 1964) 93.
10. Keyssar, *Feminist Theatre* 104.
11. Myrna Lamb, "But What Have You Done for Me Lately? or Pure Polemic," *The Mod Donna and Scyklon Z: Plays of Women's Liberation* (New York: Pathfinder, 1971) 158.
12. Keyssar, *Feminist Theatre* 73.
13. Megan Terry, *Interviews with Contemporary Women Playwrights* 394.
14. Keyssar, *Feminist Theatre* 74.
15. Megan Terry and Jo Ann Schmidman, "Babes in the Bighouse," *High Energy Musicals from the Omaha Magic Theatre* (New York: Broadway Play Publishing, 1983) 202.
16. Martha Boesing, "River Journal," *Journeys along the Matrix: Three Plays* (Minneapolis: Vanilla Press, 1978) 62.
17. Ibid. 72.
18. Ibid. 78.
19. *Brecht on Theatre* 140.
20. Joan Schenkar, "Signs of Life," *The Women's Project: Seven New Plays by Women*, ed. Julia Miles (New York: Performing Arts Journal Publications, 1980) 310.
21. Ibid. 346.
22. Vivian Patraka notes James's "artistic vampirism" and points to the parallels between James and Sloper in her "Notes on Technique in Feminist Drama: *Apple Pie* and *Signs of Life*," *Women & Performance* 1.2 (1984): 68.
23. Patraka, "Notes on Technique in Feminist Drama" 67.
24. "Alienation Effects in Chinese Acting", *Brecht on Theatre* 97–8.
25. Schenkar, *The Women's Project* 313.
26. Clare Coss, Sondra Segal, and Roberta Sklar, "Electra Speaks," *Union Seminary Quarterly Review* 35.3 and 4 (1980): 226. The full text of "Electra Speaks" is unpublished; this piece contains substantial excerpts from the play as well as an introduction by the authors and forms the basis for my analysis.
27. Ibid. 240–1.
28. Ibid. 253.
29. Ibid. 237–9.
30. Ibid. 223.
31. Denise Hamilton, "Parallax (In Honor of Daisy Bates)," *Women Heroes: Six Short Plays from the Women's Project*, ed. Julia Miles (New York: Applause, 1986) 61.
32. Megan Terry, *Approaching Simone* (Old Westbury, NY: Feminist Press, 1973). Terry's comment appears on the dust jacket of this volume.
33. Julia Miles, 'Introduction," *Women Heroes*, vii.
34. Bertolt Brecht, *The Life of Galileo*, trans. Desmond I. Vesey (London: Methuen, 1963) 108.
35. See Elin Diamond, "Refusing the Romanticism of Identity: Narrative Interventions in Churchill, Benmussa, Duras," *Theatre Journal* 37.3 (1985): 273–86, for a discussion of three European alternatives to the valorization of female identity implied in this search for heroic women.
36. Michelene Wandor, *Understudies: Theatre and Sexual Politics* (London: Methuen, 1981) 87.
37. "Roberta Sklar: Toward Creating a Women's Theatre" 27.
38. "Indirect Impact of the Epic Theatre," *Brecht on Theatre* 58.
39. Adrienne Rich, *Of Woman Born: Motherhood as Experience and Institution* (New York: Norton, 1976) 16.

40. See "On the Use of Music in an Epic Theatre," *Brecht on Theatre* 85, 86.
41. Lamb, "The Mod Donna," *The Mod Donna and Scyklon Z* 31–2.
42. Ibid. 139.
43. Megan Terry, "American King's English for Queens," *High Energy Musicals* 8.
44. Ibid. 34–5.
45. "Alienation Effects in Chinese Acting," *Brecht on Theatre* 97.
46. "Roberta Sklar: Toward Creating a Women's Theatre" 30.
47. Sarah Bryant-Bertail, "Women, Space, Ideology: *Mutter Courage und ihre Kinder*," *Brecht, Women and Politics*, ed. John Fuegi, Gisela Bahr, and John Willett (Detroit: Wayne State University Press, 1983) 45.
48. *Brecht on Theatre* 182.
49. Ibid. 40 n.

23

BRECHT, FEMINISM, AND CHINESE THEATRE

Carol Martin

Bertolt Brecht's theatrical techniques are commonly cited as a useful means for feminist revisions of theatrical realism. Two articles in particular, one historical, the other theoretical, have connected Brechtian techniques to the sources of feminist theatre, proposing an intersection between Brechtian theory and feminist theatre practice: "Brechtian Theory and the American Feminist Theatre," by Karen Laughlin (1990) and "Brechtian Theory/Feminist Theory: Toward a Gestic Feminist Criticism," by Elin Diamond (1988). Focusing on Brecht has been important for feminist theatre theory and practice, but it has also obscured the fact that the political complexities of traditional Chinese acting were already well articulated by the Chinese, especially Chinese women, long before Brecht's famous article from the 1930s "Alienation Effects in Chinese Acting" (1964). Dissenting readings of traditional Chinese acting make the alliance of feminism and Brecht worth additional consideration.[1]

Brecht spelled out his theory of *Verfremdungseffekt* (alienation effect) in "Alienation Effects in Chinese Acting," written after he saw in Moscow in 1935 an impromptu demonstration of Chinese acting – known in the West as Beijing "opera" – by Mei Lanfang (1894–1961). In his essay, Brecht articulates a relationship between actor and spectator wherein both become critical observers (not without empathy) of the actions the actor performs. Instead of "real life" Brecht saw in Mei's acting a manipulable system of signs and referents. He celebrated the Chinese theatre's ability to manufacture and manipulate *Gestus*, actions that were both themselves and emblematic, if not symbolic, of larger social practices. Brecht's particular twist on acting – driving a wedge between actor and action – opened a space in which the actor could communicate with the spectator both about the character and about the actions being performed. What Mei demonstrated for Brecht was the transparency of the relationship between actor and character. This is the crux of contemporary feminist interest in Brecht. When Brecht saw Mei perform the female (*dan*) role in Moscow, it was without costume, theatrical lighting, or any apparent interior preparation. Seeing Mei confirmed for Brecht what was already taking shape in his own thought and practice: that "character" in the theatre can and must be manipulable independent of the actor. No total amalgam or identification of actor with character need take place on stage. The Brechtian actor, like Mei, does not live the role, he demonstrates it.

Traditional Chinese actors do not pretend there is a fourth wall; they show their awareness of being watched. This awareness is shared with the audience who consequently must also abandon the illusion of being unseen (Brecht 1964: 92). Together actors and spectators acknowledge that what is taking place is real only in the theatrical sense: the awareness of representation replaces "willing suspension of disbelief." For Brecht this is not a metaphysical or mysterious process; the Chinese actor's alienation effect is "a transportable piece of technique" (1964: 95).

Brecht's reading of Chinese acting is only one possible reading. A different reading emerged from a notorious international incident involving Chinese acting and the French diplomat Bernard Bouriscot's love affair with a Chinese actress who, in fact, turned out to be a man. When questioned about confusing his lover's gender, Bouriscot responded that he had never seen what he thought was his girlfriend naked, explaining, "I thought she was very modest. I thought it was a Chinese custom" (in Worthen 1995: 987).

In *M. Butterfly* (1986) David Henry Hwang, inspired by a two-paragraph newspaper article in the *New York Times* about Bouriscot's mistake, explores Western fantasies and stereotypes and a very different reading of Chinese acting. Bouriscot did not perceive Chinese acting as a transparent medium that displayed both actor and character, but an opaque medium that presented a vision of an ideal Asian woman to the gaze of a very believing spectator. In Hwang's play, Bouriscot becomes "Gallimard" and his lover, "Song Liling." Never intending to write a docudrama, Hwang, nevertheless, used the international incident to expose an exotic, erotic, and imperialist view of the East (see Worthen 1995: 987). In the case of Bouriscot, these illusions were exploited by the Chinese actor/spy for her/his own purposes.

Brecht's reading of Chinese acting is as a lucid display of alienation; Bouriscot's reading of Chinese acting both onstage and off is as a believable portrayal of gender; Hwang's reading of Bouriscot's misreading is a critique of Western colonialism. With these competing readings it is curious that feminist theatre scholars inspired by Brechtian thought and theories have generally not looked directly at the practice, history, or theory of Chinese acting to make their own inquiries into alternative ways of constructing theatre practices and dramatic texts.[2]

What Brecht saw Mei perform – the title of the "opera" was *Dayu Shajia* (The Fisherman's Revenge) – could only give Brecht a small part of the system of signification of Chinese acting. Generally, *jingju*, the traditional style of acting that Mei mastered, stressed both techniques of representation and an inner technique of introspection. The four salient characteristics of traditional Chinese acting at the time of Mei were fluidity, plasticity, sculpturality, and conventionality. Conventionality, however, refers not only to form but also to *xie yi* which has no exact equivalent in English but which can be understood as "essence." This characterization of traditional performance via Chinese painting has been used since the beginning of the twentieth century.

While Brecht was seeing "alienation," Mei was concerned with essence, specifically the four essences: life, movement, language, and decor (costumes, general setting). Mei's technique appeared to Brecht's Western eyes as form but was to Mei, at least in part, a transcendent kind of theatre refined from life into a higher plane of human movement, lyrical language, and theatrical visuality (Wu, Huang, and Mei: 1981). Thus Mei, in the words of his contemporaries, was concerned with the "essence rather than the appearance of things" (1981: 28).

Another explanation of Mei's system of acting is that it is just the opposite of Brecht's. In his article comparing Stanislavsky, Brecht, and Mei, Sun Huizhu writes:

> The Mei Lanfang system, however, is just the reverse [of Brecht's approach] in this respect: while the external action is far removed from its natural appearance in real life – every little gesture, every utterance, is guided by convention and timed to music and rhythm – internally the actors are encouraged, however, to forget about "acting" and to move as close as possible to their characters; otherwise, the full meaning of the play will be lost on the audience. When talking about the conventionalized pantomime of smelling the flower in "Drunken Beauty" (*Guifei zuijiu*), Mei Lanfang said: "The important thing is for my heart and my eyes to see that flower (even though there is not one in sight onstage), only that will give the audience a sense of reality" (1999: 175–6).

Following Sun's explanation, Mei's pantomime and his interior process were parallel but dialectical. Highly stylized and predetermined dance, gesture, and voice work place exterior demands on the actor. Yet, the actor has also to invent an interior reality to transform the distance between the artificiality of what he is doing into the reality of what he wants to convey. Brecht seems not to have been interested in Mei's explanations of the dual structure of exterior and interior processes in Chinese acting. In Western realism the exterior and interior are thought to be congruent, and the audience takes pleasure in the invisible seam of this congruence. In Chinese acting, spectators take pleasure in the way in which the actor makes the jump between the exterior and the interior. The assumption is that performers are present in their own persons and their character. Yet they are understood to be separate, and the artistry is in making visible the spark that connects them. Its affective power and pleasure is in the simultaneity of external virtuosity and interior meaning. For Brecht there is also a separation: it is the separation of the spectator and the actor from the character that is at the core of his acting theory. The performer to some degree functions as a spectator to his own character. Both spectators and performers are invited to have a critical response to the characters' situations and choices. The theatre is a laboratory for critical observation and change. The pleasure is in seeing actors control characters even as the characters control the actors.

While Brecht was enamored with Chinese acting, theatre practitioners in China (and Japan) were enamored with appropriating Western acting and playwriting to modernize their theatre. It should be noted that Mei also performed *huaju* (spoken drama or modern theatre) and was very active in experimenting with ways to modernize classical Chinese theatre.[3] His play *Yi lu ma* (A Piece of Flax) was praised as a transitional play – a transition between traditional and modern – because it explored the traditional system of marriage in the manner of Ibsen. Mei wanted to incorporate traditional elements into the developing modern theatre but his efforts were often met with sharp criticism. Fu Sinian, the head of Beijing University commented: "Mei's use of singing, acrobatics, and tumbling reduced the modern spirit of his works since in the idealistic modern theater, all acting should be based on everyday gestures and posture" (in Chou 1997: 47). Similarly, the Chinese theatre scholar Qian Xuantong noted that the "convention of face painting [in Chinese opera] is absurd, and the traditional bare stage is primitive" (46).

Mei was in Moscow at the same time as Brecht and others not only because he was a great classical Chinese actor but also because he was a bridge figure who was interested in connecting traditional Chinese acting to what were for him newer Western ideas about acting. Often we lose sight of the fact that traditional forms are also contemporary – shaped by the forces of the times in which they are enacted.

Mei's tours included three trips to Japan (1919, 1924, and 1956); the United States (1930); and Moscow (1935). Over the years, Mei met a wide range of international artists: Ted Shawn, Ruth St. Denis, Mary Pickford, Charlie Chaplin, Cecil B. de Mille, Paul Robeson, and Rabindranath Tagore. The leading American critic Stark Young writing in the *New Republic* elegantly defined the way in which Chinese theatre was realistic:

> The Chinese theater is spoken of as completely unrealistic art, entirely ideal in character [. . .]. The theater art of Mei Lanfang is not completely without realism, not in the sense that a cubist painting would be, an abstract Arabic decoration, a geometric dance design. Its exact parallel is Chinese painting and sculpture. In these, the impression that remains in the memory is of the abstract and decorative, but we are constantly surprised at the exactitude with nature, a leaf, a bough, a bird, a hand, or a mantle has been observed and are amazed at the dazzling notation of characteristic details and at the manner in which they are made to supersede and concentrate their own actuality [. . .]. To judge even by

> their common paintings and statuettes, the delight felt by the Chinese in this dexterous realism combined with tradition, convention and abstract pattern, must be very strong. We are to remember this when we hear it said that Mei Lanfang's art is wholly unrealistic. We must also remember that one of things to learn from this Chinese theater art is not the need for unrealism or its contrary, but rather the exactness of the degree to which, in every part of it, realism is employed. The gestures, the narration, the acting, even the much discussed falsetto voice employed for the female roles, the movements and so on, all are the same distance from the actual; which is another way of saying that the whole achieves a total unity of style. (in Wu, Huang, and Mei 1981: 55–6)

Young was interested in understanding Chinese acting as a coherent aesthetic system. His comments also reveal that realism in the 1930s was for many *the* point of departure for viewing theatre *and* a contested notion that could not simply be defined as the imitation of daily life. Rather, Young's comments point out that real life – its gestures, emotions, movements – is a part of Chinese acting in a stylized and theatricalized way, just as realism on Western stages can be seen in terms of semiotic convention as well as internal conviction. Identification and illusion were encouraged in Chinese acting but the result was not anything like realism as it is understood in the West.[4]

Brecht's emphasis on the form of Chinese acting at the expense of its interior processes, and the fact that he chose to ignore the significance of men playing women, could only have occurred because he ignored two of his own main concerns: an understanding of the historical conditions that produced traditional Chinese acting, and an inquiry into the political implications of the assertion that the actor could and should quote the character played.

In actuality, the many related forms that we in the West refer to as Chinese opera were in the process of tremendous change. The development of *xin nuxing* (new woman), the term given by critics to female characters created on the modern Chinese stage from 1919 to 1949, was well underway. Radical female artists were challenging the taboo against women acting on the stage. Interestingly, in order for this to happen, *huaju*, a Chinese version of realism emerged. Modern Chinese artists were appropriating Western ideas to reform Chinese theatre. Realism, in this context, was not a reflection of everyday reality as it orginally was constructed in the West, but "the construction of a model lifestyle that was to be promoted by means of film and theatre" (Chou 1997: ix). Thus, cross-dressing, the means by which stereotypical notions of gender were encoded in China, had to be challenged.

In China in the 1930s casting women in women's roles was a radical new form of gender ideology (Chou 1997: ix). The resulting representation of gender freed women from the formalism invented by men and encoded in the performances of female impersonators. According to

Katherine Chou, "Women could now speak in their own voices and strike their own poses. In other words, realistic performance was for Chinese modernist[s] the strategy of liberation from their traditional past" (ibid.).

Since at least the nineteenth century many Chinese went to Japan to learn about and participate in the changes brought about by the 1868 Meiji restoration which paved the way for the study of Western culture (Chou 1997: 16) and the restructuring of traditional society. While in Japan, Li Shutong and Ouyang Yuqien formed the Spring Willow Dramatic Association, presenting first *Camille* (1907) and then *Uncle Tom's Cabin* (1907) (ibid.). The production of *Uncle Tom's Cabin* is considered the pioneer work of Chinese spoken drama. These ideas, however, were not solely the invention of the Spring Willow Dramatic Association, but an adaptation of Japanese *shingeki* (new drama), the Japanese modern theatre that emerged at the end of the nineteenth century modelled on Western drama. Like the New Woman movement in China, *shingeki* exploited the conventions of realism to allow women to appear on stage. Gender was not alienated but embodied, setting in motion a system of signs that transgressed the social order. What was alienated was the convention of using female impersonation – the very practice that so enchanted Brecht. Besides staging a Western drama with spoken text, amateur performers, and no music, Spring Willow's production of *Uncle Tom's Cabin* featured another important political intervention: a new ending was added in which the enslaved blacks regained their freedom by assassinating the white slave traders (17).

Whatever Brecht might have known about modern theatrical experiments in China, he did not make them relevant to his work.[5] Yet the political potential of Chinese acting was already well-articulated long before Brecht's brief encounter with Mei.

Diamond cites the centrality of *Verfremdungseffekt* as the cornerstone of Brecht's theory (1988: 122). She also points out that Brechtian technique, at least theoretically, places the physical signs of the actor and the performer's body in an historical context: "In my hybrid construction – based in feminist and Brechtian theory – the female performer, unlike her filmic counterpart, connotes not 'to-be-looked-at-ness' [taken from Mulvey 1975: 11] – the perfect fetish – but rather 'looking-at-being-looked-at-ness' or even just looking-ness. This Brechtian-feminist body is paradoxically available for both analysis and identification, paradoxically, within representation while refusing its fixity" (1988: 129).

When a spectator is able to separate familiar ideas and gestures from conventional associations, she can begin to understand the social and material construction of gender. Similarly, Laughlin notes that Megan Terry and Jo Ann Schidman furthered Brechtian acting (and feminist concerns) by casting both men and women in the role of female prisoners in *Babes in the Bighouse*, a 1974 production of Omaha Magic Theatre: "As Terry and her company observed, 'men are socialized to respond to a male voice; from an early age they seem to be trained to discount what women say.' Hence the value of 'alienating' actor and character through cross-gender casting: 'by putting a man in a dress, in the same constraints as the women characters in the play, it became clear to the men in the audience what women were up against'" (Laughlin 1990: 150).

Laughlin cites two other aspects of Brecht's thinking important for the development of a theatre attempting to resituate the experience of women: an emphasis on historical context; and an epic structuring of dramatic narratives (1990: 147). With acting that provides distance between actor and character, and spectator and subject; historical understanding; and episodic interruption of the continuity of narratives, Brechtian techniques provide feminist theatre practitioners with tools necessary to create feminist theatre.

Both Diamond and Laughlin are correct. Yet the interventions for which they credit Brecht were done more than fifty years earlier by theatre practitioners with analogous interests in the political repercussions of gender representations. The way plays situate gender can be in a dialectical relationship to how any given form of performance positions gender. For feminist theatre in the U.S., cross-gender casting has been a major means of exposing the conventions of gender. For the Chinese *xin nuxing* movement, cross-gender casting was the major means of excluding women from the stage. Women playing women was the radical new means of putting the physical signs of the actor and the performer's body in historical context.

Of course, seeing Chinese women play women on stage did not necessarily signify gender as "natural." While this act referenced daily life, it also referred to, by its very absence, the convention of men impersonating women. When women play themselves on stage as a radical act referring both to the changing needs of modern daily life and the representational apparatus of traditional theatre, realism is revealed as an enigmatic notion. In the context of a long tradition of female impersonation, women on stage may have appeared less real than their fictional representations. This is especially true if one defines the real as abstract, decorative and exact, as Young did. What was exact was precisely that which was abstract.

In writing *M. Butterfly* Hwang states that he wanted to create a "deconstructivist *Madame Butterfly*" (in Worthen 1995: 987). In the process of doing this, Hwang explored the sexual and political domination of the West over Asia in terms of fantasies concerning gender. Hwang's play exemplifies the performativity of gender identity. Song Liling is not only a man in disguise, but a Beijing "opera" performer known for his female impersonations. Song Liling's performance is both public and private. Given public knowledge about the performance conventions of Beijing "opera," Liling's public gender performance (a man playing a woman on the stage) gets confused for what he "really" is. Yet what really is "Song?" Is Gallimard wrong? Given Gallimard's fusion of his sexual and colonial desires, his "error" is actually an enactment of a social and political truth. Toward the end of *M. Butterfly*

Gallimard confesses, "I'm a man who loved a woman created by a man" (Worthen 1995: 986). His troubled love is sexual, cultural, and ahistorical.

Brecht's prominence in feminist theatre history and theory has obscured the complexities and contributions of Chinese women (and men) to twentieth-century theatre practices. We have to be increasingly mindful of histories that are seemingly not our own. Otherwise we risk being like Gallimard: ignorant of what we are looking at yet in love with what we think we see.

While feminist theorists and artists have made exemplary use of Brecht's work as a model for their ideas, we would do well to look past Brecht to his original sources. The resulting narrative would first begin by acknowledging that Mei's performances and ideas were informed by *huaju* and *xin nuxing* and then recognize the influence of Brecht on feminist theatre theorists and practitioners in the U.S. In this formulation, feminist theatre has intertextual, interhistorical, and international lineages that makes the emergence of women's rights in a variety of historical contexts pivotal in the creation of twentieth-century theatre.

Asian theatre has been theorized in ways that can no longer be ignored by Western feminist scholars. There is much more beyond Brecht's formulations of Chinese theatre. Chinese theatre and other Asian theatre should be directly, rather than through the filter of Brecht's partial understanding, investigated for their theoretical and pracitical complexities and what they can teach about the political implications of different forms of enactment in different historical contexts. As I see it the question is: What other aspects of Asian *and* Western theatre aesthetics and practices might serve feminist theatre practitioners in both parts of the world?

Brecht lived what amounted to a twenty-year exile. Everything in his life was in flux. He was a diasporic figure: a personal enactment of "alienation." Globalization has come a long way since Brecht. Colonial assumptions about the flow of information from the West to the East must be rethought in the opposite direction. This way, theatre history and theory will begin to take into account the real impact of the movement of artists and ideas in the twentieth century, without the lingering notion that historical influences are one way, or that the study of theatre exactly coincides with the borders of nation states. In short, theory must be conversant with history.

NOTES

1. This chapter was originally given as a talk to the German Department at Dartmouth College in the fall of 1998. Katherine Hui-ling Chou's research on *xin nuxing* has been instrumental to this work.
2. In the last half century, Western theatre scholars and practitioners have become increasingly aware of Asian performance. In part, this is due to the fact that the U.S, Britain, and France have fought Pacific wars bringing hundreds of thousands of ordinary people to Asia and stimulating a

great increase of interest in Asian cultures. Many Americans and Europeans have studied in Asia, learning first-hand through practice, fieldwork, and direct observation about a wide variety of Asian performance genres, ranging from traditional Chinese theatre to Indonesian, Indian, Korean, and Japanese forms. These practices have deeply affected experimental and even mainstream theatre practice – from Jerzy Grotowski and Peter Brook to Ariane Mnouchkine, Joanne Akalaitis, and Anne Bogart to name just a few of many.

3. Modern drama in China was not initially called *huaju*. Various names were used. One outstanding term was "civilized drama," as opposed to traditional drama. When Mei was doing modern plays no one knew the term *huaju*, but it is commonly used now.
4. The Indian aesthetic distinction between *lokadharmi* and *natyadharmi* is useful for understanding many forms of Asian theatre: lokadharmi is the theatrical presentation of ordinary behavior. In several Asian theatres including the Chinese, characters such as monks, servants, and commoners are often performed in a *lokadharmic* manner. The *natayadharmic*, by contrast, is a highly stylized or abstracted means of theatrical presentation. In Asian theatre, aristocrats, generals, gods, and other higher class figures are most often performed in a *natayadharmic* way. Both *lokadharmic* and *natyadharmic* representations are part of the same coherent systems of theatricalized signs.
5. For a discussion of Brecht's interest in Chinese culture, see Ding Yangzhong "Brecht's Theatre and Chinese Drama," in Tatlow and Wong 1982: 28–43.

REFERENCES

Brecht, Bertolt (1964) *Brecht on Theatre*. Trans. John Willett. New York: Hill and Wang.

Brecht, Bertolt (1964) "Alienation Effects in Chinese Acting." In *Brecht on Theatre*.

Chou, Katherine Hui-ling (1997) *Staging Revolution: Actresses, Realism & the New Woman Movement in Chinese Spoken Drama & Film, 1919–1949*. PhD diss., New York University.

Diamond, Elin (1988) "Brectian Theory/Feminist Theory:Toward a Gestic Feminist Criticism." *TDR* 32, 1 (T117): 82–94.

Laughlin, Karen (1990) "Brechtian Theory and the American Feminist Theatre." In *Re-Interpreting Brecht*, ed. Pia Kleber and Colin Visser. Cambridge: Cambridge University Press, 147–63.

Sun, Huizhu (1999) "Aesthetics of Stanislavsky, Brecht, and Mei Lanfang." In *Chinese Theories of Theater and Performance from Confucius to the Present*, ed. and trans. Faye Chunfang Fei. Ann Arbor: The University of Michigan Press.

Tatlow, Antony, and Wong, Tak-Wai (1982) *Brecht and East Asian Theatre*. Hong Kong: Hong Kong University Press.

Worthen, W.B. (1995) *Modern Drama*. New York: Harcourt Brace, Jovanovitch.

Wu, Zuguang, Huang, Zuolin, and Mei, Shaowu (1981) *Peking Opera and Mei Lanfang*. Beijing: New World Press.

INDEX